The Future of Information Architecture

The Future of Information Architecture

Conceiving a Better Way to Understand Taxonomy, Network, and Intelligence

PETER BAOFU

Chandos Publishing
Oxford · England

Chandos Publishing (Oxford) Limited
TBAC Business Centre
Avenue 4
Station Lane
Witney
Oxford OX28 4BN
UK
Tel: +44 (0) 1993 848726 Fax: +44 (0) 1865 884448
Email: info@chandospublishing.com
www.chandospublishing.com

First published in Great Britain in 2008

ISBN:
978 1 84334 470 4 (paperback)
978 1 84334 471 1 (hardback)
1 84334 470 X (paperback)
1 84334 471 8 (hardback)

British Library Cataloguing-in-Publication Data.
A catalogue record for this book is available from the British Library.

Produced from camera-ready copy supplied by the author.
Printed by Chris Fowler International Ltd, London.

To Those in the Synthetic World of Information Architecture

.

BOOKS ALSO BY PETER BAOFU

• *The Rise of Authoritarian Liberal Democracy* (2007) •

• *The Future of Aesthetic Experience* (2007) •

• *The Future of Complexity* (2007) •

• *Beyond the World of Titans, and the Remaking of World Order* (2007) •

• *Beyond Nature and Nurture* (2006) •

• *Beyond Civilization to Post-Civilization* (2006) •

• *The Future of Post-Human Space-Time* (2006) •

• *Beyond Capitalism to Post-Capitalism* (2005) •

• Volume 1: *Beyond Democracy to Post-Democracy* (2004) •

• Volume 2: *Beyond Democracy to Post-Democracy* (2004) •

• *The Future of Post-Human Consciousness* (2004) •

• *The Future of Capitalism and Democracy* (2002) •

• Volume 1: *The Future of Human Civilization* (2000) •

• Volume 2: *The Future of Human Civilization* (2000) •

CONTENTS

Part One: Introduction

Part Two: Taxonomy

Part Three: Network

Part Four: Conclusion

TABLES

FOREWORD

To question the process of sorting information into meaningful bundles is what Dr. Peter Baofu has chosen to examine here. And, for readers of his 14 prior works, he leads us through an exotic doorway to challenge our beliefs on yet a new level.

In this volume, he examines the customary ways we use to classify and arrange information to make it meaningful. To make order of information is absolutely necessary for comprehension, and Dr. Baofu recounts the traditional ways the human mind has used to accomplish this. Thereupon, he posits an alternative, quite unique way, in accordance to his "synthetic theory of information architecture," especially in relation to the "post-human" stage.

We witness here the working of a futuristic mind-set in action, causing us to speculate how near we may be to being there..

Sylvan Von Burg
School of Business
George Washington University

ACKNOWLEDGMENTS

This book, like all other previous ones of mine, is written to challenge conventional ideas and values, both past and present.

Because of this political incorrectness, it receives no external funding nor help from any formal organization or institution, and this is a common character of all my previous works.

The only reward is that extraordinary feeling of discovering something new about reality, in a way that no one else has ever understood before.

Lest I forget, Sylvan von Burg at George Washington University School of Business is greatly appreciated for his foreword written for this book.

In the end, obviously, I bear the sole responsibility for all ideas presented hereafter.

ABBREVIATIONS

ALD = Peter Baofu. 2007. *The Rise of Authoritarian Liberal Democracy: A Preface to a New Theory of Comparative Political Systems.* Cambridge, England: Cambridge Scholars Publishing, Ltd.

BCIV = Peter Baofu. 2006. *Beyond Civilization to Post-Civilization: Conceiving a Better Model of Life Settlement to Supersede Civilization.* NY: Peter Lang Publishing, Inc.

BCPC = Peter Baofu. 2005. *Beyond Capitalism to Post-Capitalism: Conceiving a Better Model of Wealth Acquisition to Supersede Capitalism.* NY: The Edwin Mellen Press.

BDPD1 = Peter Baofu. 2004. Volume 1. *Beyond Democracy to Post-Democracy: Conceiving a Better Model of Governance to Supersede Democracy.* NY: The Edwin Mellen Press.

BDPD2 = Peter Baofu. 2004. Volume 2. *Beyond Democracy to Post-Democracy: Conceiving a Better Model of Governance to Supersede Democracy.* NY: The Edwin Mellen Press.

BNN = Peter Baofu. 2006. *Beyond Nature and Nurture: Conceivng a Better Way to Understand Genes and Memes.* Cambridge, England: Cambridge Scholars Publishing, Ltd.

BWT = Peter Baofu. 2007. *Beyond the World of Titans, and the Renaking of World Order: A Preface to a New Logic of Empire-Building.* Cambridge, England: Cambridge Scholars Publishing, Ltd.

FAE = Peter Baofu. 2007. *The Future of Aesthetic Experience: Conceiving a Better Way to Understand Beauty, Ugliness and the Rest.* Cambridge, England: Cambridge Scholars Publishing, Ltd.

FC = Peter Baofu. 2007. *The Future of Complexity: Conceiving a Better Way to Understand Order and Chaos.* London, United Kingdom: World Scientific Publishing Co.

FCD = Peter Baofu. 2002. *The Future of Capitalism and Democracy.* MD: The University Press of America.

FHC1 = Peter Baofu. 2000. Volume 1. *The Future of Human Civilization.* NY: The Edwin Mellen Press.

FHC2 = Peter Baofu. 2000. Volume 2. *The Future of Human Civilization.* NY: The Edwin Mellen Press.

FIA = Peter Baofu. 2008. *The Future of Information Architecture: Conceiving a Better Way to Understand Taxonomy, Network, and Intelligence.* Oxford, England: Chandos Publishing (Oxford) Limited.

FPHC = Peter Baofu. 2004. *The Future of Post-Human Consciousness.* NY: The Edwin Mellen Press.

FPHST = Peter Baofu. 2006. *The Future of Post-Human Space-Time: Conceivng a Better Way to Understand Space and Time.* New York: Peter Lang Publishing, Inc.

• PART ONE •

Introduction

CHAPTER 1
INTRODUCTION—THE ROLE
OF INFORMATION ARCHITECTURE

> Intuitions without concepts are blind;
> concepts without intuitions are empty.
> —Immanuel Kant (WK 2007)

The Information Question

Why is information processed, stored, and applied in the way that it has, since time immemorial?

Contrary to the conventional wisdom held by many scholars in human history hitherto existing, the recurrent debate on the explanation of the most basic categories of information (e.g., space, time, causation, quality, quantity) has been misconstrued, to the effect that there exist some deeper categories and principles behind these categories of information—with enormous implications for our understanding of reality in general.

In this light, the re-asking of the question on the nature of information is by no means an idle academic exercise, since a new answer to it can shed some illuminating insights not only on the nature of data taxonomy and info network but also, even more fundamentally, on the very vital inquiry concerning the nature of intelligence, be it here on earth and out there in deep space.

After all, "Information," for some scholars, is regarded as, "together with Matter and Energy, the building blocks of the Universe." (WK 2007f) This is so, even though the word "information," in a more general sense, can also refer to any of its multiple meanings like "a pattern," "a sensory input," "something that leads to transformation," a "record," or whatnot. (WK 2007ss)

The need of this inquiry is all the more urgent, in light of the different stages of the Information and Scientific Revolutions that have fundamentally changed human lives in the last few hundred years, unto this day and age of ours—and this trend is expected to continue into the future.

A good way to start this inquiry about information so understood is to put it in the context of information architecture—with the word "architecture (from Latin, *architectura* and ultimately from Greek, αρχιτεκτων)" to be related to "a master builder," from Greek αρχι- ("chief, leader") and τεκτων ("builder, carpenter"), and therefore to mean "the art and science of designing buildings and structures." (WK 2007rr)

But this formal definition of architecture can be broadened, so it "by extension,…has come to denote the art and discipline of creating an actual, or inferring an implied or apparent plan of any…object or system." (WK 2007rr)

The information question is thus to be answered in the context of information architecture, or more technically, in relation to this art and discipline of creating an acutal (or inferring an implied or apparent) plan of any object or system—especially, though not exclusively, in relation to the nature of taxonomy and network (as will be clear in the rest of the book).

The Theoretical Debate

Historically, different schools of thought have competed for attention in the intellectual marketplace to answer this information question, but none is sufficiently persuasive to be accepted by most scholars in the literature of information architecture.

Perhaps a summary of three major theoretical approaches in the literature suffices to illustrate this disturbing state of affairs, with the fourth to be my original contribution to the theoretical debate (as shown in *Table 4.1*).

(a) Firstly, on one side of the theoretical debate is an approach, which can be called, in the absence of better terms, *the reflective argument*.

An excellent example is none other than Immanuel Kant's synthetic-a priori propositions in his "transcendental idealism," in that "[i]t is our mind…that processes…information about the world and gives it order, allowing us to comprehend it…." (WK 2007)

A good instance concerns elementary mathematics, which, "like arithmetic, is synthetic [i.e., true by revealing something about the world] a priori [i.e., true by nature of the meaning of the words involved]. Here Kant includes a priori and a posteriori concepts into his argument, and posits that it is in fact possible to have knowledge of the world that is not derived from empirical experience….He justifies this by arguing that experience depends on certain necessary conditions—which he calls a priori forms—and that these conditions hold true for the world." (WK 2007)

Thus, in accordance to his "'transcendental unity of apperception,' the concepts of the mind (Understanding) and the intuitions which garner information from phenomena (Sensibility) are synthesized by comprehension. Without the concepts, intuitions are nondescript; without the intuitions, concepts are meaningless." (WK 2007) So, Kant (1965) wrote in a classic passage: "Intuitions without concepts are blind; concepts without intuitions are empty." (WK 2007) In the end, for Kant, information about the world can therefore reflect the nature of the mind.

But Willard Quine in his influential article titled "The Two Dogmas of Empiricism" (1951) rejected Kant's synthetic-apriori propositions by questioning the very assumption in the latter's argument, that is, the synthetic-analytic distinction itself, which, upon closer examination, turns out to be untenable. (WK 2007d)

However, more and more scientists nowadays hold the view, even if they reject Kant's transcendental idealism, that "the physical nature of our brains limits how we perceive physical reality. Even if our reality is not a construction of our brains, the physical limits of our brains at least bias our perception of reality." (J. Beichler 1998)

(b) An opposing approach which stands in sharp contrast to Kant's transcendental idealism is a fashionable thesis in our time, that is, *the constructivist argument.*

The constructivist argument regards all information about the world as a byproduct of the social institutions and values that contribute to their construction, based on different vested interests and power formations.

Michel Foucault, for instance, had written different works on the multifaceted relationships between power and knowledge. As an illustration, he argued—in *The Order of Things* (1971) in English, or *L'Ordre des Choses* in French—that, "all periods of history possessed certain underlying conditions of truth that constituted what was acceptable....[And] these conditions of discourse changed over time, in major and relatively sudden shifts, from one period's episteme to another." (WK 2007c)

But the critics are quick to point out that the attempt to treat information about the world as an epi-phenomenon of social construction based on power formations and vested interests is too reductionistic indeed.

As an illustration, Noam Chomsky showed in *Logical Structure of Linguistic Theory* (1955) the structure of transformational grammars, in that "utterances (sequences of words)...have a syntax which can be (largely) characterized by a formal grammar; in particular, a context-free grammar extended with transformational rules. Children are hypothesized to have an innate knowledge of the basic grammatical structure common to all human languages (i.e. they assume that any language which they encounter is of a certain restricted kind). This innate knowledge is often referred to as universal grammar." (WK 2007e)

However, Chomsky changed a bit of his position in a later work titled *The Minimalist Program* (1995), in which he revised his original version of universal grammar by giving it a weaker form, that is, keeping only the "barest necessary elements, while advocating a general approach to the architecture of the human language faculty that emphasizes principles of economy and optimal design." (WK 2007e)

(c) In between the two extremes (viz., the reflective argument and the constructivist argument) is *the representational argument*, in the absence of better terms.

One good instance of the representational argument is Realism in epistemology, which treats information as representing some reality in the world. There are different versions of realism, however, and two main examples are "direct realism" and "indirect realism."

In "direct realism" (also known as "naïve realism" or "common sense realism"), the world of information is treated "pretty much as common sense would have it," because "when we look at and touch things we see and feel those things directly, and so perceive them as they really are…whether or not there is anyone present to observe them…." (WK 2007a)

A problem here is that the same information may be perceived differently by different people. Yet, someone like Myles Burnyeat's in "Conflicting Appearances" argued that this problem is really no problem at all, and his reasoning is that "[t]o say that something cannot really possess a property if it appears different at different times, from different perspectives and under different conditions, is logically equivalent to saying that something cannot really possess a property unless it always appears to possess that property." (WK 2007a)

And Burnyeat's point is, Why should we insist that something must always appear in a certain way at all? After all, "we would have to conclude that a stick that was really straight would have to, under all conditions and at all times, look straight. But clearly this is false; everyone would accept that straight sticks can look bent in water (owing to refraction), but no one thinks that this is because sticks aren't really straight." (WK 2007a)

In "indirect realism," however, direct realism is attacked in a different way, in that "we do not (and can not) perceive the external world directly; instead we know only our ideas or interpretations of objects in the world. Thus, a barrier or a veil of perception prevents first-hand knowledge of anything beyond it. The 'veil' exists between the mind and the existing world." (WK 2007b)

Aristotle, for instance, in "On the Soul," showed "how the eye must be affected by changes in an intervening medium rather than by objects themselves. He then speculates on how these sense impressions can form our experience of seeing and reasons that an endless regress would occur unless the sense itself were self-aware. He concludes by proposing that the mind is the things it thinks. He calls the images in the mind 'ideas.'" (WK 2007b)

But indirect realism poses some serious problems: "How well do sense-data represent external objects, properties, and events? Indirect realism creates deep epistemological problems, such as solipsism and the problem of the external world," but this does not prevent indirect realism from being influential among scholars like Bertrand Russell, Spinoza, René Descartes, and John Locke." (WK 2007b)

(4) Lastly, unlike the previous three approaches is my *synthetic argument*, in the absence of better terms.

My synthetic argument learns from the weaknesses and strengths of the previous three approaches—without, however, siding with any of them (or even integrating them in a harmonious whole, since they can be incompatible).

This constitutes my theoretical contribution to the debate, as summarized in the next section.

The Synthetic Theory
of Information Architecture

My *synthetic argument*, when put in the context of the information question, can be more precisely called *the synthetic theory of information architecture*, since it treats the processing, storage, and application of information into taxonomy and network from the four main perspectives of the mind, nature, society, and culture.

This theory of mine contains six major theses, namely, (a) the simpleness-complicadness principle, (b) the exactness-vagueness principle, (c) the slowness-quickness principle, (d) the order-chaos principle, (e) the symmetry-asymmetry principle, and (f) the post-human stage—to be analyzed in the rest of the book and summarized in Chapter Four (the concluding chapter) and *Table 4.2*.

Theory and Meta-Theory

Any theory, however, has a meta-theory (i.e., ontology and methodology) behind it, either explicitly or implicitly.

My theory is no exception, since it makes use of two distinctive meta-theories of mine (one on ontology and the other on methodology), namely, (a) existential dialectics and (b) sophisticated methodological holism.

A summary of (a) and (b) will be provided in the next section, for the convenience of the reader.

The Logic of Existential Dialectics

The ontology of existential dialectics can be summarized below—*often verbatim* (with only some minor revisions) from my previous works—as this is something that I regularly do as an introduction to some background information for the convenience of the reader (since this book, like all others of mine, is in conversation with all previous ones of mine, for the final aim to converge all of them into a larger grand project on the future of intelligent life, both here on earth and there in deep space unto multiverses).

The summary can be organized in relation to (a) the conception of existential dialectics, (b) the syntax of existential dialectics, (c) the semantics of existential dialectics, and (d) the pragmatics of existential dialectics, respectively hereafter—again *often verbatim*.

The Conception of Existential Dialectics

This ontology was originally designated as "existential dialectics" in *Beyond Capitalism to Post-Capitalism* (herein abbreviated as *BCPC*), although it was already analyzed in other books of mine like the 2 volumes of *The Future of Human Civilization* (*FHC*), *The Future of Capitalism and Democracy* (*FCD*), *The Future of Post-Human Consciousness* (*FPHC*), and the 2 volumes of *Beyond Democracy to Post-Democracy* (*BDPD*).

Lest any confusion occurs, it is important to stress at the outset that the word 'existential' in "existential dialectics" has nothing to do with Existentialism, which I rebuked in *FHC*, *FCD*, and also *FPHC*. Instead, the word merely refers to the existence of intelligent life (both primitive and advanced), in a broad sense.

The conception of existential dialectics makes use of different concepts (like "sets," "elements," "relations," "operations," "functions," "truth values," "axioms," "postulates," and "principles"—as shown in *Table 1.7*), which are important for the understanding of any logic of ontology.

That clarified—existential dialectics, as a language of ontology, can be analyzed in different ways that a language, as an analogy, is often analyzed, namely, in relation to phonology ("the study of patterns of a language's sounds"), phonetics ("the study of the physical aspects of sounds of human language"), morphonology ("the study of the internal structure of words"), syntax ("the study of how words combine to form grammatical sentences"), semantics ("the study of the meaning of words [lexical semantics] and fixed word combinations [phraseology]"), and pragmatics ("the study of how utterances are used...literally, figuratively, or otherwise...in communicative acts"). (WK 2007)

But since my theory of existential dialectics makes use of the English language for communication here, it does not propose a new way to make the patterns of a language's sounds (as in phonology), to study the physical aspects of sounds (as in phonetics), or even to strive for a new organization of the internal structure of words for the English language (as in morphonology).

For this reason, the language of existential dialectics to be analyzed hereafter is not concerned with the phonological, phonetic, and morphonological aspects of the English language. Instead, the analysis will explore the syntax, semantics, and pragmatics of existential dialectics as a language of ontology to improve our understanding of reality.

Let's consider first the syntax of existential dialectics first below, to be followed with the analysis of the semantics and pragmatics of the ontology, respectively.

The Syntax of Existential Dialectics

The syntax of existential dialectics, analogously speaking, refers here to the structure of an ontology which can be studied by way of combining ideas into complex relationships like ontological principles to depict reality in the world.

The Selection Criteria

To start, not any pair of relationship can be chosen as an ontological principle in existential dialectics; otherwise, there could be billions of them under the sky.

Four illustrations below suffice to clarify this point.

(a) Firstly, an ontological principle cannot *overlap* with other principles, in that it is too closely related with other ones.

Of course, one cannot totally rule out any relationship between two entities, especially in a complex world of everything being linked to everything else—but the comparison here is relative, not absolute.

In this sense, the flexibility-inflexibility pair cannot be an ontological principle, since it has something closely in common with other ones (like the simpleness-complicatedness principle, for instance).

As an illustration, something which is flexible in interpretation is more likely to allow multiple viewpoints and thus makes the overall picture more complicated than otherwise (simple).

(b) Secondly, an ontological principle cannot be *redundant* in relation to other principles, in that it somehow duplicates other principles.

In this sense, for instance, the directness-indirectness pair cannot be an ontological principle, because it somehow duplicates other ontological principles (like the preciseness-vagueness principle, for instance).

As an illustration, something which is direct means to be right to the point and does not need to go to an unnecessarily long loop—so it is less vague, in being clearer about the thing in quesiton.

(c) Thirdly, an ontological principle cannot be *derived* from other ones—as if it is a child-parent relationship.

In this sense, the convenience-inconvenience pair cannot be an ontological principle, because it can be derived from other ones (like the slowness-quickness principle, for instance).

For instance, something which is convenient already implies that it can be obtained quickly (rather than slowly)—all things considered.

(d) Fourthly, an ontological principle cannot be *trivial* (or *parochial*)—as if it is only one component competing with other ones for inclusion in a set.

In this sense, the consistency-inconsistency pair cannot be an ontological principle, because its validity is limited (or parochial), as it can be easily challenged and replaced by opposing major (not minor) theories (e.g., the correspondence theory of truth, the pragmatic theory of truth, the semantic theory of truth, and whatnot), not just in accordance to the consistency theory of truth (for consistency).

In this sense, the consistency argument is only one among different opposing arguments in relation to the logic of what constitutes "truth."

Although these examples are not exhaustive, they illustrative the selectiveness of any ontological principle to be existentially dialectic.

The Principles of Existential Dialectics

With these selection criteria in mind—the first three principles in the ontological logic of existential dialectics were introduced in *BCPC*. And more principles were later added to the logic in my subsequent books (like *FC*, *FAE*, and others).

More specifically, in *BCPC*, I proposed three principles (based on previous works of mine, not just something out of the blue) for the ontological logic, namely, (a) the regression-progression principle on the direction of history, (b) the symmetry-asymmetry principle on the relationships among existents, and (c) the change-constancy principle on the alteration of things—or in a more elegant term, the dynamics of space-time (in *FC*).

Then in *The Future of Complexity* (*FC*), I added three more principles, on top of the three aforementioned, namely, (d) the partiality-totality principle on the relationships between the parts and the whole, (e) the order-chaos principle on the pattern of things, and (f) the predictability-unpredictability principle on the occurrence of things—as part of the ontological logic of existential dialectics.

And in *The Future of Aesthetic Experience* (or simply *FAE*), another principle is added, namely, (g) the evolution-transformation principle (on the multiple kinds of agency).

In *FAE*, I then reclassified the 7 principles into four categories, namely, (i) in relation to method, for the partiality-totality principle and the predictability-unpredictability principle, (ii) in relation to process, for the change-constancy principle and the order-chaos principle, (iii) in relation to agency, for the symmetry-asymmetry principle and the evolution-transformation principle, and (iv) in relation to outcome, for the regression-progression principle.

In *The Rise of Authoritarian Liberal Democracy* (*ALD*), I added two more principles, namely, (h) the softness-hardness principle on the force of agency (which is to be classified in the category about agency) and (i) the same-difference principle about the metamorposis of change (which is to be classified in the category about outcome).

And in *The Future of Information Architecture* (*FIA*), I introduce three additional principles, that is, (j) the simpleness-complicadness principle on the interconnection among things, (k) the preciseness-vagueness principle on the refinement of things, and (l) the slowness-quickness principle on the speed of change—with the first two in relation to structure and the third in relation to process.

With this update, there are twelve principles so far in existential dialectics, that is, two principles for the category in relation to method (viz., the partiality-totality principle and the predictability-unpredictability principle), two principles for the category in relation to structure (viz., the simpleness-complicatedness principle and the preciseness-vagueness principle), three principles for the category in relation to process (viz., the change-constancy principle, the slowness-quickness principle, and the order-chaos principle), three principles for the category in relation to agency (viz., the symmetry-asymmetry principle, the evolution-transformation principle, and the softness-hardness principle), and two principles for the category in relation to outcome (viz., the regression-progression principle and the same-difference principle).

There are thus twelve principles in existential dialectics—so far (as summarized in *Table 1.8*).

The Dialectic Constraints Imposed by the Principles

The principles, as they constitute the syntax of existential dialectics, are dialectic in character, such that, when they are applied, they impose dialectic constraints on how reality is to be understood.

Consider, say, the symmetry-asymmetry principle as an illustration here, in order to summarize two main characters of the dialectic constraints in question (as summarized in *Table 1.9*).

Firstly, to be dialectic here is to go beyond the narrow dichotomies (and, for that matter, any rigid multi-dimensional classificatory scheme), be they about "self" vs. "world," "freedom" vs. "unfreedom," "barbarity" vs. "civilization," "individuality" vs. "communality," and so on.

One way to do so (to go beyond) is to consider them all in terms of co-existence (without favoring one over the rest). For instance, my theory of "post-civilization" (to be summarized later in the section on the pragmatics of existential dialectics) is to go beyond barbarity and civilization in terms of understanding barbarity and civilization as being co-existent.

And the same logic can be said in relation to my theories of "post-democracy," "post-capitalsm," and others (also to be introduced later in the section on the pragmatics of existential dialectics), in regard to freedom vs. unfreedom, equality vs. inequality, communality vs. individuality, spirituality vs. materiality, and so on.

But to consider them all (in the dichotomies—and, for that matter, in any rigid multi-dimensional classifactory schme) as co-existent is not the same as to imply that the opposing categories in any classificatory scheme are all equal, since, in accordance to the symmetry-asymmetry principle (as an illustration here), if they are equal in terms of being considered as co-existent, they are asymmetric in terms of being unequal in dialectic interaction (e.g., X can be more dominant than Y in case A, or Y is more dominant than X in case B).

For this reason, there are different versions of "post-democracy" and "post-capitalism" in my theories. As an illustration, in version I of the theory of post-democracy, freedom is more dominant than equality, whereas in version II of the theory of post-democracy, equality is more so than freedom.

But this "X more than Y" has to be understood in the context of dialectic logic (not in symbolic logic, as conventionally understood), in that both "X" and "Y" are important in post-democracy (in the context of dialectic logic), but in an asymmetry way. By contrast, in symbolic logic, it often favors one over the other—be it in regard to privileging freedom over equality in Fascism, favoring freedom relatively more than equality in Liberal Democracy, or favoring equality relatively more than freedom in Socialist Democracy. In regard to the latter two cases (about Liberal Democracy and Socialist Democracy), the difference between dialectic logic and symbolic logic can be one in degree, not in kind—in this sense, albeit not in other senses.

The same reasoning can be said about the relatonships between individuality and communality, between spirituality and materiality, and between formal legalism and informal legalism in the different versions of my theory of "post-capitalism."

Secondly, to be dialectic is to go beyond the narrow dichotomies (and, for that matter, any rigid multi-dimensional classificatory scheme) in another way, this time, in a transcendent way, that is, in exploring other possibilities or even other issues not considered within the narrow confines of narrow dichotomies (and, for that matter, any rigid multi-dimensional classificatory scheme).

As an analogy, in this second meaning, to go beyond the narrow dichotomy of "black" vs. "white" is not just to choose both "black" and "white" (as in the first meaning) but also to explore other options (e.g., "green," "purple," "blue," etc.—and, alternatively, "shade," "line," "curve," etc.).

By the same reasoning, to go beyond "democracy" is to transcend democracy (as in version III of my theory of "post-democracy") and to explore other possibilties of lifeforms (e.g., "floating consciousness," "hyper-spatial consciousness," etc., to live beyond the narrow obsession with freedom and equality).

This dialectic character of the principles in existential dialectics has important implications for the pragmatics of existential dialectics (as will be clear shortly, in the section on the pragmatics of existential dialectics).

The Semantics of Existential Dialectics

The syntax of existential dialectics so understood in terms of ontological principles only gives us the structure of ontology in the world, in an abstract (general) sense. These principles by themselves do not tell us the specific meanings in a given context.

In order to grasp the specific meanings of the principles in a given context, it is necessary to study the semantics of existential dialectics (as summarized in *Table 1.10*).

For this reason, I have often gone in great lengths in my previous books on different subjects to explain the specific meanings of the principles when applied in different contexts.

For instance, in *FPHST*, I used the first three principles (i.e., the change-constancy principle, the regression-progression principle, and the symmetry-asymmetry principle) to propose "the perspectival theory of space-time," for a better way to understand space and time—especially, though not exclusively, in relation to future post-human history (as summarized in *Table 1.18*, *Table 1.19*, *Table 1.20*, and *Table 1.21*). In so doing, I had to introduce concepts and theories specific to the field of physics and other related fields (e.g., "absolute space" and "absolute time" in "classical mechanics" and "relative space-time" in "the theory of relativity").

In *BNN*, I also exploited the three principles to propose the "transcendent" approach to the study of genes and memes as a new way to understand the interaction between nature and nurture. In so doing, I had to explore concepts and theories in the world of evolutionary biology (e.g., "mutation," "variation," "adaptation," "selection," and "inheritance" in evolutionary theory) and neural biology (e.g., "chromosome," "gene," "DNA," "RNA," "protein," "neuron," "neural network," and "behavior").

The Pragmatics of Existential Dialectics

Even the semantics of existential dialectics is not enough to understand reality, since semantics by itself does not tell us the nature of intentionality in relation to the matrix of power formations and human interests when existential dialectics as an ontology is applied.

For this reason, the pragmatics of existential dialectics needs to be studied too, in special relation to the inclusion of power formation and human interests in the application of the principles of existential dialectics (as summarized in *Table 1.11*).

It is thus no wonder that all my previous books have shown in different ways how and why these ontological principles and their theoretical applications can reveal the future world to come in a way that humans have never known, in a totally different battleground for competing human (and later post-human) interests by myriad groups fighting for their own versions of hegemony.

Perhaps a summary of my previous works in relation to existential dialectics and their contributions to my new theories as proposed over the years is deemed revealing here, for the further understanding of the pragmatics of existential dialectics (in close relation to the semantics of existential dialectics too).

That stressed—the following summary in the next four sub-sections is something that I often do in my previous books too, as a way to introduce the intellectual background of my ideas. So, for those reader who had read my previous works, the following sub-sections serve as a reminder, as they are repeated hereafter *often verbatim* (with only some minor changes, with the rest kept intact).

The Two-Way Street Connecting Theory and Meta-Theory

However, lest misunderstanding occurs, it is more important to remember that the pragmatics of existential dialectics is not a one-way street (that is, using the ontological principles for theoretical insights in praxis) but a two-way one, namely, (a) from meta-theory to theory, and (b) from theory to meta-theory.

(a) On one side of the street, the ontological principles can inspire some theoretical insights in praxis, that is, in relation to some specific fields.

(b) On the other (opposing) side of the street, however, the study of a subject matter in the specific fields in turn reveals some more hitherto unknown ontological principles to be discovered and identified. For this reason, three new principles were added in *FC*, one in *FAE*, two in *ALD*, and three in *FIA*, on top of the original three in *BCPC*—after some research on the specific subject matters.

Both theory and meta-theory enrich each other in all my works over the years.

The Theoretical Application of Existential Dialectics

For instance, at the beginning, in *FHC*, two examples of the theoretical application of existential dialectics are to reveal no freedom without unfreedom (as shown in *Table 1.12*) and no equality without inequality (as shown in *Table 1.13*), especially in relation to the seven dimensions of life existence first worked out in *FHC* (i.e., the technological, the everyday, the true, the holy, the sublime/beautiful, the good, and the just).

In Ch.10 of *FCD*, the relationship between these two examples of the theoretical application of existential dialectics was extended further, so as to provide some new visions to understand the future forms of political and economic systems.

In regard to politics, my vision of a path-breaking political system in future times concerns the different forms of "post-democracy" to supersede democracy unto the post-human age. My vision of post-democracy was called "the theory of post-democracy" (as summarized in *Table 4.12*, *Table 4.13*, and *Table 4.14*), whereas *Table 4.15* explains the distinctions among democracy, non-democracy, and post-democracy. And *Table 4.16* stresses the multiple causes of the emergence of post-democracy, while *Table 4.17* clarifies some possible misunderstandings in regard to post-capitalism and post-democracy.

In regard to economics, I also offered another vision, this time to understand the future forms of economic systems, that is, the different forms of "post-capitalism" to supersede capitalism unto the post-human age. My vision of post-capitalism was referred to (in *FCD*, *BDPD* and *BCPC*) as "the theory of post-capitalism" (as summarized in *Table 4.18*, *Table 4.19*, *Table 4.20*, *Table 4.21*, and *Table 4.22*). And *Table 4.23* clarifies the differences among capitalism, non-capitalism, and post-capitalism, whereas *Table 4.24* shows multiple causes of the emergence of post-capitalism. This vision on "post-capitalism" constitutes the third theoretical application of existential dialectics, this time, in that there is no wealth without poverty (or the wealth/poverty dialectics).

More importantly, these existential constraints hold true for the age of pre-modernity, modernity, post-modernity, and, in the future, what I originally suggested in *FHC* as "after-postmodernity"—as shown in *Table 1.1*, *Table 1.2*, *Table 1.3*, and *Table 1.4*.

This is all the more so, in the "post-human" age at some distant point of "after-postmodernity," long after human extinction, to be eventually superseded by post-humans of various forms. Some good candidates of the post-human lifeforms include, for instance, thinking robots, thinking machines, cyborgs, genetically altered superior beings, floating consciousness, and hyper-spatial consciousness. This post-human vision of mine was first originally worked out in *FHC* and further elaborated in both *FCD* and *FPHC*, for instance.

In the end, a most fundamental question about intelligent life now has an answer, in that, if asked, "What is the future of human civilization?"—my answer in *FCD* (89) is thus: "As addressed in Ch.7 of *FHC*, a later epoch of the age of after-postmodernity (that is, at some point further away from after-postmodernity) will begin, as what I called the 'post-human' history (with the term 'post-human' originally used in my doctoral dissertation at M.I.T., which was finished in November 1995, under the title *After Postmodernity*, still available at M.I.T. library, and was later revised and published as *FHC*). The post-human history will be such that humans are nothing in the end, other than what culture, society, and nature (with some luck) have shaped them into, to be eventually superseded by post-humans (e.g., cyborgs, thinking machines, genetically altered superior beings, and others), if humans are not destroyed long before then."

A conclusion which is shocking indeed for many contemporaries is none other than that "[t]he post-human history will therefore mark the end of human history as we know it and, for that matter, the end of human dominance and, practically speaking, the end of humans as well. The entire history of human civilization, from its beginning to the end, can be summarized by four words, linked by three arrows (as already discussed in *FHC*)":

Pre-Modernity → Modernity → Post-Modernity →
After-Postmodernity

In *BDPD*, this thesis of mine was specifically called "the theory of the evolution from pre-modernity to after-postmodernity," at the historical level.

Therefore, "[t]he end of humanity in the coming human extinction is the beginning of post-humanity. To say an untimely farewell to humanity is to foretell the future welcome of post-humanity." (P. Baofu 2002: 89) This thesis of mine was known in *BDPD* as "the theory of post-humanity," at the systemic level.

In Ch.9 of *FCD* (367-8), I further showed "that civilizational history will continue into the following cyclical progression of expansion, before it is to be superseded (solely as a high probability, since humans might be destroyed sooner either by themselves or in a gigantic natural calamity) by posthumans at some distant point in after-postmodernity (which I already discussed in *FHC*)" unto multiverses (different constellations of universes):

Local → Regional → Global → Solar → Galactic →
Clustery... → Multiversal

In *BDPD*, this thesis of mine was referred to as "the theory of the cyclical progression of system integration and fragmentation," at the systemic level.

In *BWT*, a different version of this thesis is "the theory of cyclical progression of empire-building," at multiple levels (e.g., institutional, structural, systemic, and others), in providing a better way to understand the logic of empire-building on earth and beyond.

In *BNN*, I further worked out "the theory of contrastive advantages" (which was originally proposed in *FCD*), to show the nature-nurture interactions of multiple levels in action (e.g., the biological, the psychological, the structural, the systemic, the cultural, and others) for humans and post-humans on earth and beyond, to the extent that different groups, be they on the basis of race, gender, ethnicity, class, age, or else, are not equal, on average, and have never been, nor will they be.

In fact, even greater transformations are yet to come in the post-human age. For instance, even the existence of human consciousness will be superseded one day too, with "floating consciousness" and "hyper-spatial consciousness" (as elaborated in *FPHC*) as a climax of evolution in consciousness, after the future extinction of human consciousness:

Primordial consciousness → Human consciousness →
Post-human consciousness (with floating consciousness and hyper-spatial consciousness as a climax in the evolution of consciousness)

In *BDPD*, these latest theses of mine were called "the theory of floating consciousness" and "the theory of hyper-spatial consciousness," both at the cosmological and psychological levels (as summarized in *Table 4.11* and *Table 4.10*, together with *Table 4.7* on the conceptual dimensions of consciousness, *Table 4.8* on the theoretical levels of consciousness, and *Table 4.9* on the theoretical debate on nature and nurture).

But this is not the end of the matter yet.

The Further Use of Existential Dialectics

Even more interestingly, in *BDPD* and later in *BCIV*, I further revealed a theoretical refinement of existential dialectics, this time, in arguing that there is no civilization without barbarity, with human civilization to be eventually superseded by what I originally analyzed as "post-human post-civilization" (which should not be confused with "post-human civilization"), in the context of the freedom/unfreedom and equality/inequality dialectics.

In the final analysis, civilization cannot live without barbarity and has to learn to co-exist with it in ever new ways. Preposteorus as this may seem to many contemporaries—it is no more imperative to preserve civilization than necessary to destroy barbarity, and the ideal of civilization is essentially bankrupt, to be eventually superseded by "post-civilization" (as summarized in *Tables 4.25-4.33*).

Yet, this requires some understanding of my analysis of the trinity of modernity and other ages. For instance, in both *FCD* and *FPHC*, I worked out the structure of "post-human civilization" in terms of the trinity of after-postmodernity (i.e., "free-spirited after-postmodernity," "post-capitalist after-postmodernity," and "hegemonic after-postmodernity").

Both conceptually and theoretically, the trinity of after-postmodernity is a sequential extension to the trinity of modernity (i.e., "free-spirited modernity," "capitalist modernity,"and "hegemonic modernity") and the trinity of postmodernity (i.e., "free-spirited postmodernity," "capitalist postmodernity," and "hegemonic postmodernity") as first proposed in *FHC*.

And the trinity of pre-modernity (i.e., "pre-free-spirited pre-modernity," "pre-capitalist pre-modernity" and "hegemonic pre-modernity") was later conceived in *BCIV* to complete the historical set from pre-modernity to after-postmodernity.

In *BDPD*, this thesis about the trinity of pre-modernity, modernity, postmodernity, and after-postmodernity was collectively known as "the theory of the trinity of modernity to its after-postmodern counterpart," at the cultural level (as summarized in *Table 1.1*, *Table 1.2*, *Table 1.3*, and *Table 1.4*).

At the structural level, all these trinities are subject to the existential constraints (e.g., the freedom/unfreedom and equality/inequality dialectics in the context of "the cyclical progression of hegemony"), be the historical epoch in pre-modernity,   modernity, postmodernity, or after-postmodernity in future times. Each of the historical epochs has its ever new ways of coming to terms with the ever new (different) mixtures of freedom/unfreedom and equality/inequality.

This is importantly so, not because, as is falsely assumed in conventional wisdom, one certain way is superior (or better) than another in terms of achieving more freedom and less unfreedom, or more equality with less inequality.

On the contrary, indeed, in each of the historical epochs, each increase of unfreedom greets each freedom achieved, just as each increase of inequality welcomes each equality achieved, albeit in ever new (different) ways. In *BDPD*, this thesis of mine was labeled as "the theory of the cyclical progression of hegemony," at the structural level, though it was first analyzed in *FCD*.

In *BDPD*, more theoretical applications of existential dialectics were further examined, in relation to five main features, in the context of the duality of oppression, namely, (a) that each freedom/equality achieved is also each unfreedom/inequality created, (b) that the subsequent oppressiveness is dualistic, both by the Same against the Others and itself and by the Others against the Same and themselves, (c) that both oppression and self-oppression can be achieved by way of downgrading differences (between the Same and the Others) and of accentuating them, (d) that the relationships are relatively asymmetric among them but relatively symmetric within them, even when the Same can be relatively asymmetric towards itself in self-oppression, and the Others can be likewise towards themselves, and (e) that symmetry and asymmetry change over time, with ever new players, new causes, and new forms, be the locality here on Earth or in deep space unto multiverses—as summarized in *Table.1.12*, *Table 1.13*, *Table 1.14*, and *Table 1.15*.

The same logic also holds both in relation to wealth and poverty (as addressed in *BCPC* and summarized in *Table 1.16* on the wealth/poverty dialectics) and in relation to civilization and barbarity (as addressed in *BCIV* and summarized in *Table 1.17* on the civilization/barbarity dialectics).

In *BDPD*, this thesis on existential dialectics was labeled as "the theory of existential dialectics,".

Direct and Indirect Applications of Existential Dialectics

A different way to appreciate the usefulness of existential dialectics is by way of the analysis of its (a) direct and (b) indirect applications.

(a) In direct applications, on the one hand, the logic of existential dialectics can shed some theoretical insights on diverse phenomena in the world, and good instances are the usage of the principles of existential dialectics for the theoretical insights on the freedom/unfreedom dialectics, the equality/inequality dialectics, and the wealth/poverty dialectics (as introduced above).

My books like *FPHST* and *BNN* also use the principles to reveal some theoretical insights on the perspectives of space and time (as in *FPHST*) and of nature and nurture (as in *BNN*).

(b) In indirect applications, on the other hand, the theoretical insights can further be used to reveal other phenomena directly from them (viz., the theoretical insights) and therefore indirectly from the principles themselves.

A good illustration is of course the use of the theoretical insights on the freedom/unfreedom and equality/inequality dialectics for the understanding of the civilization/barbarity dialectics.

This distinction between direct and indirect applications may sound a bit academic, since even in indirect applications, the phenomena under study can still be directly related back to the principles themselves.

In the previous example, as an illustration, the civilization/barbarity dialectics can be directly related to the principles of existential dialectics without the intermediate role of the freedom/unfreedom and equality/inequality dialectics.

Multiple Levels of Application

There is another issue to be clarified, however. In other words, the theoretical insights can be applied to multiple levels of analysis—even though, in a given example, it may refer to one level or a few only.

For instance, in the example concerning the freedom/unfreedom dialectics, it can be used at the structural level (e.g., in relation to the theory of the cyclical progression of hegemony), but it can also be exploited for other levels (e.g., the theory of post-capitalism at the institutional level).

All these levels of application should not be misleadingly construed, as I stress this before, as a one-way street (that is, to use the ontological principles for theoretical application at multiple levels of specific analysis) but a two-way one, in which theoretical insights in praxis, when studied in more specific contexts, can in turn refine the nature of existential dialectics (for example, with the addition of new principles).

Sophisticated Methodological Holism

The summary of my original meta-theory on methodology is provided below, again *often verbatim* from my previous works.

This original contribution of mine to the study of methodology takes the form of an approach known as "the theory of methodological holism" or "methodological holism" in short, as already worked out in *FPHC* (2004).

I have made good use of this methodological approach of mine for all of my previous works.

Yet, it is imperative to stress at the outset, as I have so emphasized in all my previous books, that my approach of "methodological holism" does not oppose or exclude "methodological individualism" (as some reader may be tempted to assume, as is conventionally understood) but actually includes it.

For this reason (and others too, as summarized in *Table 1.5*), my version of methodological holism is *sophisticated*—not *vulgar* as sometimes used by inapt scholars employing the same term.

The Ontological Constraints

Sophisticated methodological holism is subject to some ontological constraints, and two good examples (although there are more than two) include "the partiality-totality principle" and "the predictability-unpredictability principle" in existential dialectics (as originally introduced in previous books of mine, namely, *The Future of Complexity*, or in short *FC*, and *The Future of Aesthetic Experience*, or in short *FAE*). This issue about ontology was already summarized in the previous section.

For now, it suffices to show that sophisticted methodological holism, because of these ontological constraints on methodology, targets two major sins of methodology, namely, what I call, in the absence of better words, (a) *reductionism* and (b) *reverse-reductionism*—both of which come in all shapes and sizes, to be summarized below (and also shown in *Table 1.6*).

Against the Varieties of Reductionism

There are four versions of reductionism to be summarized here, which sophisticated methodological holism rejects, namely, (a1) conceptual, (a2) theoretical, (a3) methodological, and (a4) ontological forms of reductionism.

(a1) In methodological reductionism, a good illustration can be the debate between different versions of qualitative and quantitative methods (as already analyzed in *FC* and also *FHC*).

(a2) In ontological reductionism, an excellent instance involves another debate, this time between emergentism and reductionism in complexity theory (as addressed in *FC*) and also in psychology (as elaborated in *FPHC*, in the context of Being and Belonging).

(a3) In conceptual reductionism, a good case in point concerns myriad dualities like mind vs. body, self vs. world, democracy vs non-democracy, and the like (as already addressed in *FHC*, *FPHC*, and *BDPD*, for instance).

(a4) In theoretical reductionism, an illuminating case study is best exemplified by what I originally called "the foundation fallacy" in *FPHST*, in any attempt to naively understand space-time from the physical perspective as the foundation and, consequently, to dangerously dismiss (or belittle) other perspectives.

In *FAE*, I elaborated further these versions of reductionism in the literature on aesthetics (e.g., form vs. content, representation vs. expression, crtics vs. artists, and externalism vs. internalism).

And in *FIA*, I reveal other forms of reductionism in the literature on information architecture (e.g., the constructivist argument).

Against the Varieties of Reverse-Reductionism

The other side of the same coin is of course the reverse version of reductionism, which is what I want to call, in the absence of better words, *reverse-reductionism*. My sophisticated version of methodological holism targets against the varieties of reverse-reductionism (just as it also rejects the ones of reductionism).

Perhaps nothing expresses better the popularity of reverse-reductionim than the "anything-goes" mentality in postmodernism of our time, as shown in the following four versions.

(b1) In conceptual reverse-reductionism, any concept of "art" (e.g., fine art, applied art, outsider art, junk art) is welcome in postmodernism (as already analyzed in Ch.4 of *FHC*—and also in *FAE*).

(b2) In theoretical reverse-reductionism, a variety of art and literary theories co-exist. Take the case of literature, as there are now Literary Structuralism, Marxist Literary Criticism, New Criticism, Phenomenology, Hermeneutics, Language-Game Literary Criticism, Feminist Literary Criticism, Reception Theory, Reader Response Criticism, Poststructuralism, Semiotics, Pyschoanalytic Literary Criticism, just to cite some well-known ones, with no one being said to be better than any others (as detailedly analyzed in Ch.4 of *FHC*). (S. Raman 1997) In *BNN*, I even introduced "the compromise fallacy" as another good illustration of theoretical reverse-reductionism, in misleadingly treating both genetic and environmental approaches as equally valid.

(b3) In methodological reverse-reductionism, multiple methodologies are deemed as acceptable in postmodernism (e.g., doing art without praxis, doing art with praxis, and doing art by sublation), as analyzed in Ch.4 of *FHC*.

(b4) In ontological reverse-reductionism, no privileged ontology is allowed, and the door is open practically for anything in postmodernism (e.g., the equal status of the ontology of Being vs. that of Becoming, as already addressed in Ch.4 of *FHC*—and also in *FPHC*).

In *FAE*, I also introduced another version of reverse-reductionism, that is, "the pluralist fallacy," in the context of understanding aesthetic experience, for instance.

These dual dangers against reverse-reductionism (in this sub-section) and reductionism (in the previous sub-section) are something that sophisticated methodological holism rejects.

The Holistic Organization of an Inquiry

With these dual dangers against reductionism and reverse-reductionism in mind—sophisticated methodological holism suggests that an inquiry of any given phenomenon is more complete, if treated in the context of a comprehensive analysis at all relevant levels, which challengingly encompass all the fields of human knowledge, ranging from the natural sciences through the social sciences to the humanities.

This section is something that I had already stressed in all my previous books and repeat (*often verbatim*) hereafter. But, for those readers who had read my previous books, this serves as a reminder.

With this reminder in mind—there are multiple ways to engage in a holistic inquiry with all relevent levels of analysis. Over the years, I have proposed different ways to fulfill this holistic methodological requirement, as repeated in my previous books.

Hereafter is a summary of four major ways, namely, (i) by discipline, (ii) by domain, (iii) by subject, and (iv) by meta-analysis—all of which fulfill the holistic requirement of sophisticated methodological holism on a given issue.

(i) In a holistic organization by discipline, a good illustration is the multiple levels of analysis, namely, (i1) the micro-physical, (i2) the chemical, (i3) the biological, (i4) the psychological, (i5) the organizational, (i6) the institutional, (i7) the structural, (i8) the systemic, (i9) the cultural, (i10) the macro-physical (cosmological), and (i11) other relevant levels, which are either a combination of all these levels or the practical applications with a combination of them. This holistic organization is used in *FCD* and *BCPC*, for instance.

(ii) In a holistic organization by domain, some good candidates include the classification of different perspectives of analysis in relation to (ii1) nature, (ii2) the mind, (ii3) society, and (ii4) culture, as already worked out in *BCIV*, *FPHST*, *FC*, and *FAE*.

In this re-classification, culture in (ii4) is the same as culture in (i9). Society in (ii3) includes the organizational in (i5), the institutional in (i6), the structural in (i7), and the systemic in (i8). The mind (ii3) has more to do with the chemical in (i2), the biological in (i3), and the psychological in (i4), although it can overlap with (i1), (ii3) and (ii4), for instance. And nature in (ii1) refers to the micro-physical in (i1) and the macro-physical (cosmological) in (i10), although it can also overlap with (i2), (i3) and (i4).

(iii) In a holistic organization by subject, some excellent examples concern the analysis of consciousness in *FPHC* (i.e., on Having, Belonging, and Being), of civilization in *FHC* (i.e., the True, the Holy, the Everyday, the Technological, the Beautiful/Sublime, the Good, and the Just), of international politics in *BWT* (i.e., Hyper-Empires, Meso-Empires, and Micro-Empires), of nature and nurture in *BNN* (i.e., genes and memes), and of taxonomy and network in *FIA*—by incorporating all the relevent levels of analysis as cited above in each.

(iv) In a holistic organization by meta-analysis, two good cases in point involve the works on post-capitalism in *BCPC* and on authoritarian liberal democracy in *ALD*, with the classification of analysis in theory and meta-theory.

The essential point to remember here, as I thus stress in all my previous books, is that the multiple levels of analysis can be reorganized in many different ways, insofar as none of the levels (if relevant to an inquiry in question) is ignored or dismissed, to avoid the danger of reductionism (and for that matter, the one of reverse-reductionism, in the opposite direction).

Three Clarifications

Three clarifications are needed here, however, to avoid hasty misunderstanding.

Firstly, the entities in each classification are not mutually exclusive. For instance, in the holisitc organization by domain, nature in (ii1) can also be linked to the chemical in (i2), the biological in (i3), and the systemic in (i8). And the mind (ii3) can alternatively be related to the micro-physical in (i1) and the chemical in (i2), for example.

Secondly, there is also the important factor of luck (or uncertainty in conventional usage), but it is already implied or allowed in each of the organizations of an inquiry—especially in relation to the predictability-unpredictability principle in existential dialectics (as will be elaborated in Chapter Three).

And lastly, the comparison in a classification is not absolute, but relative, as there are often some shades of gray, not exactly black or white (figuratively speaking).

Some further clarifications and qualifications of sophisticated methodological holism are shown in *Table 1.5*.

Chapter Outline

With this summary of my two unique meta-theories (on methodology and ontology, *almost verbatim* from my previous works) in mind—this book is then organized in four main parts, namely, (a) Part I on the introduction of this book, (b) Part II on taxonomy, (c) Part III on network, and (d) Part IV on the conclusion of this book.

In Part I (on the introduction) is the introductory chapter, namely, Chapter One, titled *Introduction: The Role of Information Architecture,* which begins with the vital question concerning the role of information within the context of the larger theoretical debate in the literature, my original synthetic theory of information architecture, the summary of my previuos work on meta-theory, and some qualifications about the book project (as will be described shortly).

In Part II (on taxonomy) is Chapter Two, titled *Information Architecture and Taxonomy,* which provides a critical examination of the nature of data taxonomy from the main perspectives of culture, society, nature, and the mind.

In Part III (on network) is Chapter Three, titled *Information Architecture and Network,* which constructively investigates the world of info network from the main perspectives of culture, society, nature, and the mind.

In Part IV (on the conclusion) is the concluding chapter, namely, Chapter Eight, titled *Conclusion: The Future of Information Architecture,* which proposes six main theses in my synthetic theory of information architecture, namely, (a) the first thesis on the simpleness-complicatedness principle, (b) the second thesis on the exactness-vagueness principle, (c) the third thesis on the slowness-quickness principle, (d) the fourth thesis on the order-chaos principle, (e) the fifth thesis on the symmetry-asymmetry principle, and (f) the sixth thesis on the post-human stage.

In the end, the analysis of the role of information architecture helps us understand how and why information is processed, stored, and arranged in the way that it has since time immemorial—and the educated prediction of its future also enhances our comprehension of the multifaceted working of intelligent life, both here on earth and out there in deep space unto multiverses.

Three Notes of Caution

Nevertheless, there are three notes of caution to be made here, in order to avoid any potential misunderstanding by the reader, namely, in relation to (a) the conversation with my previous books, (b) the number of case studies and examples, and (c) the use of neologisms.

These notes are something that I often stressed in my previous books too, so these points are repeated hereafter, *often verbatim.*

In Conversation with My Previous Books

Firstly, my synthetic theory of information architecture is constructed on the theoretical foundation of my previous books (i.e., *FHC, FCD, FPHC, BDPD, BCPC, BCIV, FPHST, BNN, BWT, FC, FAE,* and *ALD*—as explicated in "The List of Abbreviations," on page xix).

Although a summary of my previous books is provided whenever necessary, as shown in the two sections above (*often verbatim*) and in different tables at the end of some chapters, I still expect the reader to read my previous books directly for more details.

Case Studies and Examples

Secondly, the case studies and examples used throughout the book are not exhaustive but solely illustrative. Nor are they necessarily mutually exclusive, as they can be reclassified in a different way. And exceptions are allowed.

One is tempted to assume, however, that, since the case studies and their examples are not exhaustive, more case studies and examples are needed. But the problem here is that just adding more of them does not necessarily change much of the conclusions to be drawn and may even lead to redundancy.

After all, the case studies and examples used in this book are chosen with care and deemed sufficient for the purpose at hand, even though they are solely illustrative.

The Use of Neologisms

And lastly, I use different neologisms in my books, mostly to introduce my original concepts and theories, and good instances include those here or elsewhere in my previous books (e.g., "the synthetic theory of information architecture," "the exactness-vagueness principle," "the simpleness-complicatedness principle," "post-democracy," "hyper-spatial consciousness," "post-capitalism," and whatnot). Needless to say, they are used here solely for our current intellectual convenience, as they will be renamed differently in different ways in future history.

As I thus wrote in *FCD* (508-9), "all these terms 'post-capitalism,' 'post-democracy'...and other ones as introduced in...[the] project (e.g.,...'posthuman elitists,' and 'posthuman counter-elitists,' just to cite a few of them) are more for our current intellectual convenience than to the liking of future humans and post-humans, who will surely invent more tasteful neologisms to call their own eras, entities, and everything else, for that matter. But the didactic point here is to use the terms to foretell what the future might be like, not that its eras and entities must be called so exactly and permanently. After all, William Shakespeare (1995: Act II, Scene II, Line 47) well said long ago: 'What is in a name? That which we call a rose by any other name would smell as sweet.'"

As I had also stressed time and again before, each of the neologisms can be re-written as a different "X," only to be re-named differently by the powers that be in different eras of future history.

With these clarifications in mind—I now proceed to Chapter Two on information architecture and taxonomy.

Table 1.1. The Trinity of Pre-Modernity

• **Pre-Free-Spirited Pre-Modernity (Pre-Modernism) and Its Internal Split**

—Competing worldviews and values both within and between linear centric (e.g., Islamic, Christian, Judaic, Imperial Roman) and cyclical-centric (e.g., Confucian, Taoist, Hindu, and Buddhist) orientations

—Compare modernism with pre-modernism here in relation to the seven dimensions of human existence like the true and the holy (e.g., different versions of epistemic dogmas and religious superstitions), the everyday and the technological (e.g.,different versions of non-technophilism and non-consumerism), the beautiful/sublime (e.g., different versions of aesthetic non-autonomy), and the good and the just (e.g., different versions of moral particularism).

• **Pre-Capitalist Pre-Modernity (Pre-Modernization) and Its Own Discontents**

—Competing versions of societal arrangements (e.g., feudalism, monarchism, and the holy order)

• **Hegemonic Pre-Modernity and Its Countervailing Forces**

—Different power centers and their enemies (e.g., the Roman Empire and the "barbarian hordes," the "Holy Crusades" and the Muslims, the Middle Kingdom and the invading tribes, different social castes in India, and warring Greek city-states)

Notes: The examples in each category are solely illustrative (not exhaustive) nor necessarily mutually exclusive, and the comparison is relative (not absolute). As generalities, they allow exceptions. Also, it does not matter what the "base" era is in the analysis of any trinity. And in the present context, the "base" era is modernity (for instance, with its "free-spirited modernity" and the other two parts). So, for pre-modernity, the trinity takes the form of, say, "pre-free-spirited pre-modernity," together with the other two parts.

Sources: From Ch.2 of *BCIV* and also the 2 volumes of *FHC*

Table 1.2. The Trinity of Modernity
(Part I)

• **Free-Spirited Modernity (Modernism) and Its Internal Split**
—*On the True and the Holy*
  • The freedom from the dogmas of the past to the better understanding of, and union with, the world and self (Ch.3 of *FHC*)
  • Alternative discourses: about the true (e.g., anti-science discourses) and the holy (non-mainstream theologies) (Ch.3 of *FHC*)
—*On the Technological and the Everyday*
  • The freedom from life harshness to the higher technophilic, consumeristic lifeform (Ch.2 of *FHC*)
  • Alternative discourses: about the everyday (e.g., transcendental mindsets) and the technological (e.g., Arcadianism) (Ch.2 of *FHC*)
—*On the Good and the Just*
  • The freedom from the theo-aristocratic tyranny to the moral universality for a just society (Ch.5 of *FHC*)
  • Alternative discourses: about the just (e.g., Communism, Anarchism) and the good (e.g., Nazism/Fascism, and Zarathustrianism) (Chs.5-6 of *FHC*)
—*On the Beautiful and the Sublime*
  • The freedom from the external distortion of aesthetic pleasure to the boundless infinity of totality in artistic autonomy (Ch.4 of *FHC*)
  • Alternative discourses: about the beautiful/sublime (e.g., kitsch and historical avant-gardism) (Ch.4 of *FHC*)

• **Capitalist Modernity (Modernization) and Its Own Discontents**
—*During the Industrial Revolution*
  • Ex: Marx on the institution of inequality (Ch.1 of *FHC*)
—*During the Modern Rational-Instrumental Epoch*
  • Ex: Weber on the politics of soft liberal institutions (Ch.5 of *FHC*)
—*During the Great Depression*
  • Ex: Keynes on the myth of the free market (Chs.1-3 of *FHC*)
—*During the Cold War*
  • Ex: Lasch on the narcissistic culture industry (Chs.2-3 of *FHC*)

(continued on next page)

Table 1.2. The Trinity of Modernity
(Part II)

- **Hegemonic Modernity and Its Countervailing Forces**
  —*The Legacies of Colonialism and Imperialism*
    - Ex: European colonization of most of the modern world (Ch.1 of *FHC*)
  —*The Struggle for Decolonialization*
    - Ex: The countervailing forces of resentment, rechantment, and regionalism (Chs.1 & 6 of *FHC*)

Notes: The examples in each category are solely illustrative (not exhaustive) nor necessarily mutually exclusive, and the comparison is relative (not absolute). As generalities, they allow exceptions.
Sources: From the 2 volumes of *FHC*—and also from *FCD*

Table 1.3. The Trinity of Postmodernity

- **Free-Spirited Postmodernity (Postmodernism) and Its Internal Split**
  —*On the True and the Holy*
    - Postmodern performative turn for knowing and its enemies (Ch.3 of *FHC*)
    - Postmodern comparative theology and its opponents (Ch.3 of *FHC*)
  —*On the Technological and the Everyday*
    - Postmodern corporate technological mindset and its adversaries (Ch.2 of *FHC*)
    - Postmodern postmaterialism and its critics (Ch.2 of *FHC*)
  —*On the Good and the Just*
    - Postmodern politics of difference and its foes (Ch.5 of *FHC*)
  —*On the Beautiful and the Sublime*
    - Postmodern deconstruction and its dissenters (Ch.4 of *FHC*)

- **Capitalist Postmodernity (Postmodernization) and Its Own Discontents**
  —*During the Post-Cold War and Beyond*
    - Ex: post-Fordism and its shortcomings (Ch.6 of *FHC*; Chs.6-7 of *FCD*)

- **Hegemonic Postmodernity and Its Countervailing Forces**
  —*The Debate on the Global Village*
    - Ex: uni-civilizationalism vs. multi-civilizationalism (Ch.6 of *FHC*)
  —*The Resistance Movement*
    - Ex: rechantment and the politics of civilizational claims (e.g., Islamic, Confucian and other ethos in relation to the Same) (Ch.6 of *FHC*; Ch.10 of *FCD*)
    - Ex: resentment and the politics of resurgence (e.g., the rising Chinese superpower, the growing EU, and other players in relation to the U.S. and her allies) (Ch.6 of *FHC*; Ch.8 of *FCD*)
    - Ex: regionalism and the politics of inequality (e.g., trans- or inter- national blocs, the North-South divide, NGO's) (Ch.6 of *FHC*; Ch.5 of *FCD*)

Notes: The examples in each category are solely illustrative (not exhaustive) nor necessarily mutually exclusive, and the comparison is relative (not absolute). As generalities, they allow exceptions.
Sources: From *FCD* and the 2 volumes of *FHC*

Table 1.4. The Trinity of After-Postmodernity

• **Free-Spirited After-Postmodernity (After-Postmodernism) and
 Its Internal Split**
 —The discourse of naked contingency (Ch.10 of *FCD*; Ch.4 of *FPHC*)

• **Post-Capitalist After-Postmodernity (After-Postmodernization)
 and Its Own Discontents**
 —Different versions of post-capitalism and post-democracy, and their
 enemies (Ch.10 of *FCD*; Chs.3-4 of *FPHC*)

• **Hegemonic After-Postmodernity and Its Countervailing Forces**
 —The Cyclical Progression of Hegemony in Multiverses (Chs.9-10 of *FCD*;
 Ch.4 of *FPHC*)

Notes: The examples in each category are solely illustrative (not exhaustive) nor
necessarily mutually exclusive, and the comparison is relative (not absolute). As
generalities, they allow exceptions.
Sources: From *FCD* and also *FHC*

Table 1.5. Sophisticated Methodological Holism
(Part I)

- "My methodological holism implies the partiality-totality principle in the ontology of existential dialectics (see the table on the partiality-totality principle for summary), which is against the varieties of (a) reductionism and (b) reverse-reductionism, in relation to (i) concept, (ii) theory, (iii) methodology, and (iv) ontology." (*FC*)

- "[M]y methodological holism here is not opposed to methodological individualism but includes it (and, for that matter, other methodologies too)...." (*FPHC*) For this reason (and others too, as summarized hereafter), my version of methodological holism is sophisticated—not vulgar as sometimes used by inapt scholars using the same term. (*FC*)

- "[M]y methodological holism does not democratically presume that all levels are equally valid, as all levels are not created equal. In other words, in relation to issue X, level A may be more relevant than level B, but in relation to Y, level B can be more relevant than level A instead." (*FPHC*) One excellent example of this vulgar democratic presumption is what I called in *BNN* "the compromise fallacy." (*FC*)

- My methodological holism does not presume that a lower level of analysis is more important than a higher level, solely because the former serves as the foundation for the latter—and vice versa, for that matter. One excellent example of this reductionistic presumption is what I called in *FPHST* "the foundation fallacy." (*FPHST, FC*)

- "[M]y methodological holism does not make any a-priori postulation that there must be a definite (and, for that matter, indefinite) number of levels" in any analysis. (*FPHC*) Nor does it dogmatically require that there must be a certain combination of levels of analysis in a given inquiry. (*FC*)

(continued on next page)

**Table 1.5. Sophisticated Methodological Holism
(Part II)**

• "[M]ethodological holism, in my usage, does not assume that all levels…can necessarily be integrated, since methodological holism is not aimed to search for the holy grail of 'an integral theory…' (as is the case for Wilber). In other words, it allows that sometimes some levels may experience irreducible gaps between them, to be understood, at best, as empirical correlations, not as causal relations…." (*FPHC*)

• "[D]ifferent levels may overlap and even interact with each other in a given context (but sometimes may not), and the fact that I even proposed different ways of re-classifying the levels (whenever needed) in *FDC* reinforces this point….The dual danger here is either forcefully making different levels interact when they are just different (or, metaphorically speaking, apples and oranges) or inappropriately ignoring their interactions when some situations instead require them." (*FPHC*)

• "[T]o understand different levels from their own (unique) perspectives (as required by my methodological holism) is not the same as trying to reduce them to a preferred level in the process of learning from other levels. This second kind of multidisciplinary work is not genuine and does no justice to the unique complexities and merits inherent at each level." (*FPHC*)

• "[My] methodological holism walks a fine line between the artificial classification (separation) of levels and the simultaneous incorporation of them, if only for the sake of human scholarly endeavor. It should be reminded that nature does not impose upon itself the academic classification of the levels of analysis as humans have. The enterprise of classification is therefore anthropocentric." (*FPHC*)

(continued on next page)

**Table 1.5. Sophisticated Methodological Holism
(Part III)**

• "[M]y methodological holism advocates neither epistemic subjectivism nor epistemic non-subjectivism (e.g., realism, idealism, and historicism), neither epistemic relativism (e.g., subjectivism, historicism) nor epistemic absolutism (e.g., realism, positivism), neither epistemic reductionism nor epistemic emergencism, and neither epistemic objectivism (e.g., realism, idealism) nor epistemic historicism....Neither does methodological holism, in my usage, accept the false meta-conceptual dichotomy between nominalism and realism....These false dichotomies...are to be transcended. In other words, methodological holism does not fully accept epistemic realism, positivism (a form of epistemic idealism), historicism, subjectivism, and reductionism in epistemology and philosophy of science but learns from the strengths and weaknesses of all of the opposing approaches without siding with any of them...." (*FPHC*)

• "Sophisticated methodological holism is subject to the constraints as imposed by the syntax of existential dialectics (e.g., the partiality-totality principle and the predictability-unpredictability principle). Even in predictability, outcomes are subject to uncertainty, the degree of which varies from case to case." (*FC*)

Sources: A summary of *Sec.1.2* in *FPHC*—and also from *BNN, FPHST, ALD*, and *FC*. See the books for more detail.

Table 1.6. On Reductionism and Reverse-Reductionism
(Part I)

• **The Partiality-Totality Principle**
—The partiality-totality principle in the ontology of existential dialectics targets against the varieties of reductionism and reverse-reductionism (as already worked out in my previous books).

• **Against the Varieties of Reductionism**
—*Methodological Reductionism*
  • A good instance concerns the debate between different versions of qualitative and quantitative methods (as already analyzed in *FC* and also *FHC*).
—*Ontological Reductionism*
  • An excellent example is the debate between emergentism and reductionism in complexity theory and also in psychology (as elaborated in *FPHC*, in the context of Being and Becoming).
—*Conceptual Reductionism*
  • Some illustrative instances involve myriad dualities like mind vs. body, self vs. world, democracy vs. non-democracy, and the like (as already addressed in *FHC*, *FPHC*, and *BDPD*, for instance).
—*Theoretical Reductionism*
  • A fascinating case study concerns what I originally called "the foundation fallacy" in *FPHST*, in any attempt to naively understand space-time from the physical perspective as the foundation and, consequently, to dangerously dismiss other perspectives.

(continued on next page)

**Table 1.6. On Reductionism and Reverse-Reductionism
(Part II)**

• **Against the Varieties of Reverse-Reductionism**
—*Methodological Reverse-Reductionism*
  • There is the "anything-goes" mentality in postmodernism (e.g., doing art without praxis, doing art with praxis, and doing art by sublation), as analyzed in Ch.4 of *FHC*.
—*Ontological Reverse-Reductionism*
  • There are likewise no privileged ontology, and the door is open for anything in postmodernism (e.g., the equal status of the ontology of Being vs. that of Becoming, as already addressed in Ch.4 of *FHC*—and also in *FPHC*).
—*Conceptual* Reverse-Reductionism
  • Any concept of "art" (e.g., fine art, cave art, outsider art, junk art) is deemed acceptable in postmodernism (as already addressed in Ch.4 of *FHC*).
—*Theoretical Reverse-Reductionism*
  • There are a plurality of art and literary theories (e.g., New Criticism, Romanticism, Expressionism, Feminist Art Theory) in the postmodern scene, with no one being said to be better than any others (as also addressed in Ch.4 of *FHC*). In *BNN*, I introduced "the compromise fallacy" as another good example of theoretical reverse- reductionism, in misleadingly treating the genetic and environmental approaches as equally valid.

Sources: A summary of my previous books, especially though not exclusively *FHC, FCD, FPHC, BDPD, BCPC, BNN, FPHST, BCIV, FC, FAE*, and *ALD*

Table 1.7. The Concepton of Existential Dialectics
(Part I)

• **Sets and Elements**
   —Sets
      • Ex: the Same
      • Ex: the Others
   —Elements
      • Ex: whites in 20th century America (in the set of "the Same")
      • Ex: Iraq during the U.S. invasion in 2003 (in the set of "the Others")

• **Relations, Operations, Functions**
   —Relations (e.g., "belongs," "equals to," "is greater than")
      • Ex: symmetric interactions within the Same (or the Others)
      • Ex: asymmetric interactions between the Same and the Others
   —Operations (e.g., "and," "or," "not," "if...then")
      • Ex: if the Same oppresses the Others, it will also oppress itself.
      • Ex: the Same is not the Others.
   —Functions (e.g., goals)
      • Ex: the Same is hegemonic in relation to the Others.

• **Truth Values**
   —"1" if True (in Symbolic Logic)
      • Ex: the proposition that imperial Japan was hegemonic to China
         during WWII
   —"0" if False (in Symbolic Logic)
      • Ex: the proposition that Grenada invaded France in 2003
   —"1" & "0" if Both True and False (in Dialectic Logic)
      • Ex: the proposition that the rabbit-duck picture refers to a duck
   —"~1" & "~0" if Neither True Nor False (or N/A)
      • Ex: the proposition that God really exists

(continued on next page)

Table 1.7. The Conception of Existential Dialectics
(Part II)

• **Axioms, Postulates, Theorems, Principles**
   —Axioms
      • Ex: the reflexive axiom—"any quantity is equal to itself"
   —Postulates
      • Ex: the SSS postulate—"if the three sides of a triangle are congruent
        to their corresponding parts, then the triangles are congruent"
   —Theorems (and Principles) in Existential Dialectics
      • In Relation to Method
         –Ex: the partiality-totality principle
         –Ex: the predictability-unpredictability principle
      • In Relation to Structure
         –Ex: the preciseness-vagueness principle
         –Ex: the simpleness-complicatedness principle
      • In Relation to Process
         –Ex: the change-constancy principle
         –Ex: the order-chaos principle
         –Ex: the slowness-quickness principle
      • In Relation to Agency
         –Ex: the evolution-transformation principle
         –Ex: the symmetry-asymmetry principle
         –Ex: the softness-hardness principle
      • In Relation to Outcome
         –Ex: the regression-progression principle
         –Ex: the same-difference principle

Notes: The categories and examples in each are solely illustrative (not exhaustive). The comparison is also relative (not absolute), nor are they mutually exclusive. As generalities, they allow exceptions.
Sources: From Ch.6 of *BCPC* and also from other books of mine.

**Table 1.8. The Syntax of Existential Dialectics I:
The Principles
(Part I)**

• **In Relation to Method**

—*The Partiality-Totality Principle*
  (On the Relationships between Whole and Parts)
  • Any inquiry about a phenomenon in the work is to guard against the varieties of (a) reductionism and (b) reverse-reductionism.
  • Reductionism and reverse-reductionism can be (i) conceptual, (ii) theoretical, (iii) methodological, and (iv) ontological.
  • Sources: Especially from *FC*. See also *FHC, FCD, FPHC, BCPC, FPHST, BCIV, BNN, BWT, FAE*, and *ALD*.

—*The Predictability-Unpredictability Principle*
  (On the Occurrence of Events)
  • Both predictability and unpredictability have a major role to play in the occurrence of things, so that neither determinism nor indeterminism wins the centuries-old fight.
  • There are events which are predictable, just as there are those which are not. Or what is regarded as unpredictable at one point in time may turn out to be predictable later, and, conversely, what is deemed as predictable may turn out to not be so predictable. Even in predictability, outcomes are subject to uncertainty, the degree of which varies from case to case.
  • Sources: Especially from *FC*. See also *FHC, FCD, FPHC, BCPC, FPHST, BCIV, BNN, BWT, FAE*, and *ALD*.

(continued on next page)

Table 1.8. The Syntax of Existential Dialectics I:
The Principles
(Part II)

• **In Relation to Structure**

—*The Simpleness-Complicatedness Principle*
  (On the Interconnection among Things)
  • Both simpleness and complicatedness are vital, without favoring one over the other, in that each is utilized, depending on the basis of the perspectives of nature, the mind, culture, and society. And even when a combination of them is preferred, the dilemma is only shifted to a combinational degree of concern.
  • In relation to taxonomy, simpleness has its heuristic usefulness, just as complicatedness has its realistic representation, for instance. And in relation to network, simpleness has its economical attractiveness, just as complicatedness has its practical reliability, for instance.
    • Sources: Especially from *FIA*

—*The Preciseness-Vagueness Principle*
  (On the Refinement of Things)
  • Both preciseness and vagueness are important, not that one is better than the other, but that both are used, in different degrees of preference, in accordance to the contextual application from the perspectives of nature, the mind, culture, and society. Even when both are used in a combination, the dilemma is shifted instead to one of combinational concern.
  • In relation to taxonomy, preciseness has its taxonomic clarity, just as vagueness has its classificatory flexibility, for instance. And in relation to network, vagueness has its explorative liberty, just as preciseness has its conceptual definitiveness, for instance.
    • Sources: Especially from *FIA*

(continued on next page)

Table 1.8. The Syntax of Existential Dialectics I:
The Principles
(Part III)

• **In Relation to Process**

—*The Slowness-Quickness Principle*
  (On the Speed of Change)
  • Both slowness and quickness co-exist, with their own internal tension, to the extent that each fights for its own relevance with the other, in accordance to the perspectives of nature, the mind, culture, and society, without one being the victor and the other being the vanquished in the long haul. Even when both are chosen in other cases, this dilemma is only transferred into something else with a combinational character.
  • In relation to taxonomy, quickness has its efficient usability, just as slowness has its aesthetic appeal, for instance. And in relation to network, quickness has its adventurous readiness, just as slowness has its risk-adverse convenience, for instance.
  • So, in the end, the dilemma still remains, and the dialectic continues its relevance, with the two co-existing in ever new ways, but the window of transcending into something else of interest is opened.
  • Sources: Especially from *FIA*

—*The Order-Chaos Principle*
  (On the Pattern of Things)
  • Both order and chaos are vital in the process of change in the world. The preference for order is biased, since it does not give sufficient attention to the vital role of chaos in the transformation of the world (without somehow reducing it for the understanding of order).
  • The scientific search for order in the world is often a hidden bias in its ontological obsession with order, since chaos is often treated as the "bad" guy, with order as the "good" guy (for the end goal of science).
  • Neither order nor chaos is the final end of the world, and one is not to be treated as the means for the other in the transformation of things. Both are fundamental in their recurrent dialectical interactions with each other over time, without reducing one for the other.
  • Sources: Especially from *FC*. See also *FHC, FCD, FPHC, BCPC, FPHST, BCIV, BNN, BWT, FAE,* and *ALD.*

(continued on next page)

**Table 1.8. The Syntax of Existential Dialectics I:
The Principles
(Part IV)**

• **In Relation to Process (cont'd)**

—*The Change-Constancy Principle*
(On the Alteration of Things)
  • Change occurs over time, although constancy is also allowed.
  • Asymmetry undergoes changes over time, so does symmetry.
  • Old players fade away, and new ones emerges, with ever new causes and ever new forms.
  • Sources: First named in *BCPC*. Especially from *FHC*, *FCD*, and *FPHC*. See also *BDPD*, *FPHST*, *BCIV*, *BNN*, *BWT*, *FC*, *FAE*, and *ALD*.

• **In Relation to Agency**

—*The Evolution-Transformation Principle*
(On the Multiple Kinds of Agency)
  • This principle (and the symmetry-asymmetry principle) are both about *the agency of change*. The word "agency," in a formal definition, refers to "a person or thing through which power is exerted or an end is achieved." (MWD 2007b) It therefore does not have to necessarily involve an intelligent lifeform.
  • Because of this dual meaning in agency, the evolution-transformation principle is more concerned with *the multiple kinds of agency*, that is, both about the *evolution* in the state of nature (e.g., an object of natural beauty) and the *transformation* in the world of intelligent lifeforms (e.g., a work of art).
  • And the transformative part of the principle precisely refers to the other dimension in the dual meaning of agency, in giving technology a major role to play in the change of the world, which is something that I extensively analyzed in *FHC* in the context of the technophilic lifeworld, espeically though not exclusively since modern times.
  • Sources: Especially from *FAE*. See also *FHC*, *FCD*, *FC*, and the rest.

(continued on next page)

Table 1.8. The Syntax of Existential Dialectics I:
The Principles
(Part V)

• **In Relation to Agency (cont'd)**

—*The Softness-Hardness Principle*
(On the Force of Change)
  • This has to do with *the force of change* under the category about agency in existential dialectics, in that any change by an agent, be it organic (like humans) or non-organic (like natural objects), can occur in a forceful (aggressive) or gentle (pacific) way, which can come in all shapes and sizes, of course.
  • Sources: Especially from *ALD*. See also *FHC*, *FCD*, *FPHC*, *BCPC*, *FPHST*, *BCIV*, *BNN*, *BWT*, and *FAE*.

—*The Symmetry-Asymmetry Principle*
(On the Relationships among Existents)
  • The relationships are relatively asymmetric between the Same and the Others but relatively symmetric within the Same (or the Others). There is no asymmetry without symmetry. This is true, even when the Same can be relatively asymmetric towards itself in self-oppression, just as the Others can be likewise towards themselves.
  • The subsequent oppressiveness is dualistic, as much by the Same against the Others and itself, as by the Others against the Same and themselves.
  • Both oppression and self-oppression can be achieved by way of downgrading differences between the Same and the Others and of accentuating them.
  • Sources: From all my books, starting with *FHC*. First named in *BCPC*.

(continued on next page)

Table 1.8. The Syntax of Existential Dialectics I:
The Principles
(Part VI)

• **In Relation to Outcome**

—*The Regression-Progression Principle*
   (On the Direction of History)
   • Neither the cyclical nor the linear views are adequate for explaining many phenomena at all levels.
   • History progresses to more advanced forms, but with a regressive touch. Examples include no freedom without unfreedom, no equality without inequality, and no civilization without barbarity.
   • This is not an inevitable law, but merely a highly likely empirical trend.
   • Sources: From all my books, starting with *FHC*. First named in *BCPC*.

—*The Same-Difference Principle*
   (On the Metamorphosis of Change)
   • This has to do with *the metamorphosis of change* under the category about outcome in existential dialectics, in that an entity, as it evolves over time, can be both different from and similar to its opposing alternatives and does not have to be solely more different from them over time.
   • Opposites are not absolute in a black-or-white fashion; so, an entity can become relatively more similar to (or more different from) its opposite over time.
   • Sources: Especially from *ALD*. See also *FHC, FCD, FPHC, BCPC, BDPD, FPHST, BCIV, BNN, BWT, FC,* and *FAE*.

Notes: The features in each principle are solely illustrative (not exhaustive). The comparison is also relative (not absolute), nor are they mutually exclusive. As generalities, they allow exceptions.

Table 1.9. The Syntax of Existential Dialectics II:
The Dialectic Constraints Imposed by the Principles
(Part I)

• **Co-Existent and Asymmetric**

—The principles, as they constitute the syntax of existential dialectics, are dialectic in character, such that, when they are applied, they impose dialectic constraints on how reality is to be understood. Consider, say, the symmetry-asymmetry principle as an illustration here, in order to summarize two main characters of the dialectic constraints in question.

—Firstly, to be dialectic here is to go beyond the narrow dichotomies (and, for that matter, any rigid multi-dimensional classificatory scheme), be they about "self" vs. "world," "freedom" vs. "unfreedom," "barbarity" vs. "civilization," "individuality" vs. "communality," and so on.

—One way to do so (to go beyond) is to consider them all in terms of co-existence (without favoring one over the rest). For instance, my theory of "post-civilization" (to be summarized later in the section on the pragmatics of existential dialectics) is to go beyond barbarity and civilization in terms of understanding barbarity and civilization as being co-existent. And the same logic can be said in relation to my theories of "post-democracy," "post-capitalsm," and others (also to be introduced later in the section on the pragmatics of existential dialectics), in regard to freedom vs. unfreedom, equality vs. inequality, communality vs. individuality, spirituality vs. materiality, and so on.

—But to consider them all (in the dichotomies—and, for that matter, in any rigid multi-dimensional classifactory schme) as co-existent is not the same as to imply that the opposites in any classificatory scheme are all equal, since, in accordance to the symmetry-asymmetry principle (as an illustration here), if they are equal in terms of being considered as co-existent, they are asymmetric in terms of being unequal in dialectic interaction (e.g., X can be more dominant than Y in case A, or Y is more dominant than X in case B).

—For this reason, there are different versions of "post-democracy" and "post-capitalism" in my theories. As an illustration, in version I of the theory of post-democracy, freedom is more dominant than equality, whereas in version II of the theory of post-democracy, equality is more so than freedom.

(continued on next page)

Table 1.9. The Syntax of Existential Dialectics II:
The Dialectic Constraints Imposed by the Principles
(Part II)

—But this "X more than Y" has to be understood in the context of dialectic logic (not in conventional logic), in that both "X" and "Y" are important in post-democracy (in the context of dialectic logic), but in an asymmetry way. By contrast, in conventional logic, it often favors one over the other— be it in regard to privileging freedom over equality in Fascism, favoring freedom relatively more than equality in Liberal Democracy, or favoring equality relatively more than freedom in Socialist Democracy. In the latter two cases (about Liberal Democracy and Socialist Democracy), the difference between dialectic logic and conventional logic can be one in degree, not in kind—in this sense, albeit not in other senses.

—The same logic can be said about the relatonships between individuality and communality, between spirituality and materiality, and between formal legalism and informal legalism in the different versions of my theory of post-capitalism.

• **Transcendent**
  —Secondly, to be dialectic is to go beyond the narrow dichotomies (and, for that matter, any rigid multi-dimensional classificatory scheme) in another way, this time, in a transcendent way, that is, in exploring other possibilities or even other issues not considered within the narrow confines of narrow dichotomies (and, for that matter, any rigid multi-dimensional classificatory scheme).

  —As an analogy, to go beyond the narrow color dichotomy of "black" and "white" is not just to choose both "black" and "white" (as in the first meaning) but also to explore other color options (e.g., "green," "purple," "blue," etc.—and, alternatively, "shade," "line," "curve," etc.). By the same logic, to go beyond "democracy" is to transcend democracy (as in version III of the theory of "post-democracy") and to explore other possibilties of lifeforms (e.g., floating consciousness, hyper-spatial consciousness, etc., to live beyond the narrow obsession with freedom and equality).

  —This dialectic character of the principles in existential dialectics has important implications for the pragmatics of existential dialectics (as will be clear shortly, in the section on the pragmatics of existential dialectics).

(continued on next page)

Table 1.9. The Syntax of Existential Dialectics II:
The Dialectic Constraints Imposed by the Principles
(Part III)

Notes: The examples here are solely illustrative (not exhaustive). The comparison is also relative (not absolute), nor are they mutually exclusive. As generalities, they allow exceptions.

Sources: From my previous books like *FHC*, *FCD*, *FPHC*, *BDPD*, *BCPC*, *BNN*, *FC*, *FAE*, etc.

Table 1.10. The Semantics of Existential Dialectics

• **Abstract Structure vs. Specific Meanings**
—The syntax of existential dialectics so understood in terms of ontological principles only gives us the structure of ontology in the world, in an abstract (general) sense. These principles by themselves do not tell us the specific meanings in a given context.
—In order to grasp the specific meanings of the principles in a given context, it is necessary to study the semantics of existential dialectics. For this reason, I have often gone in great lengths in my previous books on different subjects to explain the specific meanings of the principles when applied in different contexts.

• **Specific Meanings in Specific Fields**
—For instance, in *FPHST*, I used the first three principles (i.e., the change-constancy principle, the regression-progression principle, and the symmetry-asymmetry principle) to propose "the perspectival theory of space-time," for a better way to understand space and time—especially, though not exclusively, in relation to future post-human history (as summarized in *Table 3.6*, *Table 3.7*, *Table 3.8*, and *Table 3.9*). In so doing, I had to introduce concepts and theories specific to the field of physics and other related fields (e.g., "absolute space" and "absolute time" in "classical mechanics" and "relative space-time" in "the theory of relativity").
—In *BNN*, I also exploited the three principles to propose the "transcendent" approach to the study of genes and memes as a new way to understand the interaction between nature and nurture. In so doing, I had to explore concepts and theories in the world of evolutionary theory (e.g., "mutation," "variation," "adaptation," "selection," and "inheritance" in evolutionary theory) and neural biology (e.g., "chromosome," "gene," "DNA," "RNA," "protein," "neuron," "neural network," and "behavior").

Notes: The categories and examples in each are solely illustrative (not exhaustive). The comparison is also relative (not absolute), nor are they mutually exclusive. As generalities, they allow exceptions.
Sources: From all of my previous books

Table 1.11. The Pragmatics of Existential Dialectics
(Part I)

- **The Two-Way Street Connecting Theory and Meta-Theory**
  —The pragmatics of existential dialectics is not a one-way street (that is, using the ontological principles for theoretical insights in praxis) but a two-way one, that is, (a) from meta-theory to theory, and (b) from theory to meta-theory.
  —(a) On one side of the street, the ontological principles can inspire some theoretical insights in praxis, that is, in relation to some specific fields.
  —(b) On the other (opposing) side of the street, however, the study of a subject matter in the specific fields in turn reveals some more hitherto unknown ontological principles to be discovered and identified. For this reason, three new principles were added in *FC*, one in *FAE*, and two in *ALD*, on top of the original three in *BCPC*—after some research on the specific subject matters.

- **Direct and Indirect Applications**
  —*Direct*
    - The logic of existential dialectics can shed some theoretical insights on diverse phenomena in the world, and good instances are the pertinent use of the principles of existential dialectics for the theoretical insights on the freedom/unfreedom dialectics, the equality/inequality dialectics, and the wealth/poverty dialectics in my previous works.
    - My latest books like *FPHST* and *BNN* also use the principles to reveal some theoretical insights on the perspectives of space and time (as in *FPHST*) and of nature and nurture (as in *BNN*).
  —*Indirect*
    - The theoretical insights can further be used to reveal other phenomena directly from them (viz., the theoretical insights) and therefore indirectly from the principles themselves. A good instance is the use of the theoretical insights on the freedom/unfreedom and equality/inequality dialectics for the understanding of the civilization/barbarity dialectics.
    - Even in indirect applications, however, a phenomenon under study can still be directly related back to the principles themselves. In the example as cited above, the civilization/barbarity dialectics can be directly related to the principles of existential dialectics without the intermediate role of the freedom/unfreedom and equality/inequality dialectics.

(continued on next page)

Table 1.11. The Pragmatics of Existential Dialectics
(Part II)

• **Multiple Levels of Application**

—The theoretical insights can be applied to different levels of analysis, even though in a given example, it may refer to one level only. For instance, in the example concerning the freedom/unfreedom dialectics, it can be used at the structural level (e.g., in relation to the theory of cyclical progression of hegemony), but it can be exploited as well for other levels (e.g., the theory of post-capitalism at the institutional level).

Notes: The categories and examples in each are solely illustrative (not exhaustive). The comparison is also relative (not absolute), nor are they mutually exclusive. As generalities, they allow exceptions.

Sources: From Ch.6 of *BCPC* and also from *FHC, FCD, FPHC, BDPD, BNN, FC, FAE,* and *ALD*

Table 1.12. The Freedom-Unfreedom Dialectics
(Part I)

- **On Having**
  - *—In Relation to the Technological*
    - (1) if freer from submission to Nature, then less free from ecological degradation (Deep and Social Ecology), even if in a hi-tech form
    - (2) if freer from technological inconvenience / backwardness, then less free from technological control and the loss of privacy
    - (3) if freer from technological (material) backwardness, then less free from the abusive (barbaric) maltreatment of the primitive Others
  - *—In Relation to the Everyday*
    - (1) if freer from abject poverty, then less free from artificial needs/discontents (Frankfurt School)
    - (2) if freer from sensual suppression, then less free from violent sublimation (Freud)
    - (3) if freer from the snobbishness of high culture, then less free from the shabbiness (leveling-off effect) of mass culture (Tocqueville)
    - (4) if freer from the inefficiency of traditional "compassionate economy," then less free from the bondage of a "ruthless [competitive] economy" (Keynes)
    - (5) if freer from anarchy in the state of nature (system fragmentation), then less free from government regulations and controls in system integration

- **On Belonging**
  - *—In Relation to the Good and the Just*
    - (1) if freer from disciplinary society, then less free from society of control (Foucault)
    - (2) if freer from the tyranny of one or a few, then less free from the tyranny of the majority (or sometimes, minority veto)
    - (3) if freer from elitist decision making, then less free from political gridlock/cleavage
    - (4) if freer from arbitrary (discretionary) administration, then less free from bureaucratic irrationality (Weber) and legal trickery (loopholes)

(continued on next page)

Table 1.12. The Freedom-Unfreedom Dialectics
(Part II)

• **On Being**
  —*In Relation to the True*
  (1) if freer from unscientific dogmas, then less free from instrumental abyss (nihilism). Or conversely, if freer from meaninglessness, then less free from dogmas.
  (2) if freer from the bondage of partiality/partisanship (e.g., prejudice, discrimination), then less free from the danger of impartiality and neutrality (e.g., opportunism, unrealisticness, lack of compassion, inaction)
  (3) if freer from making generalizations, then less free from being unable to understand much of anything
  —*In Relation to the Holy*
  (1) if freer from collective conscience, then less free from social loneliness
  (2) if freer from religious absoluteness, then less free from spiritual emptiness
  —*In Relation to the Beautiful/Sublime*
  (1) if freer from artistic non-autonomy, then less free from aesthetic disillusion (deconstruction)

Notes: The examples in each category are solely illustrative (not exhaustive), and the comparison is relative (not absolute), nor are they necessarily mutually exclusive. And some can be easily re-classified elsewhere. As generalities, they allow exceptions.

Sources: A reconstruction from Ch.10 of *FCD*, based on *FHC*

Table 1.13. The Equality-Inequality Dialectics
(Part I)

• **On Having**
  —*In Relation to the Technological*
    (1) if more equal in treating Nature with spiritual unity, then less equal in suppressing the dominant drive to transcend it altogether
  —*In Relation to the Everyday*
    (1) if more equal in building social plurality, then less equal in leveling-off effects (e.g., the subsequent relative intolerance of high/intellectual ethos in mass culture industry)
    (2) if more equal in socioeconomic distribution beyond a certain point, then less equal in efficiency (e.g. resentment, the erosion of work ethics)
    (3) if more equal in urging an affirmative action program, then less equal in creating victim mentality (in oneself), stigma (from others), reverse discrimination (against the once privileged), and mediocracy (against the more able)

• **On Belonging**
  —*In Relation to the Good and the Just*
    (1) if more equal in banning monarchic/oligarchic exclusion, then less equal in producing "the tyranny of the majority" or of "minority veto"
    (2) if more equal in encouraging participatory decision making, then less equal in inducing political divisiveness (gridlock/cleavage in power blocs) and organizational oligarchy
    (3) if more equal in institutionalizing a decentralized bureaucracy, then less equal in falling into more territorial/turf politics (intrigues)

(continued on next page)

Table 1.13. The Equality-Inequality Dialectics
(Part II)

- **On Being**
  - *—In Relation to the Beautiful/Sublime*
    - (1) if more equal in accepting diverse styles ("anything goes" mentality), then less equal in artistic good quality (in leveling-off effects against the best)
  - *—In Relation to the True*
    - (1) if more equal in tolerating multiple viewpoints (no matter how extreme), then less equal in epistemic standards
  - *—In Relation to the Holy*
    - (1) if more equal in celebrating any cults and sects (no matter how questionable), then less equal in spiritual depth and authenticity

Notes: The examples in each category are solely illustrative (not exhaustive), and the comparison is relative (not absolute), nor are they mutually exclusive. And some can be easily reclassified elsewhere. As generalities, they allow exceptions.

Sources: A reconstruction from Ch.10 of *FCD*, based on *FHC*

**Table 1.14. The Duality of Oppression in Existential Dialectics:
Oppression and Self-Oppression
(Part I)**

• **From the Same to the Others and Itself**
  —*The Oppression by the Same against the Others*
    • By way of downgrading differences
        −Ex: on judiciary caprice for corporate crimes (*Sec.2.2.1.2.1*)
        −Ex: on the deceptive politics of liberation (*Sec.3.5*)
        −Ex: on the humanitarian mystique (*Sec.4.4*)
        −Ex: on the fad of emotional intelligence (*Sec.5.3*)
    • By way of accentuating differences
        −Ex: on the legal sophistry of self-defense (*Sec.2.3*)
        −Ex: on the legal semantics of proportionality (*Sec.2.4*)
        −Ex: on the tricky politics of external threat (*Sec.3.4*)
        −Ex: on the appeal of the Far Right for democracy (*Sec.5.4*)
        −Ex: on the democratic axis of evil (*Sec.5.5*)
        −Ex: on the democratic way of brutality and revenge (*Sec.5.6*)
        −Ex: on democratic autocracy (*Sec.6.4*)
  —*The Oppression by the Same against Itself*
    • By way of downgrading differences
        −Ex: on the politics of fear (*Sec.2.2*)
        −Ex: on the trickery of compassionate conservatism (*Sec.3.2*)
        −Ex: on the deceptive politics of patriotism (*Sec.3.3*)
    • By way of accentuating differences
        −Ex: on the caprice of due process on domestic suspects (*Sec.2.2*)
        −Ex: on the false security/freedom dilemma (*Sec.6.5.2*)

(continued on next page)

Table 1.14. The Duality of Oppression in Existential Dialectics:
Oppression and Self-Oppression
(Part II)

• **From the Others to the Same and Themselves**
—*The Oppression by the Others against the Same*
  • By way of downgrading differences
      –Ex: on judiciary caprice in the reverse direction (*Sec.2.2.1.2.2*)
      –Ex: on equal pay (*Sec.6.2.1.1*)
      –Ex: on equal representation (*Sec.6.2.1.2*)
      –Ex: on affirmative action program (*Sec.6.3.1.1*)
      –Ex: on same-sex marriage (*Sec.6.3.1.2*)
  • By way of accentuating differences
      –Ex: on sexual harassment (*Sec.6.2.2.1*)
      –Ex: on physical violence (*Sec.6.2.2.2*)
      –Ex: on sexual exploitation (*Sec.6.2.2.3*)
—*The Oppression by the Others against Themselves*
  • By way of downgrading differences
      –Ex: on the reverse-class mystique (*Sec.4.2*)
      –Ex: on the reverse-black mystique (*Sec.4.3*)
      –Ex: on self-discrimination by downgrading (*Sec.6.3.2.2*)
  • By way of accentuating differences
      –Ex: on self-discrimination by accentuating (*Sec.6.3.2.1*)

Notes: The examples are solely illustrative (not exhaustive), nor are they mutually exclusive. As generalities, they allow exceptions. Also, both forms of oppression co-exist in all of the examples, so the listing of them are only meant in a relative, not absolute, sense.
Source: A summary of the sections (as cited) in Chs.2-6 of *BDPD*. See text for more info and references.

Table 1.15. The Structure of Existential Dialectics I:
The Freedom/Unfreedom and Equality/Inequality Dialectics

• Each freedom and equality produces its own unfreedom and inequality, regardless of whether the pair occurs in political society (with the nation-state), in civil society (with some autonomy from the state), or elsewhere (e.g., in the private sphere of individual homes)—and regardless of whether freedom and equality are understood as "negative" or "positive."

• Oppression is dualistic, as much by the Same against the Others and itself, as by the Others against the Same and themselves.

• Both forms of oppression and self-oppression can be achieved by way of downgrading differences (between the Same and the Others) and of accentuating them.

• The relationships are relatively asymmetric between the Same and the Others and relatively symmetric within them. This is true, even when the Same can be relatively asymmetric towards itself in self-oppression, just as the Others can be likewise towards themselves.

• Symmetry and asymmetry change over time, with ever new players, new causes, and new forms.

Notes: The examples in each category are solely illustrative (not exhaustive) nor necessarily mutually exclusive, and the comparison is relative (not absolute). As generalities, they allow exceptions. "Negative" freedom is freedom "from" (e.g., freedom from poverty), whereas "positive" freedom is freedom "to" (e.g., freedom to the state of enlightenment). "Negative" equality is "procedural" equality (e.g., equality of opportunity), while "positive" equality is "substantive" equality (e.g., equality of outcome). Existential dialectics impose constraints on freedom and equality in democracy, non-democracy, and post-democracy. There is no utopia, in the end; even should there be one, dystopia would exist within it.
Sources: From *Table 1.5* of *BDPD*—and also from *FHC, FCD,* and *FPHC*

Table 1.16. The Structure of Existential Dialectics II:
The Wealth/Poverty Dialectics

• There is no wealth without poverty, just as there is no poverty without wealth.

• The wealth/poverty dialectics occurs in the realms of having, belonging, and being, in relation to the material, relational, and spiritual.

• The wealth/poverty dialectics also expresses itself at the multiple levels of analysis in accordance to methodological holism, be they about the microphysical, the chemical, the biological, the psychological, the organizational, the institutional, the structural, the systemic, the cultural, and the cosmological.

• The wealth/poverty dialectics is a different manifestation of existential dialectics in general, subject to the principles in its logic of ontology—just as the freedom/unfreedom and equality/inequality dialectics are likewise.

• There is no economic utopia, in the end; even should there be one, dystopia would exist within it.

Notes: The main points here are solely illustrative (not exhaustive) nor necessarily mutually exclusive, and the comparison is relative (not absolute). As generalities, they allow exceptions.

Sources: From *BCPC*. See also *FCD* and *FHC*.

Table 1.17. The Structure of Existential Dialectics III:
The Civilization/Barbarity Dialectics

• There is no civilization without barbarity.

• The civilization/barbarity dialectics applies in the four civilizing processes (e.g., the rationalizing process, the pacifying process, the stewardizing process, and the subliming process).

• The civilization/barbarity dialectics is another (different) manifestation of existential dialectics in general, subject to the principles in its logic of ontology—just as the freedom/unfreedom and equality/inequality dialectics and the wealth/poverty dialectics are likewise.

• There is no utopia, in the end; even should there be one, dystopia would exist within it.

Notes: The main points here are solely illustrative (not exhaustive) nor necessarily mutually exclusive, and the comparison is relative (not absolute). As generalities, they allow exceptions.
Sources: From *BCIV*. See also *FCD*, *FHC*, and *BDPD*.

**Table 1.18. The Theoretical Debate on Space-Time
(Part I)**

• **Isaac Newton's Absolutist (Substantivist) Theory of Space-Time**
  —space and time are independent from each other. The structure of space-time is $E3 \times E1$ (with the structure of space, P, as the set of spatial locations in a three-dimensional Euclidean space, $E3$, and the structure of time as the set of temporal moments, T, in the one-dimensional real time, $E1$).
  —space and time are also independent from the effects of matter and events. The existence of space and time is possible even in a world absent of matter (and, for that matter, even in a world absent of events), as if they were material objects but with their total unchangingness thorough time.

• **Albert Einstein's Relativist Theory of Space-Time**
  —space and time are interchangeable (not absolute), just as matter and energy are equivalent (not independent) with the famous equation, $E = mc^2$ (as in the special theory of relativity in 1905).
  —space-time and matter-energy are also relative in a grand union (as in the general theory of relativity in 1915). Thus, each pair affects the other pair, as "matter 'tells' spacetime how to curve [in a non- Euclidean geometry] and curved spacetime 'tells' matter how to behave....Space contracts near mass and dilates away from it. Time dilates near mass and contracts away from it. Clocks positioned farther away from the mass of the earth run faster than clocks closer to the earth." (L. Shlain 1991: 328-330)

(continued on next page)

Table 1.18. The Theoretical Debate on Space-Time
(Part II)

• **Peter Baofu's Perspectival Theory of Space-Time**

—space and time can be understood from multiple perspectives, be they in relation to culture, society, nature, and the mind, with each perspective revealing something about the nature of space- time and simultaneously delimiting its view. This is subject to "the regression-progression principle" in existential dialectics.

—each perspective of space and time exists in culture, society, nature, and the mind with good reasons, with some being more successful and hegemonic (dominant) than others. This is subject to "the symmetry-asymmetry principle" in existential dialectics.

—space and time will not last, to be eventually superseded (altered) by post-humans in different forms (e.g.,stretching/shrinking space-time, engineering more dimensions of space-time, and manipulating multiverses), be they here in this universe or in multiverses. Thus, even the physical existence of space-time cannot last forever, with ever more transformations in the process. This is subject to "the change-constancy principle" in existential dialectics.

—the conventional wisdom (especially by physicists) of treating the physical perspective of space and time as the foundation of all other perspectives (of space and time) and of regarding them as much less important is a form of reductionism, committing what I call the foundation fallacy, in misleadingly dismissing the multiple perspectives of space and time in relation to culture, society, nature, and the mind.

Notes: The examples in each category are solely illustrative (not exhaustive), and the comparison is relative (not absolute), nor are they necessarily mutually exclusive. Some can be easily re-classified elsewhere. As generalities, they allow exceptions.

Source: A summary of *Sec.1.1*, *Sec.1.2*, and *Sec.1.3* of *FPHST*—and, for that matter, the rest of *FPHST*

Table 1.19. The Technological Frontiers of the Micro-World

• **Type I-Minus**
—Ex: building structures and mining

• **Type II-Minus**
—Ex: playing with the genetic makeups of living things

• **Type III-Minus**
—Ex: manipulating molecular bonds for new materials

• **Type IV-Minus**
—Ex: creating nanotechnologies on the atomic scale

• **Type V-Minus**
—Ex: engineering the atomic nucleus

• **Type VI-Minus**
—Ex: restructuring most elementary particles

• **Type Ω-Minus**
—Ex: altering the structure of space-time

Notes: As already indicated in *Sec.4.4.2.2* of *FPHC*, the problem with this micro-classification (from Barrow's work) is that the civilization types (with the exception of Type Ω-Minus, for example) are not quite distinct, since many of them can be achieved more or less in a civilization, to the extent that Type II-minus and Type III-minus, just to cite two plausible types, can be historically contemporaneous, relatively speaking, unlike the vast historical distance between, say, Type O and Type I (or Type I and Type II) civilizations. In other words, the micro-classification here is not very useful to understand civilization types but is revealing to see the technological frontiers of the micro-world.

Sources: A reconstruction from J.Barrow (1998:133), as originally shown in *Table 4.7* of *FPHC*. See *FPHC* for more info.

Table 1.20. Theoretical Speculations of Multiverses

• **"Baby Universes" (Ex: Andre Linde and others)**
 —Ex: In a flat universe theory, "even if our part of it eventually collapses,...some spots in the cosmos would suddenly start inflating on their own, creating brand-new 'baby universes.'" (P. Baofu 2000: 623)

• **"Parallel Universes" (Ex: Stephen Hawking and others)**
 —Ex: In quantum cosmology, there allows the existence of infinite numbers of parallel universes, with tunneling among them. (M. Kaku 1994: 256) Hawking later revised his views on this.

• **"Pocket Universes" (Ex: Alan Guth)**
 —Ex: "As the pocket universes live out their lives and recollapse or dwindle away, new universes are generated to take their place....While life in our pocket universe will presumably die out, life in the universe as a whole will thrive for eternity." (A. Guth 1997: 248; P. Baofu 2002: 482)

• **"Brane Worlds" (Ex: Warren Siegel, Lisa Randall, and others)**
 —Ex: Our universe is stuck on a membrane of space-time embedded in a larger cosmos, with different brane worlds connecting and/or colliding with each other.

Notes: These examples are solely illustrative (not exhaustive), and some of the items can be reclassified somewhere else. Nor are they always mutually exclusive. Since they are generalities, exceptions are expected.
Source: From *Table 4.8* of *FPHC*

Table 1.21. Main Reasons for Altering Space-Time

• **The Need to Make New Energy-Matter**
  —Ex: manipulating molecular bonds for new materials
  —Ex: creating nanotechnologies on the atomic scale
  —Ex: engineering the atomic nucleus
  —Ex: restructuring most elementary particles
  —Ex: inventing new forms of matter and energy

• **The Need to Create New Space-Time**
  —Ex: creating "warp drive" (as in science fiction) for space travel
  —Ex: creating "pocket universes"

• **The Need to Conquer the Cosmos unto Multiverses**
  —Ex: spreading floating consciousness and hyper-spatial consciousness, besides other forms that humans have never known, in the cosmos and beyond unto multiverses for ultimate conquest

Notes: The examples in each category are solely illustrative (not exhaustive) nor necessarily mutually exclusive, and the comparison is relative (not absolute). As generalities, they allow exceptions. Also, it should be stressed that the three reasons are all related, in that they all contribute to the evolution of intelligent life in the cosmos unto multiverses in the most distant future beyond our current knowledge.
Sources: A summary of *Sec.6.2* of *FPHST*. See also *FHC*, *FCD*, and *FPHC*.

• PART TWO •

Taxonomy

CHAPTER 2
INFORMATION ARCHITECTURE AND TAXONOMY

> [O]ur classifications are human impositions
> [that] shape our thoughts and deeds in ways
> that we scarcely perceive because we view
> our categories as "obvious" and "natural."
> —Stephen Jay Gould (1996)

The Nature of Taxonomy

Information that we receive daily is processed, stored, and applied in a certain way. But what does this say about the nature of intelligent life (like humans and, for that matter, post-humans in the future)?

A good point of departure is the analysis of the nature of taxonomy as a case study for illustration.

As a start, the word "taxonomy," which etymologically derives from the Greek τάξις (*taxis* = "order") and νόμος (*nomos* = "law" or "science"), therefore means "the practice and science of classification." (WK 2007g)

Any classification (or "taxonomic scheme") is customarily constructed into "taxonomic units known as *taxa* (singular *taxon*), or kinds of things that are arranged frequently in a hierarchical structure," with "subtype-supertype relationships...." (WK 2007g)

The subtype-supertype relationships can take different forms, be they in a simple parent-child hierarchy (e.g., "car" in relation to "vehicle"), a complex children-with-multi-parents relationship (e.g., "car" in relation to "vehicle" and "steel mechanisms"), a simple organization of things in the form of an alphabetical list (e.g., a listing of cars starting from A to Z in accordance to the sequential listing of the plate letters), or else in other manners. (WK 2007g)

With this preliminary definition of taxonomy in mind—the nature of taxonomy can be more deeply analyzed from the four main perspectives of (2.2) nature, (2.3) the mind, (2.4) society and (2.5) culture, respectively hereafter.

Taxonomy and Nature

Consider taxonomy from the perspective of nature first in this section.

The world of nature has had a major impact on how and why information is processed, stored, and applied in the way that it has, since time immemorial.

With this goal in mind, the analysis of taxonomy from the perspective of nature can be divided into three domains (and summarized in *Table 4.3*), namely, (2.2.1) in chemistry, (2.2.2) in micro-physics, (2.2.3) in macro-physics (or cosmology), and (2.2.4) in biology (animal).

It should be stressed that biology (animal) in *Sec. 2.2.4* overlaps with the issue of biology (human) in relation to the mind, which is further analyzed in the next section on taxonomy and the mind in *Sec. 2.3*.

Taxonomy and Chemistry

In chemistry, taxonomy has a special label, namely, "chemotaxonomy," from chemistry and taxonomy, as a novel way to classify organisms from the perspective of nature.

Chemotaxonomy

Chemotaxonomy, also known as "chemosystematics," attempts "to classify organisms (originally plants), according to differences in their biochemical makeup. Mostly the amino acid sequences of proteins are used for comparison." (WK 2007nn)

The goal here is to study "the demonstrable differences and similarities in the biochemical compositions of the organisms to be identified....John Griffith Vaughan was one of the pioneers of chemotaxonomy." (WK 2007nn)

This novel approach seems to bring good results. For instance, Dr. Charles Vairappan used chemotaxonomy to lead his "researchers in MBRI to determine the taxonomy of various species of seaweed rapidly and accurately." (BMRI)

The reason is that chemotaxonomy can "elucidate the taxonomic affinities of various organisms due to the amount of metabolites that may be obtained compared to the minute amount of DNA that is available in a cell." (BMRI)

An Alternative Approach

Yet, chemotaxonomy is by no means the only approach in taxonomy for organisms.

Of course, chemotaxonomists often "argue that, because proteins are more closely controlled by genes and less subject to natural selection than are anatomical features, they are more reliable indicators of genetic relationships." (EB 2007) In this way, it produces quick and reliable results.

But there are weaknesses in the approach. Just consider three illustrations.

Firstly, it is not easy to collect all the data as needed to understand the biochemical compositions of all the organisms in question, and the research process can be slowed down, because of the lack of good data.

It is for this reason, among others, that alternative taxonomic schemes have not disappeared, and good instances are "the classical comparison of phenotypical descriptions (morphological and physiological traits)," contemporary DNA sequencing, or else. (V. Boivin-Jahns 1995; R. Korf 2005)

Secondly, if the data used for a chemotaxonomy are not correct, the classification is not worth much.

And thirdly, what is true at the biochemical level (say, in chemotaxonomy) does not say much about other levels of classification, which are important in their own right, not to be reduced to the biochemical level.

Richard Korf (2005) has a wise observation to share with us, in that all of the different taxonomic schemes have suffered from an over-exaggerated promise of their potential as a research tool: "We have seen many new tools, have their brief day in the sun, each in turn touted as 'cutting edge.' These include technologies, e.g., electron microscopy (first TEM, then SEM), isozymes, RFLPs—then RAPDs and cognate approaches such as AFLPs, and now DNA sequence polymorphisms particularly in the nuclear ribosomal DNA repeat. These tools include schools of analysis, such as phenetics, cladistics, and recently Bayesian statistics."

The dilemma here is not to be missed: The search for quick results in chemotaxonomy has its own unspoken vices (as illustrated above).

Taxonomy and Micro-Physics

In micro-physics, taxonomy takes a novel turn, which is not less problematic.

Consider, say, the classification of particles in physics (as summarized in *Table 2.1*).

Particle Taxonomy

The classification of particles is more complicated, as the knowledge of physics advances.

For instance, in the older days, things were classified in terms of "elements" (e.g., iron, hydrogen). (J. Brewer 1994) Then, elements were further classified in terms of "nuclei" with its constituents (e.g., "protons, neutrons").

Yet, nowadays, the classification of particles is more complicated. For instance, particles can be classified as either "elementary" (viz., not composed of other particles) or "composite" (viz., composed of other particles). (WK 2007pp)

Let's elaborate elementary and composite particles a bit more below.

Elementary Particles

Elementary particles in turn are further classified into "fermions" (half-integer spin) and "bosons" (integer spin). (WK 2007pp)

On the one hand, fermions are sub-classified into six types of "quarks" and six types of "leptons." (WK 2007pp) Quarks are then further sub-classified into six "flavors" (e.g., up, down, strange, charm, bottom, top), with their antiparticles as "antiquarks." And leptons are further sub-classified into six types, with their respective antiparticles (or "antileptons")—i.e., electrons and positrons, electron neutrinos and electron antineutrinos, muons and antimuons, muon neutrinos and muon antineutrinos, Tau leptons and Tau antitepons, and Tau neutrinos and Tau antineutrinos.

On the other hand, bosons are sub-classified into six types, with the first five about the four fundamental forces of nature, namely, photos (for electromagnetic force), W and Z bosons (for weak nuclear force), gluons (for strong nuclear force), graviton (for gravitational force), and Higgs bosons. (WK 2007pp)

Composite Particles

Other particles, unlike elementary particles, are composite and classified into "hadrons," "atoms," "atomic nuclei," and "molecules." (WK 2007pp)

And hadrons are further sub-classified into "composite fermions" (or, alternatively, "baryons") and "composite bosons" (or, alternatively, "mesons").

Where Will This End?

One good question to ask here concerns the cycle of further classification and sub-classification in particle taxonomy. Where will this business of particle classification end after all?

Jess Brewer (1994) thus rightly asked: "Is this just another round of simplification followed by more complexity at a deeper level? Possibly. It has been proposed that quarks and leptons may themselves be composite particles, and further that every particle must have a 'supersymmetric' (or SUSY) partner of the opposite sort of statistics—for each fermion there must be a supersymmetric boson, and vice versa. There is no shortage of new theories, nor is arrogance in short supply—one model called 'superstrings' has been touted as a TOE (Theory Of Everything) by the New York Times (which loves to get into these debates)."

To confuse the reader further, some physicists even propose alternative classifications. Consider the following four alternative possibilities.

Firstly, one alternative classification concerns "hypothetical particles," and good examples include "superpartners" in supersymmetric theories—such as "photinos" (spin-½) as the superpartners of photons, "gluinos" (spin-½) as the superpartners of "gluons," "gravitinos" (spin-3⁄2) as the superpartners of "gravitons," etc. (WK 2007pp)

Secondly, another alternative classification concerns "condensed matter" for "quasi-particles" (e.g., "phonons" in "vibrational modes in a crystal lattice," "excitons" in "bound states of an electron and a hole," "plasmons" in "coherent excitations of a plasma," etc.). (WK 2007pp)

Thirdly, the next alternative classification concerns the factor of speed. For instance, a "tardyon or bradyon travels slower than light and has a non-zero rest mass. A luxon travels at the speed of light and has no rest mass. A tachyon…is a hypothetical particle that travels faster than the speed of light and has an imaginary rest mass." (WK 2007pp)

And fourthly, still another classification includes the rest which cannot be neatly fitted into any of the above taxonomic schemes. For example, a "WIMP (weakly interacting massive particle) is any one of a number of particles that might explain dark matter (such as the neutralino or the axion). The pomeron… used to explain the elastic scattering of hadrons and the location of Regge poles in Regge theory. The skyrmion, a topological solution of the pion field, used to model the low-energy properties of the nucleon, such as the axial vector current coupling and the mass." (WK 2007pp)

Challenging Thoughts

And the list can go on, of course. But the lessons to learn from this illustrative case study are two-fold.

Firstly, the more complicated the classification becomes, the more likely something is messed up in the conundrum. This is a major reason for the appearance of alternative classifications to challenge the standard one, as there is some uneasiness in the community of physicists about the current messy particle classification.

Secondly, the more precise the classification is, the less room there is for later additions, without substantially revising the whole taxonomic scheme. But physicists love preciseness in their measurement, so there is no end to this recurrent revision of particle taxonomy for the future to come.

Taxonomy and Macro-Physics (or Cosmology)

But this only takes us to a related field of physics, namely, macro-physics (or cosmology).

The business of particle taxonomy in micro-physics brings us to a related topic in macro-physics (or cosmology), albeit in a different focus—since one can ask the origins of all these particles, which then raise the issue concerning the nature of the cosmos.

For instance, were all of these particles formed in the early time of the cosmos? If so, what happened before the beginning?

Initial and Eternal Cosmologies

In the history of cosmology, there has been an endless debate concerning the beginning and end of the cosmos. Thus, the cosmological taxonomy looks quite complicated and even confusing, indeed.

Rudiger Vaas (2003) once took the trouble to list the major views concerning the beginning and end of the cosmos in a cosmological taxonomy classified by (a) "initial cosmologies" (viz., with a beginning) and (b) "eternal cosmologies" (viz., without a beginning)—as summarized in *Table 2.2 & Table 2.3*.

(a) Firstly, those who argue for "eternal cosmologies" can be further classified into sub-categories, namely, (i) "eternal substance" (for "transformations, aggregations, or recurrence"), (ii) "eternity: no beginning and no transience/destructibility" (for "matter, motion, the celestial sphere, or deity"), (iii) "eternity of the world, but emanation of the deity"), (iv) "timelessness of creation," (v) *"creatio continua"* ("continuous maintenance and re-creation of the world"), (vi) "no beginning and no end," (v) "no beginning, but an end," (vi) "cyclic universe," (vii) "self-creating universe," and (viii) "pseudo-beginning"—as more detailedly summarized in *Table 2.2*. (R. Vaas 2003)

(b) Secondly, those who argue for "initial cosmologies" can also be further classified into sub-categories, namely, (i) "absolute beginning, creation," (*"creatio ex nihilo"*), (ii) "beginning, no end," and (iii) "beginning and an end"—as also summarized in more detail in *Table 2.3*. (R. Vaas 2003)

Explanatory Problems

But the list reveals some obvious problems in the taxonomy, in that all of them suffer, in a way or another, from serious explanatory problems.

Firstly, the "eternal cosmologies" have the recurrent problem of how to explain "the infinite past."

Rudiger Vaas (2003) thus concisely put it: "Eternal cosmologies need not assume a first cause or accident, but they shift the burden of explanation into the infinite past. Although every event might be explicable by earlier events and causal laws, eternal cosmologies cannot even address why a temporally infinite cosmos exists and why it is the way it is. And there might be even deeper problems: Because we are able to assign a symbol to represent infinity and can manipulate such a symbol according to specified rules, one might assume that corresponding infinite entities (e.g. particles or universes) exist. But the actual (i.e. realized in contrast to potential or conceptual) physical (in contrast to the mathematical) infinite has been criticized vehemently being not constructible, implying contradictions etc....If this would be correct it should also apply to an infinite past." (D. Hilbert 1964; R. Spitzer 2000; W. Stoeger 2004)

Secondly, the "initial cosmologies" do not fare any better in relation to their own unique problems (e.g., how to explain something out of nothing).

Vaas (2003) thus rightly observed: "Initial cosmologies, on the other hand, run into deep metaphysical troubles to explain how something could come out of nothing and why is there something rather than nothing at all....Even the theological doctrine of *creatio ex nihilo* does not start with nothing at all but with something, that is God, so the principle *ex nihilo nihil fit* still holds. And contemporary secularized *ex-nihilo* initial cosmologies usually claim, as Alexander Vilenkin said..., that there were at least the laws of physics even if there was nothing more at all....Concerning this model, Vilenkin admitted that '[t]he concept of the universe being created from nothing is a crazy one,' and his analogy with particle pair creation only deepens the problem, because matter-antimatter particles do not pop out of nothing but are transformations of energy which is already there." (R. Nozick 1981; A. Vilenkin 1982)

Other thinkers share a comparable skepticism towards "initial cosmologies." For example, "Heinz Pagels subscribed to some kind of platonism with respect to physical laws: 'This unthinkable void converts itself into the plenum of existence—a necessary consequence of physical laws. Where are these laws written into that void? What 'tells' the void that it is pregnant with a possible universe? It would seem that even the void is subject to law, a logic that exists prior to space and time." (R. Vaas 2003)

Stephen Hawking (1988) also said: "Even if there is only one possible unified theory, it is just a set of rules and equations. What is it that breathes fire into the equations and makes a universe for them to describe? The usual approach of science of constructing a mathematical model cannot answer the question of why there should be a universe for the model to describe. Why does the universe go to all the bother of existing?"

But then, as Vaas (2003) further observed, "if one does not subscribe to an origin of something (or everything) from really nothing, one need not accept platonism with respect to the ontological status of physical laws....They might simply be seen as the outcome of invariant properties of nature. If so, they do not govern nature but are instantiated from it. They are abstract descriptions— like a model or theory of reality...not to be confused with reality itself."

So, what does this teach us about the nature of taxonomy?

Taxonomic Headache

In the end, these problems give cosmological taxonomy a serious headache, which in turn can teach us something.

Consider three illustration in what follows.

Firstly, the more complicated a taxonomy is by including everything, the more messy it looks, as illustrated by the taxonomy of eternal and initial cosmologies above (as also summarized in *Table 2.2* and *Table 2.3*).

Secondly, on the other hand, the more simplified a taxonomy is constructed (to avoid the mess of complication), the more unrealistic it is in failing to consider alternative views (as in the narrow-minded views on cosmology in antiquity, without the hindsights of modern and contemporary cosmology).

Thirdly, the more precise the terms in a taxonomy are defined, the more inclusive it is in excluding alternative conceptual possibilities. For instance, Vaas (2003) identified different meanings of the term "universe" by different scholars in the history of cosmological taxonomy, with each having its own conceptual limit. (R. Vaas 2001 & 2003; J. Wheeler 1983; J. Barrett 1999; M. Gell-Mann 1990 & 1993; B. DeWitt 1973; M. Tegmark 2004)

Here are some illustrative definitions which have been used over time for the term "universe," namely, (a) "everything (physically) in existence, ever, anywhere," (b) "the observable region we inhabit (the Hubble volume, roughly 27 billion light years in diameter), plus everything that has interacted (for example due to a common origin) or will ever or at least in the next few billion years interact with this region," (c) "any gigantic system of causally interacting things that is wholly (or to a very large extent or for a long time) isolated from others," be it in terms of a "multi-domain universe" or a "multiverse," (d) "any system that *might* well have become gigantic, etc., even if it does in fact recollapse while it is still very small," (e) "other branches of the wavefunction (if it never collapses...) in unitary quantum physics, i.e. different histories of the universe...or different classical worlds which are in superposition," and (f) "completely disconnected systems consisting of universes in one of the former meanings, which do or do not share the same boundary conditions, constants, parameters, vacuum states, effective low energy laws, or even fundamental laws, e.g. different physically realized mathematical structures." (R. Vaas 2003)

Illustrative though these problems are here, the point is that the dilemmas concerning preciseness vs. vagueness and simpleness vs. complicatedness show themselves once more in the history of taxonomy.

Taxonomy and Biology (Animal)

Another good way to start here is none other than the classification of living organisms—although taxonomy, as it should be stressed at the outset, can target all kinds of things, be they about "animate objects, inanimate objects, places, concepts, events, properties, and relationships." (WK 2007g)

Two case studies are in order, namely, (2.2.4.1) Linnaean taxonomy and (2.2.4.2) phylogenetic taxonomy—to be analyzed hereafter, respectively.

Linnaean Taxonomy

One of the most influential taxonomic schemes to classify living organisms is the one proposed by Carl Linnaeus (1707-1778), considered by many as the "father of modern taxonomy." (WK 2007j & 2007k)

Three Main Features of Linnaean Taxonomy

Linnaeus 's most well-known contribution to taxonomy was the original idea in his classical work *Systema Naturae* (1758) that all living organisms could be classified in accordance to the observable principle of "shared physical characteristics," with the use of "binomial nomenclature," into seven main levels of hierarchical ranking (i.e., "Kingdom, Phylum or Division, Class, Order, Family, Genus [or plural Genera], and Species"). (WK 2007h, 2007j, 2007k & 2007l)

In other words, the Linnaean taxonomy has three main features, namely, (a) the observable principle of "shared physical characteristics," (b) the use of "binomial nomenclature," and (c) the appeal to seven levels of hierarchical ranking.

In (a), the main criterion for classification is the search for "shared physical characteristics" among the living organisms in question. For instance, lions and tigers are classified as big cats, but snakes are not, because the latter have less in common with the former in terms of observable shared physical characteristics.

In (b), the trick to label a living organism is by way of a system of binomial names, which uses "the combination of a *genus* name and a single specific epithet to uniquely identify each *species* of organism. For example, the human species is uniquely identified by the binomial *Homo sapiens*. No other species of animal can have this binomial." (WK 2007j)

In other words, "a species is assigned a two-part name, treated as Latin. The genus is listed first (with its leading letter capitalized), followed by a second term." (WK 2007l) In another example, "gray wolves belong to the species *Canis lupus*, coyotes to *Canis latrans*, golden jackals to *Canis aureus*, etc...." (WK 2007l)

And in (c), there are seven main levels of hierarchical ranking, but not more, as a way to prevent any taxonomic scheme from being trapped in the problem of endless subdivisions for more and more preciseness.

Preciseness needs to have an end somewhere.

Main Weaknesses

The Linnaean classification remains to this day useful, especially though not exclusively in the biological sciences.

Yet, the Linnaean taxonomy is not without its inherent weaknesses, and a good illustration concerns its three main features.

Just consider four examples below.

Firstly, in regard to (a), much has changed since his time in relation to the principle of "shared physical characteristics." (WK 2007K) After all, one can ask, Why should a scientist be limited by the observable principle (of shared physical characteristics) in classification? Can a scientist also look into unobservable ones too?

For instance, what was not known or available in Linnaeus' time is in our more scientifically developed time very important instead, and a good example is of course "DNA sequencing," which is "unavailable in Linnaeus' time [but] has proven to be a tool of considerable utility for classifying living organisms and establishing their relationships to each other." (WK 2007k)

Secondly, also in regard to (a), are there other principles which can be appeal to in doing taxonomy—besides the principle of shared physical characteristics?

The answer is yes, since there are other principles which have been used for the classification of living organisms, and a good example is the taxonomic scheme to classify animals in accordance to "their mode of movement," although it is not very popular in our time but used to be more fashionable in the old days. (2007j)

Thirdly, in regard to (b), the nomenclature is limited to be binomial. But one can ask, Why binomial? Why not trinomial? Or even better, why not something else altogether?

This is like asking, Why do phone numbers have 7 digits in Boston, U.S.A.— but only 6 in Karaganda, Kazakhstan and only 5 in Gilgit, Pakistan? In fact, as will be clear in the next sub-section, an emergent alternative is known as the "phylogenetic nomenclature," to replace Linnaeus 's binominal nomenclature.

And fourthly, in regard to (c), the number of "seven" levels in Linnaean taxonomy seems to be a bit superstitious. Why seven, one may ask?

Nowadays, for instance, some scientists add another level called "Domain," which is above "Kingdom." (WK 2007j) Other scholars even proposed an additional level known as "Life," to be above the one of "Domain." (WK 2007l) Still others wanted to add one more level, "Sub-Genus," to be between "Genus" and "Species." (WK 2007l)

Even then, some researchers are not happy, and this is especially so in some fields of study which require more preciseness in classification than others as science advances over time.

For this reason, even more levels of classification have been proposed, and good examples are "such entities as phyla, superclasses, superorders, infraorders, families, superfamilies and tribes....There are [even] ranks below species: in zoology, subspecies and morph; in botany, variety (varietas) and form (forma). Many botanists now use 'subspecies' instead of 'variety' although the two are not, strictly speaking, of equivalent rank, and 'form' has largely fallen out of use." (WK 2007j)

And "[m]any of these extra hierarchical levels tend to arise in disciplines such as entomology, whose subject matter is replete with species requiring classification. Any biological field that is species rich, or which is subject to a revision of the state of current knowledge concerning those species and their relationships to each other, will inevitably make use of the additional hierarchical levels, particularly when fossil forms are integrated into classifications originally designed for extant living organisms, and when newer classification tools such as cladistics are applied to facilitate this." (WK 2007j)

So, the total number of levels can be 8, 9, 10, or many more in our times—not 7 as Linnaeus originally proposed. For example, *Lupinus texensis,* which is a plant known as "the Texas bluebonnet," can be classified in relation to the 11 main levels as shown below: (G. Diggs 1999)

———

- Superkingdom = Eukaryota
- Kingdom = Plantae
- Division = Magnoliophyta
- Class = Dicotyledonae
- Subclass = Rosidae
- Order = Fabales
- Family = Fabaceae
- Subfamily = Papilionoideae
- Tribe = Genisteae

- Genus = *Lupinus*
- Species = *texensis*

———

This continued contention in classification raises an interesting question concerning how precise or vague a taxonomic scheme is supposed to be, for later addition or revision, when knowledge accumulates over time in scientific research.

Phylogenetic Taxonomy

For this reason, there have been calls for a new taxonomic scheme to replace Linnaean taxonomy.

Two Crucial Features of Phylogenetic Taxonomy

A good starting point to understand this problem is the analysis of a related (but competing) taxonomy in the field of evolutionary theory—namely, phylogenetic taxonomy.

After all, "our understanding of the relationships between living things has changed. Linnaeus could only base his scheme on the structural similarities of the different organisms. The greatest change was the widespread acceptance of evolution as the mechanism of biological diversity and species formation. It then became generally understood that classifications ought to reflect the phylogeny of organisms, by grouping each taxon so as to include the common ancestor of the group's members (and thus to avoid polyphyly). Such taxa may be either monophyletic (including all descendants) such as genus *Homo*, or paraphyletic (excluding some descendants), such as genus *Australopithecus*." (WK 2007j)

Edwin Goodrich in 1916 and Jacques Gauthier in 1986, just to cite two scholars (among others), were credited for circulating the use of phylogenetic nomenclature. (WK 2007n)

Two most crucial features which separate phylogenetic nomenclature from Linnaean nomenclature are (a) "the use of phylogenetic definitions of biological taxon names" and (b) "the lack of obligatory ranks"—as explicated below. (WK 2007n)

In regard to (a), the word *phylogentics* is composed of *phyle* ("tribe" or "race" in Greek) and *genetikos* ("relative to birth," from *genesis* = "birth")— and thus refers to "the study of evolutionary relatedness among various groups of organisms (e.g., species, populations)," that is, in relation to their lineage connection. (WK 2007o)

In regard to (b), this lineage connection in evolution is more concerned with evolutionary classification without any obligatory ranks. (WK 2007o) This is so, since phylogentic classification acknowledges some basic constraints on its understanding of the world, to the extent that hierarchical ranking is not obligatory. Why?

A major reason is that the world is understood to be more complex, since "populations are altered over time and may speciate into separate branches, hybridize together again, or terminate by extinction." (WK 2007o) In addition, it is also acknowledged that "genetic data is only available for the present, and fossil records (osteometric data) are sporadic and less reliable. Our knowledge of how evolution operates is used to reconstruct the full tree." (WK 2007o)

With these constraints in mind, the lineage-connected individuals without any obligatory ranks in phylogenetic classification can be either (i) node-based, (ii) branch-based, and (iii) apomorphy-based. (WK 2007n)

In (i), the classification is "node-based," in that it includes "the most recent common ancestor [abbreviated as MRCA] of A and B (and C etc. as needed), and all its descendants," and this group is called a "clade" (meaning = "a group of biological taxa...as species...that includes all descendants of one common ancestor), and this clade is in fact "the smallest clade that includes A and B (and C etc.)." (MWD 2007; WK 2007n)

In (ii), the classification is "branch-based," which is more complicated, in that "all organisms or species...share a more recent common ancestor with A (and B, C, etc. as needed) than with Z (and with Y, X, etc. as needed)." (WK 2007n)

In (iii), the classification is "apomorphy-based," where the term *apomorphy* (meaning = "separate form") is to contrast with *plesiomorphy* (meaning = "close form")." (WK 2007p) In other words, it is a more neutral term to denote "advanced" as opposed to "primitive" in meaning. (WK 2007p)

An apomorphy-based classification simply refers to "the first organism or species [which is] to possess apomorphies M (and N etc. as needed) as inherited by A (and B etc. as needed), and all its descendants," so that "the clade" is known "by the presence of M (and N etc.) as inherited by A (and B etc.)." (WK 2007n)

The Example of an Evolutionary Tree

In fact, the illustration of an evolutionary tree can show more details about the nature of phylogenetic taxonomy in action.

In an evolutionary tree, the classification is phylogenetic, because it shows "the evolutionary interrelationships among various species or other entities that are believed to have a common ancestor. In a phylogenetic tree, each node with descendants represents the most recent common ancestor of the descendants, with edge lengths sometimes corresponding to time estimates. Each node in a phylogenetic tree is called a taxonomic unit." (WK 2007i)

Surely, the idea of an evolutionary tree has some affinity to "the idea of a 'tree of life'" which "arose from ancient notions of a ladder-like progression from lower to higher forms of life (such as in the Great Chain of Being)," but it was Charles Darwin (1859) who "first illustrated and popularized the notion of an evolutionary 'tree' in his seminal book *The Origin of Species*. Over a century later, evolutionary biologists still use tree diagrams to depict evolution because the floral analogy effectively conveys the concept that speciation occurs through the adaptive and random splitting of lineages." (WK 2007i)

An evolutionary tree can be (i) rooted or (ii) unrooted in phylogenetic classification, for instance.

In (i), it is "a directed tree with a unique node corresponding to the (usually imputed) most recent common ancestor of all the entities at the leaves of the tree. The most common method for rooting trees is the use of an uncontroversial outgroup—close enough to allow inference from sequence or trait data, but far enough to be a clear outgroup." (WK 2007i)

In (ii), however, it shows "the relatedness of the leaf nodes without making assumptions about common ancestry. While unrooted trees can always be generated from rooted ones by simply omitting the root, a root cannot be inferred from an unrooted tree without some means of identifying ancestry." (WK 2007i)

In either way, both "rooted and unrooted phylogenetic trees can be either bifurcating or multifurcating....A bifurcating tree has a maximum of two descendants arising from each interior node, while a multifurcating tree may have more than two...but there are always more multifurcating than bifurcating trees,...and more rooted than unrooted trees." (WK 2007i)

<u>Some Limitations in Phylogenetic taxonomy</u>

But phylogenetic nomenclature has its limits, just as Linnaean one has its own.

The reasons are not hard to understand. Here are a few examples.

Firstly, "[p]hylogenetic trees do not necessarily (and likely do not) represent actual evolutionary history," and there are plenty of reasons for this false representation: "The data on which they are based is noisy; horizontal gene transfer, hybridisation between species that were not nearest neighbors on the tree before hybridisation takes place, convergent evolution, and conserved sequences can all confound the analysis." (WK 2007i)

Secondly, "basing the analysis on a single gene or protein taken from a group of species can be problematic because such trees constructed from another unrelated gene or protein sequence often differ from the first, and therefore great care is needed in inferring phylogenetic relationships amongst species. This is most true of genetic material that is subject to lateral gene transfer and recombination, where different haplotype blocks can have different histories." (WK 2007i)

And thirdly, another problem occurs with the inclusion of extinct species: "When extinct species are included in a tree, they should always be terminal nodes, as it is unlikely that they are direct ancestors of any extant species. Scepticism must apply when extinct species are included in trees that are wholly or partly based on DNA sequence data, due to evidence that 'ancient DNA' is not preserved intact for longer than 100,000 years." (WK 2007i)

In sum, taxonomic schemes—be they phylogenetic, Linnaean, or else—are often torn in between preciseness and vagueness, on the one hand, and simpleness and complicatedness, on the other hand—all depending on contingent circumstances which construct them in the first place.

Taxonomy and the Mind

Taxonomy, when analyzed from the perspective of the mind (and summarized in *Table 4.4*), yields a fascinating story which is not less problematic, however.

A good point of departure is an analysis on the role of the mind in processing information from the outside world, especially in relation to (2.3.1) biology (human) and (2.3.2) psychology—respectively hereafter.

Taxonomy and Biology (Human)

It is a conventional wisdom that "most people need peace and quiet" to process information efficiently; otherwise, they could easily be distracted.

Neural Representational Instability in Info Processing

But a new study at the Massachusetts Institute of Technology (M.I.T.) suggests the opposite, with profound implications on how information is processed in the human brain for taxonomy.

Teaching and Tickering

In the M.I.T. study published in the May 24, 2007 issue of the journal *Neuron*, Sebastian Seung, Uri Rokni, and Emilio Bizzi experimented with monkeys and "found that neural activities in the brain gradually change, even when nothing new is being learned. Challenging the monkeys to adjust their task triggered systematic changes in their neural activities on top of this background 'noise.'" (HHMI 2007)

Sebastian Seung, professor of physics and computational neuroscience at M.I.T., thus said: "What surprised us most was that the neural representation of movement seems to change even when behavior doesn't seem to change at all. This was a surprising degree of instability in the brain's representation of the world." (HHMI 2007) This degree of instability has a peculiar role to play in processing information from the outside world.

To understand this, the researchers relied on an earlier work on "neural activities in the motor cortex while monkeys manipulated a handle to move a cursor to targets on a screen. In control experiments, the monkeys had to move the cursor to targets in the same way they had been trained. In learning experiments, the monkeys had to adapt their movements to compensate for novel forces applied to the handle. The scientists found that even when the monkeys were performing the familiar control task, their neural activities gradually changed over the course of the session." (HHMI 2007)

But why? Would it be possible that some background changes accounted for the change in neural activities? Or, may there be something else instead? Rokni then adjusted any background changes in the experiment to "distinguish learning-related neural changes from the background changes that occurred during the control experiments. From this analysis, Rokni developed a working theory that combined the concepts of a redundant neural network and that of a 'noisy' brain." (HHMI 2007)

Rokni offered this analogy to understand the new theory of a redundant neural network: "A good analogy to redundant circuitry, which accomplishes the same behavior by different wiring configurations, would be a piece of text, in which you can say the same thing with different words. Our theory holds that the learning brain has the equivalent of a 'teacher' and a 'tinkerer'—a learning signal and noise in the learning process, respectively." (HHMI 2007)

Here is how the brain intervenes in processing information in both chaotic and orderly way: "In producing a specific piece of text, the tinkerer just randomly changes the words, while the teacher continually corrects the text to make it have the right meaning. The teacher only cares about the meaning and not the precise wording. When the teacher and tinkerer work together, the text keeps changing but the meaning remains the same. For example, the tinkerer may change the sentence 'John is married' to 'John is single,' and the teacher may correct it to 'John is not single.'" (HHMI 2007)

Thus, by analogy, "learning in the brain has two components—error-correction and noise—so that even though the neural representation keeps changing, the behavior remains fixed. We think the tinkerer, that is the noise, is not merely a nuisance to the teacher but is actually helping the teacher explore new possibilities it wouldn't have considered otherwise." (HHMI 2007)

The surprising discovery of "redundant networks" and "noisy learning" has practical implications, as Rokni himself well said: "I don't think this concept of redundancy—that the brain can say the same thing in different ways—has really been fully appreciated until now....More practically, people who are constructing devices that translate brain signals to operate such external devices as neural prostheses will have to take such constantly changing neural representations into account." (HHMI 2007)

Some Problems for Thought

Impressive though the finding is, there is still a long way to go for the understanding of some deeper issues.

A first problem concerns how exactly this representational instability affects the way that information is processed in a certain way for taxonomy.

For instance, in what detailed way does the brain impose chaos in info processing, even if it is meant to explore different possibilities of analyzing the same thing?

This has further confirming implications for one of the ontological principles that I already proposed in an earlier book of mine titled *The Future of Complexity* (2007), namely, what I originally called "the order-chaos principle."

Secondly, to what extent does this representational instability affect the preciseness (or conversely, vagueness) and simpleness (or conversely, complicatedness) in information classification?

More works need to be done on this. And this biological issue can be further illuminated in relation to the works on taxonomy and psychology below (as the two sections overlap a bit).

Taxonomy and Psychology

In the field of psychology, taxonomy can be shown in a fascinating way, and two good case studies concern the analysis of (2.3.2.1) gender differences in info processing, and (2.3.2.2) political genetic differences in info processing—respectively hereafter.

Gender Differences in Info Processing

Joshua New of Yale University, in a article in the August 23, 2007 issue of the *Proceedings of the Royal Society*, interestingly showed gender differences in solving spatial problems. (ET 2007)

Spatial Problem Solving and Hunting-Gathering

In his study of shopping at a farmer's market, Dr. New was able to confirm that "men are better than women at solving certain sorts of spatial problems, such as remembering the locations of topographical landmarks. Many researchers suggest such skills may have been important in the past for man-the-hunter, who needed to be able to find his way round the landscape. If that is the case, then woman-the-gatherer might have been expected to develop complementary skills not shown by males." (ET 2007)

Dr. New revealed these complementary skills in women, by showing (a) that "women remember the locations of food resources more accurately than men do" and (b) that "the more nutritionally valuable a resource is, the more accurately its location will be remembered." (ET 2007)

In order to prove (a), Dr. New first "recruited 41 women and 45 men and led each of them individually on a merry dance around the chosen market. In the course of this peregrination, each participant visited six of the 90 food stalls in the market. At each of those stalls, participants were given a piece of food to eat. They were asked their preference for the taste of the food, how often they ate that food in normal life, how attractive they found the stall and how often they had made purchases from that stall in the past. After visiting all six stalls, they were taken to the centre of the market and asked to point toward those stalls, one at a time, using an arrow on a dial. In addition, they were asked to rate their own sense of direction." (ET 2007)

The result was thus: "On average, women were 9° more accurate than men at pointing to each stall—a significant deviation if you have to walk some distance to get to a place. This was not because those women had more experience of visiting the market than the men had. Nor did the women rate themselves as having a better sense of direction—indeed the men rated their own navigating skills more highly." (ET 2007)

In other words, "these results show women are better than men at the particular task of relocating sources of food. That contrasts with the idea that men are better at navigation in general. In other words, women's minds are specialised for their ancestral task of gathering the sort of food that cannot run away." (ET 2007)

In order to prove (b), Dr. New found in his results that "[t]he higher the calorific value of the food sold by a stall, the more accurately Dr. New's volunteers were able to point towards it. And that result applied to both sexes, though women still did better than men." (ET 2007)

It should be stressed, however, that in Dr. New's study, "[h]ow much the participants liked the food did not have an effect on this accuracy. Indeed none of the secondary attributes of the food or stall in question (taste preference, the frequency of an item in a volunteer's normal diet, the appearance of the stall and how often a volunteer used that stall in daily life) were found to affect pointing accuracy. Only the calorific value of the item in question was relevant." (ET 2007)

Some Difficult Questions for Taxonomy

Dr. New's results indeed raise some difficult questions concerning gender differences in information processing, especially in relation to taxonomy.

For instance, if men are better, on average, than women in processing information concerning topographical landmarks, and if women are better, on average, than men in processing information concerning locations of food resources—then this respective competence should also show up in classifying information in regard to topograhical landmarks and, conversely, in regard to locations of food resources.

In other words, more can be said in regard to how exactly men classify information in relation to topographical landmarks to make them easier to be found and how exactly women classify information in relation to sources of food to make them likewise easier to be found again.

This question seems to have a helpful answer from another study published in *Current Biology*, this time, by Anya Hurlbert and Yazhu Ling of Newcastle University in England. (ET 2007)

In the study, "volunteers were men and women of British and Chinese origin who were in their early 20s," and they were asked to use "coloured patches flashing on a computer screen to find the preferences of their set of volunteers." (ET 2007)

What is interesting in the study is that "the two researchers found that people of different sexes and from different continents did not differ in their colour preferences. But there was one exception. Among both the British and the Chinese, women preferred reddish hues such as pink to greenish-blue ones. Among men it was the other way round." (ET 2007)

To go one step further, Dr. Hurlbert and Dr. Ling wanted to know "how masculine or feminine the brains of their participants were," so they "used what is known as the Bem Sex Role Inventory, which asks about personality traits more often associated with one sex than the other. This showed that the more feminine a brain was, regardless of the body it inhabited, the more it liked red and pink." (ET 2007)

The conclusion here suggests "a biological, rather than a cultural, explanation for colour preference. And Dr. Hurlbert and Dr. Ling have produced one. They suggest that their result may be connected with the fact that the colour of many fruits is at the red end of the spectrum. An evolved preference for red, pink and allied shades—particularly in contrast with green—could thus bring advantage to those who gather such things. And if they can also remember which tree (or stall) to go and visit next time, then so much the better." (ET 2007)

In this sense, women tend to classify info more on the basis of certain color preferences (like red and pink) than on the basis of something else (like green and blue) for men.

Political Genetic Differences in Info Processing

But there is another difference in information processing, this time, in relation to political genetic endowment.

Whether Political Divides Are Hard-Wired

It is part of conventional wisdom that, for instance, "[c]onservatives tend to crave order and structure in their lives, and are more consistent in the way they make decisions. Liberals, by contrast, show a higher tolerance for ambiguity and complexity, and adapt more easily to unexpected circumstances." (M. Hood 2007)

So, New York University political scientist David Amodio and colleagues were curious enough to decide "to find out if the brains of liberals and conservatives reacted differently to the same stimuli," and their findings were published in the September, 2007 issue of the British journal *Nature Neuroscience.* (M. Hood 2007)

To start, they organized a "group of 43 right-handed subjects" who "were asked to perform a series of computer tests designed to evaluate their unrehearsed response to cues urging them to break a well-established routine." (M. Hood 2007)

For instance, as Amodio explained, "[p]eople often drive home from work on the same route, day after day, such that it becomes habitual and doesn't involve much thinking. But occasionally there is road work, or perhaps an animal crosses the road, and you need to break out of your habitual response in order to deal with this new information." (M. Hood 2007)

In the study, Amodio then used "electroencephalographs, which measure neuronal impulses," to study "activity in a part of the brain—the anterior cingulate cortex—that is strongly linked with the self-regulatory process of conflict monitoring." (M. Hood 2007)

They then discovered that "[t]he brain neurons of liberals and conservatives fire differently when confronted with tough choices, suggesting that some political divides may be hard-wired." (M. Hood 2007)

This is so, because "respondents who had described themselves as liberals showed 'significantly greater conflict-related neural activity' when the hypothetical situation called for an unscheduled break in routine. Conservatives, however, were less flexible, refusing to deviate from old habits 'despite signals that this...should be changed.'" (M. Hood 2007)

And more, "[t[he neural mechanisms for conflict monitoring are formed early in childhood," as Amodio suggested. (M. Hood 2007)

<u>Some Skeptical Notes</u>

But this study should be taken with care.

Firstly, for instance, Amodio and his team did not answer the question "of which comes first, the patterns in neuron activity or the political orientation." (M. Hood 2007)

Secondly, as Amodio added, "even if genes may provide a blueprint for more liberal or conservative orientations, they are shaped substantially by one's environment over the course of development." (M. Hood 2007)

Thirdly, the talk of causal links can be messy, since "the brain is malleable and neural functions can change as a result of new experiences." (M. Hood 2007)

But the merit of the research is to show us that some individuals (like the Liberals) are more likely, on average of course, to classify info which allows vagueness (ambiguity), disorder (chaos), and complicatedness—whereas others (like the Conservatives) are more likely to demand preciseness, order, and simplicity.

Taxonomy and Culture

But taxonomy can be affected in a different way, this time from the perspective of culture, especially in relation to four major domains, namely, (2.4.1) morality, (2.4.2) epistemology, (2.4.3) religion, and (2.4.4) aesthetics—to be analyzed respectively hereafter (and summarized in *Table 4.5*).

Taxonomy and Morality

A most fascinating account of the impact of morality on taxonomy is none other than the issue concerning moral taxonomy.

The idea of the genealogy of morals by Friedrich Nietzsche is a telling story of the origins of moral taxonomy to share here.

The Genealogy of Moral Taxonomy

It is quite common for people in different moralities to know that there is a serious distinction to be made between two opposite categories, or a vital dichotomy to be classified in terms of two binary opposites, namely, the "good" and the "evil."

Those who favor one opposite stand on one side of the moral divide, whereas those who favor the other opposite stand on the other side. And they seldom see each other eye-to-eye with any substantive approval.

What then is the genealogy of this moral taxonomy?

The Classification of the "Good" vs. the "Bad"

Nietzsche offered his own answer, in that to understand the moral classification of the "good" vs. the "evil" categories requires an understanding of the prior classification of the "good" vs. the "bad" alternatives in historical genealogy. (F. Nietzsche 1969)

In the older days of Western history, for Nietzsche, what was understood as the "good" was applied primarily for the "aristocrats" (the upper social stratum), who ruled over the lower one like the "plebeians," or any comparble name. (F. Nietzsche 1969; S. DeLue 2002; R. Wedgwood 1998) The aristocrats stood for the conquering Aryans who subdued the aboriginal population and enthroned themselves as the master race.

The distinction between the "good" and the "bad' was then institutionalized for the two groups.

On the one hand, the aristocrats were classified as the "good" for their noble qualities: well-born, courageous, arrogant, dignified, confident, optimist, life-affirming, and the like.

On the other hand, the plebeians received the lesser classificatory label known as the "bad" for their lower qualities: born of inferior background, cowardly, humble, cunning, pessimist, life-denying, and the like.

The "good" was reserved for the nobility and the aristocracy—whereas the "bad" was for the slaves and the commoners.

The Classification of the "Good" vs. the "Evil"

Then, something with great historical significance happened, which overthrew this distinction and in the process offered an entirely new moral taxonomy, this time, the distinction between the "good" and the "evil." (F. Nietzsche 1969; S. DeLue 2002; R. Wedgwood 1998)

The group which Nietzsche singled out for attention is the Jews in the moral history of the West. This group was of the lower origin, who wandered for a permanent home from one place to another—be it ancient Egypt, Babylon, the Roman Empire, or later, the rest of Europe.

They came up with a new system of morality (Judaism), which required rigid allegiance to some commandments allegedly given by God, to be further strengthened by some disciplinary routines, for the equality of everyone under

God. Thus, the very classificatory idea of the superior aristocrats over the inferior plebeians was regarded as most unacceptable to them.

The Christians, with the help of Jesus Christ, took over the monotheism of Judaism and their monastery lifestyle and championed the new classification of the "good" vs. the "evil" as "a slave revolt" against the aristocratic classification of the "good" vs. the "bad"—by turning the latter upside down, in two strikes simultaneously.

On the one hand, the "good," in this Christian reversed moral taxonomy, now treated the aristocrats as "evil"—in special regard to their once respectable values (e.g., confident, life-affirming, proud, rank-conscious, etc.). The aristocrats were even re-classified into condemned categories comparable to the evil "blood beasts" or "predatory lions," by comparison.

On the other hand, the "bad" for the plebeians in the older days was now re-classified instead as the "good"—in special regard to their once despised values (e.g., diffident, life-denying, humble, equalitarian, etc.).

This revolt of the plebeians against the aristocrats stood for the recurrent fight in human history between the masters and the slaves, the strong and the weak, the elites and the masses, the loner and the herd, and any comparible dichotomies.

Some Disturbing Questions

Nietzsche's insightful historical account of the origins of the moral taxonomic schemes concerning the "good" vs. the "evil"—and the "good" vs. the "bad"—is praised, even by his critics.

Yet, some disturbing questions can be raised in regard to his analysis. Consider four illustrative examples below.

Firstly, Jacques Derrida (1984: 24) once pondered about this thoughtful question: "One may wonder why the only teaching institution or the only beginning of a teaching institution that ever succeeded in taking as its model the teaching of Nietzsche on teaching will have been a Nazi one."

Secondly, is the genealogy of morals in regard to the classificatory distinctions between "good" and "evil" (and "good" and "bad") really empirically true in European culture—let alone other civilizations?

Thirdly, does the Nietzschean critique reflect the wishful, consoling thought of a man who suffered from ill health (and later died of insanity), was not successful with women, and lived a rather uneventful life (of low-paced action)?

And finally, should we choose only between the two classificatory schemes (i.e., "good"-"bad" and "good"-"evil")? Are there any other moral classificatory schemes to seriously consider? For instance, should we consider the Buddhist yearning for the primordial oneness—going beyond all classificatory distinctions?

So, this only raises a larger question concerning the nature of taxonomy. For instance, is the Nietzschean account of moral taxonomy and its historical origins simplistic (e.g., looking at things mostly from the European historical perspective)? And, is his account not precise enough (e.g., lumping everything into only two major taxonomic schemes concerning the "good"-"bad" and "good"-"evil" distinctions)?

In this sense, the taxonomic dilemmas concerning preciseness and vagueness, on the one hand, and simpleness and complicatedness, on the other hand, remain.

Taxonomy and Epistemology

In the case of taxonomy and its relation with epistemology—there is something interesting about Michel Foucault on taxonomy from the perspective of culture

Taxonomy and the Epistemic Orders

In his 1971 book titled *The Order of Things*, Foucault made a comment about "a certain Chinese encyclopedia," which, so he claimed, "breaks up all the ordered surfaces of our thoughts [meaning = Western thought in the modern era]. The encyclopedia divides animals into the following categories: '(a) belonging to the Emperor, (b) embalmed, (c) tame, (d) sucking pigs, (e) sirens, (f) fabulous, (g) stray dogs, (h) included in the present classification, (i) frenzied, (j) innumerable, (k) drawn with a very fine camelhair brush, (l) et cetera, (m) having just broken the water pitcher, (n) that from a long way off look like flies,'" and the rest. (K. Windschuttle 1997)

This Chinese animal taxonomy looked quite strange, indeed, when contrasted with the Western equivalent. Yet for Foucault, "the wonderment of this taxonomy" helped us understand not only "the exotic charm of another system of thought" but also "the limitation of our own." (K. Windschuttle 1997)

As Keith Windschuttle (1997) explained, "[w]hat the taxonomy or form of classification reveals is that, in Foucault's own parlance, 'there would appear to be, then, at the other extremity of the earth we inhabit, a culture . . . that does not distribute the multiplicity of existing things into any of the categories that make it possible for us to name, speak and think.' The stark impossibility of our thinking in this way…demonstrates the existence of an entirely different system of rationality."

One way to reveal this cultural construction of rationality is through the inner working of a language, which makes up the cultural fabric of a knowledge system.

In other words, for Foucault, "knowledge is a derivative of the taxonomy that language parcels up our experience. Language is the cultural fabric of knowledge systems. Knowing oneself, or knowing one's own culture is only possible given the taxonomical structure of knowledge of the knower (or the language users of a society). Knowing a country necessitates knowing how the language structures political relationships between people in the country. Knowledge becomes difficult if not impossible if one does not know the culture's language or language game." (R. Carlson 1989)

More specifically, "[l]inguistic taxonomies are developed in order that a given society can accomplish particular purposes and goals. All linguistic taxonomies and their derivative knowledge systems connote implied political relations. Examples of linguistic taxonomies which have obvious political implications are 'professor'/'student,' 'doctor'/'mental patient,' 'speaker'/'audience,' 'host'/'guest,' 'underdeveloped countries'/'developed countries.' Each of the above examples has implied political power relations and certain behavioral expectations on the part of actors." (R. Carlson 1989)

An Omitted Note of Clarification

But the problem with Foucault's interpretation is that, as Keith Windschuttle (1997) reminded us, "[t]here is, however, a problem rarely mentioned by those who cite the Chinese taxonomy as evidence for these claims. No Chinese encyclopedia has ever described animals under the classification listed by Foucault. In fact, there is no evidence that any Chinese person has ever thought about animals in this way. The taxonomy is fictitious. It is the invention of the Argentinian short-story writer and poet Jorge Luis Borges."

Yet, over the years, researchers have found out some cultural differences in the classification of basic elements in the universe. Good examples include the Hindu tradition (e.g., the *Pancha Mahabhuta*, or "five great elements"—earth, water, fire, air or wind, and aether), the Buddhist tradition (e.g., the *catudhatu* or "four elements"—earth, water, fire and air), the Japanese tradition (e.g., the *go dai* or "five great"—earth, water, fire, wind, and void), the Platonic tradition (e.g., air, fire, earth, and water), the Maori (Polynesian) tradition (e.g., earth, water, wind/air, flora and fire), and the Chinese tradition (e.g., light, darkness, water, fire, and earth). (WK 2007oo)

Some Deeper Questions

Yet, this omission does not discourage others from citing Foucault's work for the cultural deconstruction of certain taxonomic paradigms.

As an illustration, it is illuminating to contrast Foucault's idea of epistemic orders with Thomas Kuhn's notion of paradigmatic changes, in understanding how much our taxonomic schemes culturally shape the way that we think.

Firstly, "[w]hereas Kuhn's paradigm is an all-encompassing collection of beliefs and assumptions that result in the organization of scientific worldviews and practices, Foucault's episteme is not merely confined to science but to a wider range of discourse (all of science itself would fall under the episteme of the epoch)." (WK 2007q)

Secondly, "[w]hile Kuhn's paradigm shifts are a consequence of a series of conscious decisions made by scientists to pursue a neglected set of questions, Foucault's epistemes are something like the 'epistemological unconscious' of an era; the configuration of knowledge in a particular episteme is based on a set of fundamental assumptions that are so basic to that episteme so as to be invisible to people operating within it." (WK 2007q)

Thirdly, "Kuhn's concept seems to correspond to what Foucault calls theme or theory of a science, but Foucault analysed how opposing theories and themes could co-exist within a science." (WK 2007q)

And finally, or fourthly, "Kuhn doesn't search for the conditions of possibility of opposing discourses within a science, but simply for the (relatively) invariant dominant paradigm governing scientific research (supposing that one paradigm always is pervading, except under paradigmatic transition). Like Althusser, who draws on the concept of ideology, Foucault goes deeper through discourses, to demonstrate the constitutive limits of discourse, and in particular, the rules enabling their productivity." (WK 2007q)

And these rules for the production of taxnomic schemes (e.g., "doctor"/"patient," "professor"/"student," "guard"/"prisoner," etc.) often serve "the political-social purposes of the explaining culture." (R. Carlson 1989)

Consequently, the recurrent taxonomic dilemmas in relation to preciseness vs. vagueness, and simpleness vs. complicatedness, are relevant here too, although this time, in the current context, they are much contingent on the specific formation of power and vested interests at the cultural level.

Taxonomy and Religion

Another way to look at the cultural contingency of taxonomic schemes is the analysis of the partiality involved in religious classification.

On the Basis of Organizational and Client Involvement

Some sociologists like Rodney Stark and William Sims Bainbridge preferred to classify religious organizations on the basis of three types of cults, in accordance to the levels of organizational and client (or adherent) involvement.

Firstly, there are (a) "audience cults, that have hardly any organization because participants/consumers lack significant involvement," (b) "client cults, in which the service-providers exhibit a degree of organization in contrast to their clients," and (c) "cult movements, which seek to provide services that meet all of adherents' spiritual needs (although they differ significantly in the degree to which they use mobilize adherents' time and commitment)." (WK 2007r)

As an illustration of the above three types, "the Church of Scientology originated from an audience cult ([L. Ron] Hubbard's books) and a client cult (Dianetics [the organization]) to a cult movement [the more institutionalized church]," as Paul Schnabel once suggested. (WK 2007r)

But how good is this classification?

On the Basis of Movement's Views on, and Relationships with, the World

The previous classification is precise and simple in one sense (e.g., on the basis of organizational and client involvement) but vague and not complicated enough in a different way (e.g., on the basis of movement's views on, and relationships with, the world).

One good example of alternative taxonomy is Roy Wallis's innovative way to classify religious organizations on the basis of something else, this time, of movement's views on and relationships with the outside world.

Hereafter are three categories in his alternative classification.

Firstly, there are the "[w]orld-rejecting movements," which are to "view the prevailing social order as having departed from God's prescriptions and from the divine plan. Such movements see the world as evil, or at least as materialistic. They may show millenarian tendencies. ISKCON, the Unification Church and the Children of God exemplify world-rejecting movements." (WK 2007r)

Secondly, there are the "[w]orld-accommodating movements," which "draw clear distinctions between the spiritual and the worldly spheres. They have few or no consequences for the lives of adherents. These movements thus adapt to the world, but they do not reject or affirm it." (WK 2007r)

And thirdly, there are the "[w]orld-affirming movements," which "may have no rituals and no official ideology. They may lack most of the characteristics of religious movements. They affirm the world and merely claim that they have the means to enable people to unlock their 'hidden potential.' As examples of world-affirming movements [are]...Erhard Seminars Training and Transcendental Meditation." (WK 2007r)

So, which classification is better—the one based on organizational and client involvement, or the one based on movement's views on and relationships with the world?

A Wise Advice

These alternative classifications raise the more difficult question concerning the universality of classificatory schemes.

John A. Saliba (2003), for one, has an interesting advice to give, in that "the many attempts to draw a classification or typology of cults and/or sects" only reveal all the more convincingly that "the divergences that exist in these groups' practices, doctrines, and goals do not lend themselves to a simple classification that has universal approval. He argues that the influx of Eastern religious systems (which do not fit within the traditional distinctions between church, sect, denomination and cult) have compounded classificatory difficulties." (WK 2007r)

Culture thus shows its multiple faces in taxonomy, in relation to religion— so the taxonomic dilemmas in relation to preciseness vs. vagueness, and simpleness vs. complicatedness, reveal themselves once more here.

Taxonomy and Aesthetics

Culture also shows its multiple faces in taxonomy, this time, in relation to aesthetics. An excellent example concerns how to classify the arts in the Western tradition.

The Taxonomy of the Arts

The taxonomy of the arts in the history of aesthetic ideas in the Western tradtion serves as a good case study of how and why it has failed to produce any lasting classification which satisfies the critics.

Taxonomy in the Classical Era

Consider, first, the classical era, with its six different versions of taxonomy of the arts, each with its own rationale.

Firstly, there were the Sophists, who classified the arts on the basis of their "aims." (DHI 2007)

The aims of the arts can be understood in terms of two criteria, namely, (a) their "utility" (for life) and (b) the "pleasure" (for entertainment). (DHI 2007)

Secondly, there was later the Platonic classification of the arts, on the basis of "the relation between arts and reality." (DHI 2007)

The relation between arts and reality can come in two different versions of relating to "real objects," that is, for the production of either (a) "real things" (e.g., architecture) and (b) "images" (e.g., painting). (DHI 2007)

Later, his student, Aristotle, refined the Platonic classification a bit by saying the same thing in a slightly different way, that is, in classifying the arts on the basis of those which (a) "complete" nature and (b) "imitate" it. (DHI 2007)

Thirdly, there was the classical Greek classification of the arts on the basis of the degree of "physical effort" in producing it. (DHI 2007)

This classification thus distinguished two forms of arts, with one (the use of mental effort) being superior to the other (the use of physical effort). Because of the Greek contempt for physical labor in an aristocratic society, the "liberal" or "intellectual" arts (e.g., music and rhetoric) were regarded as superior to the "vulgar" arts (e.g., sculpture).

Galen, the physician of the second century A.D., for instance, regarded the "liberal" arts as "encylic" (or encyclopedic), which means "forming a circle," to refer to the obligation of what an educated man needed to learn. (DHI 2007)

Fourthly, there was the Quintilian classification of the arts on the basis of their "products." (DHI 2007)

In accordance to this classification, the arts were divided into three groups, namely, (a) "theoretical" arts, only for "studying things" (e.g., astronomy), (b) "practical" arts, only for acting (e.g., dance), and (c) "productive" (or "poietic") arts, only for producing objects (e.g., painting). (DHI 2007)

Fifthly, there was the classification of the arts by Cicero, on the basis of their "value." (DHI 2007)

On this basis of value, the arts were classified into three groups, namely, (a) "*arts maximae*" or "major arts" (e.g., political and military arts), (b) "*artes mediocres*" or "median arts" (e.g., science, poetry, and eloquence), and (c) "*artes minores*" or "minor arts" (e.g., painting, sculpture).

And finally, then came the classification of the arts by Plotinus on the basis of the "degree of spirituality." (DHI 2007)

In this way, Plotinus divided the arts into five groups, namely, (a) "arts which produce physical objects" (e.g., architecture), (b) "arts which help nature" (e.g., medicine and agriculture), (c) "arts which imitate nature" (e.g., painting), (d) "arts which improve or ornament human action" (e.g., rhetoric and politics), and (e) arts which are purely intellectuals (e.g., geometry).

Taxonomy in the Middle Ages

By contrast, the taxonomy of the arts in the Middle Ages was broader in a way.

For instance, the medieval classification of the arts included all kinds of artistic activities, ranging from handicrafts through the sciences to fine arts—insofar as they were governed "by fixed canons and by rules of the guilds." (DHI 2007) Thomas Aquinas and Duns Scotus, for instance, favored the use of fixed canons and rules for the classification of the arts.

In so doing, the medieval taxonomy was more inclusive and did not, say, "depreciate" non-liberal arts as "vulgar" (as the Greeks did) but relabeled them as "mechanical arts." (DHI 2007)

The medieval taxonomy divided the arts into seven groups, namely, (a) "lanificium" (viz., "supplying men with wearning apparel"), (b) "armatura" (viz., "supplying men with shelter and tools"), (c) "agricultura" (viz., producting food), (d) "venatio" (viz., "supplying food"), (e) "navigatio" (viz., navigating ships), (f) "medicina" (viz., curing diseases), and (g) "theatrica" (viz., entertaining). (DHI 2007)

Taxonomy in the Modern Era

The analysis of the history of aesthetic taxonomy in the modern era can be divided into three smaller eras.

Firstly, in the early modern era, especially during the Renaissance, the classification of the arts was still very much based on the ideas proposed before, especially in relation to the rebirth of the classical ideas.

Yet, the most distinctive contribution of the Renaissance to the taxonomy of the arts was its attempt to separate some arts like architecture, sculpture, dancing, painting, music, and poetry as something distinctive from other arts (like the sciences and handicrafts). (DHI 2007)

Different names had been proposed to call them, and examples included "ingenious arts" by C. G. Manetti, "musical arts" by Marsilio Ficino, "noble arts" by G. P. Capriano, "commemorative arts" by L. Castelvetro, "metaphorical arts" by E. Tesauro, and "figurative arts" by C. F. Menestrier. (DHI 2007)

Secondly, in the later period of the modern era (like the 18th century), gradually but steadily, however, these six distinctive arts were later unified under the label of "fine arts," on the basis of "beauty." (DHI 2007)

But the problem here is that "the traditional idea of beauty was very broad, successful works of industry and handicraft were also called beautiful. However, the narrower meaning of the work permitted one to separate poetry, music, dance, painting, sculpture, and architecture as a peculiar group of *beaux arts,* 'fine arts.' This is often believed to be an achievement of the eighteenth century." (DHI 2007)

Thirdly, in the later period of the modern era (like the second half of the 18th century onwards), the classification of the "fine arts" raised some new problems. Consider two examples below.

The first problem concerned how to classify the fine arts within the larger domain of human activities. In 1790, Kant provided an interesting answer, in that there were three major human activities (i.e., the cognitive, the moral, and aesthetic), so "fine arts" were classified as the products of the third (aesthetic activity). (DHI 2007)

The second problem went one step further and concerned how to classify the sub-fields of the fine arts. Kant, again, offered several answers, one of which was to further divide the fine arts into three groups, in relation to (a) words (e.g., poetry, oratory), (b) images (e.g., architecture, sculpture, and painting), and (c) tones (e.g., music). (DHI 2007)

But do the Kantian answers satisfy the critics?

Taxonomy in the Contemporary Era

At the turn of the 20th century, however, and especially until now, the 21st century, the business of aesthetic taxonomy has become more and more messy, to the point that Max Dessoir once said that "there appears to be *no* system that satisfies all claims." (DHI 2007)

Let's recapture what has been discussed so far.

The history of aesthetic taxonomy in the Western tradition can therefore be summarized in this concise way, in that "the meaning of the classification of arts has changed; in antiquity the classification of arts was a division of all human abilities; during the Middle Ages it was a division between purely intellectual (artes liberales) and mechanical arts; in the Renaissance attempts were made to divide arts into 'fine arts' and others; since the eighteenth century it has been a division among fine arts themselves." (DHI 2007)

Then, by the twentieth century, aesthetic taxonomy seemd to be settled in terms of three assumptions, namely, (a) "there exists a closed system of arts," (b) "there is a difference between arts and crafts and sciences," and (c) "the arts are distinguished by the fact that they seek and find beauty." (DHI 2007)

As time progressed, it became clear to many that none of these three assumptions were tenable.

As an illustration, in relation to (a), it has been said that "new arts were born—photography and cinema—which had to be included in the system. The same applied to those arts which have been practised before but were not covered by the system, like town planning. Moreover, the character of arts included in the system has changed: a new architecture, abstract painting and sculpture, music in a twelve-tone scale, and the anti-novel have appeared." (DHI 2007)

In relation to (b), it has also been observed that "[d]oubts arose whether one really ought to contrast crafts with arts. As recently as the end of the nineteenth cenutry William Morris argued that there can be no nobler art than good craft. And ought one to contrast science with art? Indeed, many twentieth-century artists regard their work as cognitive, similar to science, or even science itself." (DHI 2007)

And in relation to (c), some scholars have questioned whether or not "seeking beauty is essential in art and represents its *diffrentia specifica*....Is not the concept of beauty too vague to be useful in defining art? One can say of many works of art that beauty was not their objective." (DHI 2007) For some, "a work of art can be judged by more than one standard." (L. Hein 2002)

But this brief history of unsettled aesthetic taxonmoy in the Western tradition (as summarized in *Table 2.4*) only brings us back to square one, in that the dilemmas concerning preciseness vs. vagueness and simpleness vs. complicatedness remain here.

For instance, how precise should an aesthetic taxonomy be for acceptance— and, conversely, how vague should it be for inclusion? And how simple should its construction be for conciseness—and, conversely, how complicated should its analysis be for comprehensiveness?

Taxonomy and Society

But society has its own powerful impact on the evolution of taxonomy too. And four good illustrations are the ones from the perspectives of (2.5.1) social organizations, (2.5.2) social institutions, (2.5.3) social structure, and (2.5.4) social systems—to be analyzed hereafter, in that order (and summarized in *Table 4.6*).

Taxonomy and Social Organizations

Taxonomy, when examined from the perspective of a social organization, reveals a different outlook on information organization.

Take the case of information organization (from some research findings in library science), for instance.

"Traditional" Library Science Classification

In a traditional library science classification, the taxonomic schemes are more based on a precise and hierarchical organizing structure (for the service of different social organizations).

Classificatory Features of DDC and LCC

For instance, the Dewey Decimal System (DDC) and Library of Congress System (LCC) both are built around a "'correct' (or, at least, agreed upon) place somewhere in a single, large, hierarchically organized classification system...and in the case of books in a physical library, one 'correct' place in the stacks," although they also allow "cross-referencing among the terms in classification systems [which] helps information seekers." (KMC 2007)

In the case of DDC, the preciseness can take the form of ten main classes or categories, "each divided into ten secondary classes or subcategories," with each divided further into subdivisions (as summarized in *Table 2.5*): (WK 2007s & WK 2007t)

———

000 – Computer science, information, and general works
100 – Philosophy and psychology
200 – Religion
300 – Social sciences
400 – Language
500 – Science
600 – Technology
700 – Arts and recreation
800 – Literature
900 – History and geography

———

In the case of LCC, the taxonomic schemes are divided into broad categories as shown below (and summarized in *Table 2.5*): (WK 2007u)

———

A – General works
B – Philosophy. Psychology. Religion
C – Auxillary sciences of history
D – History: General and old World
E – History: America
F – History: America
G – Geography. Anthropology. Recreation
H – Social sciences
J – Political science
K – Law
L – Education
M – Music and books on Music
N – Fine arts
P – Language and literature
Q – Science
R – Medicine
S – Agriculture
T – Technology
U – Military science

V – Naval science

Z – Bibliography. Library science. Information resources.

———

A more critical question to ask concerns the contrastive advantages and disadvantages of traditional library science classification. (WK 2007t)

Although much can be said about the advantages and disadvantages between them, an illustrative summary can be provided below, in special relation to DDC and LCC.

Advantages and Disadvantages Between DDC and LCC

On the one hand, there are four main advantages of DDC over LCC (as summarized in *Table 2.6*).

Firstly, DDC is better in terms of its "simplicity. Thanks to the use of pure notation, a mnemonics system and a hierarchical decimal place system, it is generally easier to use for most users." (WK 2007t)

Secondly, DDC is more consistent than LCC, since in the latter "each area is developed by an expert according to demands of cataloging." (WK 2007t)

Thirdly, LCC is "highly U.S.-centric (more so than DDC) because of the nature of the system, and compared to DDC...it has been translated into far fewer languages." (WK 2007t)

And fourthly, LCC is "more complicated to use, and unlike DDC cannot be customised for the needs of a smaller library collection." (WK 2007t)

On the other hand, there are two main disadvantages of DDC over LCC (as summarized in *Table 2.6*).

Firstly, DDC is "less hospitable to the addition of new subjects, as opposed to Library of Congress Classification which has 21 classes at the top level. Another side effect of this is that DDC notations can be very much longer compared to the equivalent class in other classification systems." (WK 2007t)

And secondly, DDC "was developed in the 19th century, by essentially one man [John Dewey], and was built on a top down approach to classify all human knowledge which made it difficult to adapt to changing fields of knowledge. In contrast, the Library of Congress Classification system was developed based mainly on the idea of literary warrant; classes were added (by individual experts in each area) only when needed for works owned by the Library of Congress." (WK 2007t)

The point here is not that the comparison and contrast are exhaustive, but that they are illustrative of the promises and pitfalls which befall any taxomonic schemes.

So, which one is better, overall? Alternatively, is neither better, all things considered? Or is there something else to choose from, instead?

Faceted Classification

Precisely here, there is a third option, which can be analyzed here as an exploration of new possibilities which are otherwise not paid much attention to yet in everyday discourse.

A good instance is none other than the increasing use of "faceted classification."

Main Characteristics of Faceted Classification

Unlike traditional library science classification, faceted classification does not require the rigid preciseness and long hierarchy as exemplied in the former.

Bohdan Wynar (1976) once thus wrote in *Introduction to Cataloging and Classification*: "A faceted classification differs from a traditional one in that it does not assign fixed slots to subjects in sequence, but uses clearly defined, mutually exclusive, and collectively exhaustive aspects, properties, or characteristics of a class or specific subject. Such aspects, properties, or characteristics are called facets of a class or subject, a term introduced into classification theory and given this new meaning by the Indian librarian and classificationist S.R. Ranganathan and first used in his Colon Classification in the early 1930s." (KMC 2007)

In addition, as Wynar continued, "a faceted structure relieves a classification scheme from the procrustean bed of rigid hierarchical and excessively enumerative subdivision that resulted in the assignment of fixed 'pigeonholes' for subjects that happened to be known or were foreseen when a system was designed but often left no room for future developments and made no provision for the expression of complex relationships and their subsequent retrieval." (KMC 2007)

This flexibility in faceted classification can be revealed through an example.

As an illustration, "a traditional restaurant guide might group restaurants first by location, then by type, price, rating, awards, ambiance, and amenities. In a faceted system, a user might decide first to divide the restaurants by price, and then by location and then by type, while another user could first sort the restaurants by type and then by awards. Thus, faceted navigation, like taxonomic navigation, guides users by showing them available categories (or facets), but does not require them to browse through a hierarchy that may not precisely suit their needs or way of thinking." (WK 2007aa)

A typical faceted classification system can be identified in terms of the following eight main features. Of course, one should keep in mind that the features listed hereafter are to be treated as merely illustrative, not exhaustive, for the purpose of illustrating a typical faceted classificaiton system.

———

- "A faceted system focuses on the important, essential or persistent characteristics of content objects, helping it to be useful for fine-grained rapidly changing repositories."
- "You don't have to know the name of the category (or categories) into which a document is placed. In a business world in which terminology changes faster than you can blink, this is a big asset."
- "The absence of polyhierarchy is implied, at least, by having mutually orthogonal facet hierarchies. The ordering principle in a facet is not necessarily hierarchical (general-specific, whole-part, etc.), although that will be true in most cases. It might even be alphabetical."
- "It's easy to add a new facet at any time."
- "Flexibility [is sought for] in general. Makes few assumptions about the scope and organization of the domain. So it's hard to 'break' a faceted classification schema."
- It "[s]hould be easier to construct the facet hierarchies."
- "Combining elements from separate facets using a defined syntax—for example, to express the functions of a product, make assertions, or frame questions in a structured way—is an extremely powerful method of precise retrieval."
- "Adding persistent (even 'typed') relationships between elements in different facets—for example, John Smith (in the Person facet) <relationship: is an employee of> Generic Company (Organization facet) provides substantial useful representation of knowledge in the faceted classification schema itself."

———

Like all taxonomic schemes, faceted classification provides benefits with costs too. Consider a few examples below.

A Cost-Benefit Analysis of Faceted Classification

Firstly, the main virtue of faceted classification is its focus on efficiency (e.g., getting precise info quickly). This then means that it is less concerned with "systematization," which may be more important for "scholarly research." (KMC 2007)

Secondly, the focus on efficiency also means that it somehow sacrifices "depth...." (KMC 2007)

And thirdly, it also means that faceted classification is not much concerned with "all possible ways of posing a query." (KMC 2007)

In fact, the problems in regard to "systematization," "depth," and comprehensiveness can all be classified under the broader heading concerning the lack of complicatedness in faceted classification, in its favor of simpleness.

The tradeoffs in different classificatory schemes can be even more elaborated from a closely related perspective, this time, from the perspective of social institutions (not just social organizations).

Taxonomy and Social Institutions

The comparison and contrast in relation to traditional library science classification and faceted classification (in the previous subsection) can be all the more illuminated, when the social institutional concerns are factored into the analysis.

A good instance is, of course, the business environment of a social organization, that is, from the business institutional standpoint.

Info Designing Principles

Social organizations, when contextualized within the fast moving pace of business institutions, require certain info designing principles in information architecture.

Consider two main contrastive examples for illustration below.

Firstly, there are the "user-centered design principles." (WK 2007v) Businesses with a user-centered design principle in their info architecture are more concerned with the virtue of "usability" (e.g., gathering precise info, providing simple interfaces, and getting things done quickly).

Surely, there are different versions of these principles, and Donald Norman in his 1986 book titled *The Design of Everyday Things* (or originally called *The Psychology of Everyday Things*) introduced different user-centered design principles like the Scandinavian "cooperative-design" ("involving designers and users on an equal footing"), the North American "participatory design" ("focusing on the participation of users"), and the "contextual design" (paying more attention to the actual context). (WK 2007w)

Secondly, an alternative to user-centered design principles is to appeal more to the emotional aspects of info architecture (not paid much attention to by user-centered design principles).

Just as user-centered design principles have different versions, so do emotional design principles. Norman himself published another book titled *Emotional Design* to address this aspect of info architecture which he earlier neglected, and Patrick Jordan (2000) in *Designing Pleasurable Products* did likewise.

Good examples include the consideration of "aesthetic" issues in info architecture (e.g., to make info design more visually beautiful, not just functionally efficient as in user-centered info architecture), the inclusion of "pleasure" in the designs so as to make pleasurable for users to use, and the attention to "consistency," especially for traditional and academic ways of info organization. (WK 2007w)

So, which one is better—user-centered or emotions-based?

Choosing among Conflicting Approaches

The answer lies in the understanding that these opposing approaches, be they user-centered or emotions-based in info architecture, give us different classificatory schemes, which alternate in their construction among conflicting needs and interests (e.g., the business focus on usability and the alternative attention to emotions).

Even when they are to be combined, their conflicting criteria are not eliminated, only being shifted to different degrees of combination.

Since this issue overlaps with the one on network in info architecture, a more detailed analysis is postponed until the next chapter on information architecture and network, especially in the relation to the section on network and society.

Taxonomy and Social Structure

Taxonmoy can also take a different face, when examined from the perspective of social structure.

The Primitive Forms of Classification

Émile Durkheim (1858–1917) and Marcel Mauss (1872–1950) proposed an interesting thesis in a 1903 paper titled "On Some Primitive Forms of Classification." (W. Schmaus 2007)

Based on some ethnographic studies from Australia and North America, Durkheim and Mauss linked the "classificatory concepts such as genus and species" with the formation of "human social groupings." (W. Schmaus 2007)

For instance, "the Australian native considers everything in the universe to belong to his or her tribe. The entire tribe thus provided the archetype for the category of totality, the class that includes all other classes. Just as the members of the tribe are divided into phratries that are subdivided into clans, each thing in nature has its place in this nested hierarchy of phratries and clans." (W. Schmaus 2007)

In accordance to this ethnocentric category of totality, "all living and nonliving objects, including the sun, the moon, the stars, the seasons, and even weather phenomena, belong to a particular clan as well as to a more inclusive phratry." (W. Schmaus 2007)

The important point to remember here is that "[t]his system of social organization [in favor of the tribe] thus serves as the origin and the prototype of the concept of classifying things by genera and species. What has come to be known as the Durkheim–Mauss thesis thus states, 'the classification of things reproduces the classification of men.'" (W. Schmaus 2007)

The hidden social structure behind the classification of things is thus to serve the interests of the tribe for its social cohesion, in opposition to all others who compete against it. The classification of things thus has a social-structural origin in the preservation of the survival of the tribe, to compete with other tribes who offer competing classifications for their own survival too.

This thesis concerning the classification of things and its reproduction of the classification of men is not without controversy, however. Durkheim, for one, had been criticized in regard to his thesis on the classification of things, although the criticisms can be directed against Mauss too, since both wrote the paper together.

Four examples for illustration suffice hereafter.

Firstly, the Durkheimian approach "has been accused of 'reductionism' for [the] identification of religion [or, in general, the classification of things] as a symbolic expression of social experience." (D. Nielsen 2007)

Secondly, "his general emphasis on society as a reality sui generis, one that transcends the individual, has led to the accusation of 'social realism,' a 'group mind' theory, and even 'scholasticism.'" (D. Nielsen 2007)

Thirdly, "the validity of his evidence" has been questioend. For instance, "[t]he ethnography of his day (e.g., the work of Spencer and Gillen on Australia) is now viewed as inadequate. Durkheim's own (admittedly brilliant) use of the evidence also has been questioned, in particular his heavy reliance on the (probably untypical) Australian test case and his tendency to explain empirical deviations from his theory of primitive totemism by reference to allegedly later evolutionary developments in the societies under examination." (D. Nielsen 2007)

And finally, "Durkheim's logical method is criticized for often assuming the antecedent validity of the theory he is attempting to demonstrate and proving his own theory's validity by critically eliminating its competitors." (D. Nielsen 2007)

These criticisms in regard to the Durkheimian approach can be put in perspective, when contrasted with another one, this time, the Marxist classification of social class.

The Marxist Classification of Social Class

The weakness in the Durkheimian thesis on the classification of things can be all the more revealed, when contrasted with the Marxist classification of social class—although in the process, the Marxist version of classification has its own problems too.

Unlike the Durkheimian interest in primitive tribes, Karl Marx was more interested in classifying social groups in terms of class, that is, by way of the "control over the means of production. In Marxist terms a class is a group of people defined by their relationship to the means of production. Classes are seen to have their origin in the division of the social product into a necessary product and a surplus product." (WK 2007y)

In this sense, "Marxists explain the history of 'civilized' societies in terms of a war of classes between those who control production and those who actually produce the goods or services in society (and also developments in technology and the like)....For Marxists, class antagonism is rooted in the situation that control over social production necessarily entails control over the class which produces goods—in capitalism this is the exploitation of workers by the bourgeosie." (WK 2007y)

The Marxist way of classification thus entails a power structure in the categories of classification, which produces class conflict and class struggle. In the traditional European case, Marx, for instance, identified "the ruling class ('We rule you'), supported by the religious ('We fool you') and military ('We shoot at you') élites, but the French Revolution had already shown that these classes could be removed" by those below them (e.g., the workers, the peasants, etc.). (WK 2007y)

Yet, the Marxist insight on class conflict also reveals its Achilles' heel, in that it commits a different form of reductionism, that is, class reductionism. Max Weber, for instance, offered an alternative classification of social groups on a more diverse basis (e.g., class, status, party). (A. Giddens 1985)

And French sociologist Mattei Dogan in "From Social Class and Religious Identity to Status Incongruence in Post-Industrial Societies" in *Comparative Sociology* (2004) argued that "the relevance of social class has declined, giving way to a different form of social identification that is largely cultural and religious, and which raises identity conflicts called status incongruence. This can be observed in particular in the developing countries, but even in many post-industrial societies." (WK 2007y)

Taxonomy and Social Systems

Taxonomy can take even more powerful expressions, when analyzed from the perspective of social systems.

The Role of Technology on Taxonomy

An excellent example is the impact of technology on the classification of things. And the change of teaching methodology in our times can be used here as a good case study.

As a start, in the older days, the "traditional teaching approaches are generally teacher-directed and follow cookbook steps of activities and demonstrations." (P. Harris 2006)

A typical taxonomy for traditional learning includes three main skills which are to master what Benjamin Bloom called "knowledge" (e.g., the "[r]ecall of specific facts"), "comprehension" (e.g., "[g]rasping or understanding meaning of informational materials"), and "application" (e.g., "[m]ake use of the knowledge").

But the traditional approach does not emphasize more difficult, higher-level skills and therefore, as D. Udovic (2002) and others argued, "may not provide students with valuable skills or even with a body of knowledge that lasts much beyond the end of the term." (P.Harris 2006)

And these more difficult higher-level skills for learning often require "non-traditional strategies such as active, cooperative, collaborative and problem-based learning." (P. Harris 2006)

The recent advances in Information and Communication Technology (ICT) in the last few decades have made a new taxonomy for learning possible, which emphasizes these more difficult higher-level skills in learning for what Bloom referred to as "analysis," "synthesis," and "evaluation." (M. Bailey 2002 & D. Jonassen 2000)

The non-traditional taxonomy for learning now includes the transition from lower levels to higher levels in six categories, as shown below (and summarized in *Table 2.7*): (M. Bailey 2002 & D. Jonassen 2000)

- Lower Levels
    - Storage, or Remembering (e.g., the use of PDF files and Powerpoint presentation)
    - Exploration, or Comprehension (e.g., the use of the Internet)
    - Application (e.g., the use of database software like the Mighty M & M)

- Higher Levels
    - –Analysis (e.g., the use of word processing tools, whiteboards, and graphic organizer windows)
    - –Synthesis (e.g., the use of hypermedia programs like HyperStudio and web design environments like GoLive)
    - –Evaluation (e.g., the use of Web-based environments like Netmeeting)

The transition from lower-level skills (in a traditional taxonomy of the older days) to higher-level ones (in a non-traditional taxonomy of our times), as shown in the tools provided in each level, is clearly based on the advances of ICT.

In this sense, the taxonomy for learning can now be constructed in a different way, thanks to the advances in ICT.

But then, a good question to ask is, What is wrong with this new taxonomy of learning, which incorporates new advances in ICT?

The Controversy Surrounding the Non-Traditional Taxonomy

But this technology-driven non-traditional taxonomy is not without criticisms. Here are a few examples for illustration.

Firstly, some scholars on the taxonomy of educational objectives questions the cognitive domain in Bloom's Taxonomy, especially in regard to "the existence of a sequential, hierarchical link." (R. Paul 1993; WK 2007z)

Secondly, even Bloom himself, in a later (revised) edition of his book on the taxonomy of educational objectives, changed his mind and moved "Synthesis in higher order than Evaluation." (WK 2007z)

Thirdly, others simply treat "the three lowest levels as hierarchically ordered, but the three higher levels as parallel." (WK 2007z)

And finally, even more confusedly, still some scholars think that "it is sometimes better to move to Application before introducing Concepts [in Remembering]. This thinking would seem to relate to the method of Problem Based Learning." (WK 2007z)

This hierarchical controversy reveals all the more the contentious battle to be fought out among different groups for their own preferences and interests. Some win sometimes (like those for the traditional taxonomy in the older days), and others win at other times (like those for the non-traditional taxonomy in our times)—in an asymmetric way, with each group being dominant in their happier (or rather, lucky) moments.

Surely, if they ever become comparatively equal in popularity, symmetry in their contention is possible too (as in the transitional period from the traditional taxonomy to the non-traditional one).

But this also shows the relevance of another ontological principle, namely, what I originally called "the symmetry-asymmetry principle," which was already introduced in my earlier books (like *Beyond Capitalism to Post-Capitalism*, or abbreviated as *BCPC*—and other subsequent ones).

The Challenge of Taxonomy

The tedious exploration of the different ways of classifiying information in the world surrounding us—be they from the perspectives of the mind, nature, culture, or society—reveals something challenging and yet interesting, in the higher order of ontology, but in a non-reductionistic way.

Taxonomy and Ontological Principles

In other words, there can be some principles which reveals the underlying structure of things, in special regard to the interactions between different conflicting requirements.

Some good examples concern the three pairs, namely, preciseness and vagueness (like the debates on Linnaean taxonomy in *Sec. 2.2.4.1*, phylogenetic taxonomy in *Sec. 2.2.4.2*, political genetic differences in info processing in *Sec. 2.3.2.2*, and library science taxonomy in *Sec. 2.5.1*), simpleness and complicatedness (like the debates on Linnaean taxonomy in *Sec. 2.2.4.1*, phylogenetic taxonomy in *Sec. 2.2.4.2*, political genetic differences in info processing in *Sec. 2.3.2.2*, and faceted classification in *Sec. 2.5.1*), and slowness and quickness (like the debates on political genetic differences in info processing in *Sec. 2.3.2.2* and info-designing taxonomy in *Sec. 2.5.2*).

This is true, on top of other ontological pairs already introduced in earlier books of mine like the one on symmetry and asymmetry (in the context of the debate on the taxonomy of educational objectives in *Sec. 2.5.4*) and on order and chaos (in the context of the debate on neural representational differences in info processing in *Sec. 2.3.1*).

A Cautious Note

It should be stressed, of course, that the sub-sections as cited for the illustration of each principle above are not exhaustive or mutually exclusive, as other sections can overlap, in the process of illustrating other principles too.

In any event, more of these principles will be analyzed in the concluding chapter, namely, Chapter Four on the future of information architecture.

In the meantime, this is not the end of the story, as something else needs to be analyzed to tell us more about the nature of information architecture, this time, in relation to network.

With this in mind—I now proceed to Chapter Three on information architecture and network.

Table 2.1. The Taxonomy of Particle Physics
(Part I)

• **Elementary Particles**
  —ferminons (half-integer spin)
    ▪ quarks and antiquarks
        –up
        –down
        –strange
        –charm
        –bottom
        –top
    ▪ leptons and antileptons
        –electrons and positrons
        –electron neutrinos and electron antineutrinos
        –muons and antimuons
        –muon neutrinos and muon antineutrinos
        –Tau leptons and Tau antiteptons
        –Tau neutrinos and Tau antineutrinos
  —bosons (integer spin)
    ▪ photos (for electromagnetic force)
    ▪ W bosons (for weak nuclear force)
    ▪ Z bosons (for weak nuclear force)
    ▪ gluons (for strong nuclear force)
    ▪ graviton (for gravitational force)
    ▪ Higgs bosons

• **Composite Particles**
  —hadrons
    ▪ composite fermions (or, alternatively, baryons)
    ▪ composite bosons (or, alternatively, mesons).
  —atoms
  —atomic nuclei
  —molecules

(continued on next page)

Table 2.1. The Taxonomy of Particle Physics
(Part II)

• **Other Classifications**
  —superpartners (in supersymmetry theories)
    ▪ ex: photinos (spin-½) as the superpartners of photons
    ▪ ex: gluinos (spin-½) as the superpartners of gluons
    ▪ ex: gravitinos (spin-3/2) as the superpartners of gravitons
  —condensed matter (for quasi-particles)
    ▪ ex: phonons (in "vibrational modes in a crystal lattice")
    ▪ ex: excitons (in "bound states of an electron and a hole")
    ▪ ex: plasmons (in "coherent excitations of a plasma")
  —particles with different rates of speed
    ▪ ex: tardyons or bradyons (slower than light, with non-zero rest mass)
    ▪ ex: luxons (at the speed of light, with no rest mass)
    ▪ ex: tachyons (faster than the speed of light, with an imaginary rest mass)
  —the rest
    ▪ ex: WIMP's (weakly interacting massive particles)
        —neutralinos or axions (for dark matter)
    ▪ ex: pomerons ("the elastic scattering of hadrons and the location of Regge poles in Regge theory")
    ▪ ex: skyrmions ("a topological solution of the pion field, used to model the low-energy properties of the nucleon, such as the axial vector current coupling and the mass")

Sources: A summary of *Sec. 2.2.3*. For more info, see WK (2007pp).

Table 2.2. The Taxonomy of Eternal Cosmologies
(Part I)

Types	*Thinkers*
"Eternal substance"	Thales, Anaximander, Xenophanes, Empedocles, Anaxagoras, Leucippus, Demokritus, Heraclitus, Parmenides, Plato, Stoa
"Eternity of the world, but emanation of the deity"	Plotinus, Proclus, Origen, Abu Nasr Al-Faràbi (Alfarabius), Abù'Alì al-Husayn Ibn Sinna (Avicenna)
"Timlessness of creation"	Johannes Scotus Eurigena, Meister Eckhart
"*Creatio continua,* continuous maintenance and re-creation of the world"	Anaximenes, Stoa, Cicero, Augustine of Hippo, Gregor the Great, Thomas Aquinas, Henry of Gent, Petrus Aureoli, René Descartes
"Absolute beginning, creation, *creatio ex nihilo*"	Johannes Philoponos, Augustine of Hippo, Yaaqub ibn Ishaq Al-Kindi (Alkindus); Hugo & Richard & Bernard of St. Viktor, Bernard & Thierry of Chartres, Wilhelm of Conches, Clarenbaldus of Arras, Abù Hamìd Muhammad Al-Ghazàli, Moses Maimonides, Albertus Magnus, Wilhelm of Auvergne, Robert Grosseteste, Roger Bacon, Bonaventura, Matthew of Aquasparta, Henry of Gent, John Pecham, Richard of Middleton, Peter Aureol, William of Alnwick, Henry Totting of Oyta, Marsilius of Inghen

(continued on next page)

Table 2.2. The Taxonomy of Eternal Cosmologies
(Part II)

Types	Thinkers
"Eternity: no beginning and no transience/destructibility"	Aristotle, Averroes, Thomas Aquinas, Siger of Brabant, Boetius of Dacia, Wilhelm Ockham, Giles of Rome, Godfrey of Fontaines, Henry of Harclay, Thomas of Wylton, Thomas of Strassburg; Pietro D'Abano, Johannes Jandunus, Pietro Pomponazzi, Giordano Bruno, Baruch de Spinoza
"No beginning and no end (static. vs. evolutionary vs. revolutionary)"	• "static universe" by Albert Einstein (1917) • "empty expanding universe" by Willem de Sitter (1917) • "eternal expansion out of a static universe" by Arthur S. Eddington (1930) • "steady state" by Hermann Bondi, Thomas Gold & Fred Hoyle • "quasi-steady state" by Fred Hoyle, Geoffrey Burbidge & Jayant V. Narlikar • "chaotic inflation (global!)" by Andrei Linde (1983) • "Planckian cosmic egg (global!)" by Mark Israelit & Nathan Rosen (1989) • "big bounce" by Hans-Joachim Blome (1991) & Wolfgang Priester • "ekpyrotic and cyclic universe (global!)" by Paul Steinhardt & Neil Turok et al.

(continued on next page)

Table 2.2. The Taxonomy of Eternal Cosmologies
(Part III)

Types	*Thinkers*
"no beginning, but an end"	• "collapse out of a static universe" by Arthur S. Eddington (1930)

Source: From Ch.2 of *FIA*. The table is reconstructed, based on the data from the work of Rudiger Vaas (2003).

Table 2.3. The Taxonomy of Initial Cosmologies
(Part I)

Types	Thinkers
"Beginning and an end"	▪ "classical big bang/big crunch" by Alexander Friedmann, Stephen Hawking & Roger Penrose ▪ "quantum tunnel effect" by Alexander Vilenkin (1982) ▪ "no boundary instanton" by Stephen Hawking & James Hartle (1983)
"Beginning, but no end"	▪ "classical big bang/big whimper" by Alexander Friedmann, Georges Lemaître (1927), Stephen Hawking & Roger Penrose ▪ "phoenix universe (global!)" by Georges Lemaître (1933) & Richard C. Tolman (1934) ▪ "quantum tunnel effect and eternal inflation" by Alexander Vilenkin (1982) ▪ "cosmic Darwinism" by Lee Smolin (1992) ▪ "no boundary instanton" by Stephen Hawking & Neil Turok (1998) ▪ "transcendentalism idealism" by Immanuel Kant
"time-loop with/without end "	▪ "self-creating universe" by John Richard Gott III & Li-Xin Li (1998)

(continued on next page)

Table 2.3. The Taxonomy of Initial Cosmologies
(Part II)

Types	Thinkers
"pseudo-beginning with/without a local end "	*–background-dependent*: • "soft bang/emergent universe" by Eckard Rebhan (2000), George F. R. Ellis & Roy Maartens et al. • "quantum fluctuation, de Sitter instability, etc." by Edward Tryon, Robert Brout et al. (1978), Alexei A. Starobinsky, David Atkatz (1982) & Heinz R. Pagels, John Richard Gott III (1982), Mark Israelit (2002) • "pre-big bang" by Gabriele Veneziano & Maurizio Gasperini *–background-independent*: • "pregeometry" by John A. Wheeler, Peter W. Atkins (1981), & Stephen Wolfram (2002) • "loop quantum cosmology" by Abhay Ashtekar & Martin Bojowald et al.
"cycle (recurrence)"	• "oscillating universe (local!)" by Mark Israelit & Nathan Rosen (1989), & Redouane Fakir (1998) • "cyclic universe (local!)" by Paul Steinhardt & Neil Turok et al. (2002) • "circular time in a rotating universe" by Kurt Gödel (1949) • "big brunch/time-reversal" by Claus Kiefer & H. Dieter Zeh

(continued on next page)

Table 2.3. The Taxonomy of Initial Cosmologies
(Part III)

Source: From Ch.2 of *FIA*. The table is reconstructed, based on the data from the work of Rudiger Vaas (2003).

Table 2.4. The Taxonomy of the Arts:
A Brief History of the Western Tradition
(Part I)

* **Aesthetic Taxonomy in the Classical Era**
  —On the basis of "all human abilities"

* **Aesthetic Taxonomy in the Medieval Era**
  —On the basis of the division "between purely intellectual (artes liberales) and mechanical arts"

* **Aesthetic Taxonomy in the Renaissance**
  —On the basis of "the fine arts and other arts"

* **Aesthetic Taxonomy in the Eighteenth Century and Afterwards**
  —On the basis of the division "among the fine arts themselves"

* **Aesthetic Taxonomy in the Early 20th Century**
  —On the basis of the three assumptions, namely, (a) "there exists a closed system of arts," (b) "there is a difference between arts and crafts and sciences," and (c) "the arts are distinguished by the fact that they seek and find beauty"

* **Aesthetic Taxonomy in Late 20th Century Until Now (the Early 21st)**
  —On the basis of no universal criteria. There is no taxonomy which satisfies everyone.

Sources: A summary of *Sec. 2.4.4.* For more info, see DHI (2007).

**Table 2.5. The Traditional Library Science Taxonomy:
The Case of LCC & DDC
(Part I)**

• **Library of Congress System (LCC)**

    A – General works
    B – Philosophy. Psychology. Religion
    C – Auxillary sciences of history
    D – History: General and old World
    E – History: America
    F – History: America
    G – Geography. Anthropology. Recreation
    H – Social sciences
    J – Political science
    K – Law
    L – Education
    M – Music and books on Music
    N – Fine arts
    P – Language and literature
    Q – Science
    R – Medicine
    S – Agriculture
    T – Technology
    U – Military science
    V – Naval science
    Z – Bibliography. Library science. Information resources.

(continued on next page)

Table 2.5. The Traditional Library Science Taxonomy:
The Case of LCC & DDC
(Part II)

• Dewey Decimal System (DDC)
     000 – Computer science, information, and general works
     100 – Philosophy and psychology
     200 – Religion
     300 – Social sciences
     400 – Language
     500 – Science
     600 – Technology
     700 – Arts and recreation
     800 – Literature
     900 – History and geography

Sources: Data from WK (2007s), WK (2007t) & WK (2007u)

Table 2.6. Advantages and Disadvantages in Taxonomy:
The Case of LCC & DDC

• **In Favor of the Dewey Decimal System (DDC)**
—DDC is better in terms of its "simplicity. Thanks to the use of pure notation, a mnemonics system and a hierarchical decimal place system, it is generally easier to use for most users." (WK 2007t)
—DDC is more consistent than LCC, since in the latter "each area is developed by an expert according to demands of cataloging." (WK 2007t)
—LCC is "highly U.S.-centric (more so than DDC) because of the nature of the system, and compared to DDC...it has been translated into far fewer languages." (WK 2007t)
—LCC is "more complicated to use, and unlike DDC cannot be customised for the needs of a smaller library collection." (WK 2007t)

• **In Favor of the Library of Congress System (LCC)**
—DDC is "less hospitable to the addition of new subjects, as opposed to Library of Congress Classification which has 21 classes at the top level. Another side effect of this is that DDC notations can be very much longer compared to the equivalent class in other classification systems." (WK 2007t)
—DDC "was developed in the 19th century, by essentially one man [John Dewey], and was built on a top down approach to classify all human knowledge which made it difficult to adapt to changing fields of knowledge. In contrast, the Library of Congress Classification system was developed based mainly on the idea of literary warrant; classes were added (by individual experts in each area) only when needed for works owned by the Library of Congress." (WK 2007t)

Sources: Data from WK (2007t)

Table 2.7. The Non-Traditional Taxonomy of Learning:
The Case of the Use of Information & Communcation Technology (ICT)

• **Lower Levels**
—Storage, or Remembering (e.g., the use of PDF files and Powerpoint presentation)
—Exploration, or Comprehension (e.g., the use of the Internet)
—Application (e.g., the use of database software like the Mighty M & M)

• **Higher Levels**
—Analysis (e.g., the use of word processing tools, whiteboards, and graphic organizer windows)
—Synthesis (e.g., the use of hypermedia programs like HyperStudio and web design environments like GoLive)
—Evaluation (e.g., the use of Web-based environments like Netmeeting)

Sources: Data from M. Bailey (2002) & D. Jonassen (2000)

• PART THREE •

Network

CHAPTER 3
INFORMATION ARCHITECTURE AND NETWORK

A wise man learns from experience; a wiser
man learns from the experience of others.
—A Chinese proverb (WK 2007ii)

The Impact of Network

The taxonomic schemes for information classification as discussed in Chapter Two constitute only one main aspect of information architecture. The other one concerns information network.

The term "network" is often used to refer to "a fabric or structure of cords or wires that cross at regular intervals and are knotted or secured at the crossings," or "an interconnected or interrelated chain, group, or system." (MWD 2007a)

In the context of information network, it is meant here an interconnected group or system of data.

In other words, "taxonomy" (as discussed in Chapter Two) differs, in meaning, from "network" (as will be addressed hereafter in this chapter).

The reason is that the business of "taxonomy" (as in Chapter Two) is to classify things into a listing of some sort, whereas the business of "network" (as in this chapter) is to interconnect different things into a group or system.

But both (taxonomy and network) have one thing in common, in that neither provides any explanatory power by itself (unless a theoretical framework is introduced, especially in a hidden way)—other than some degree of descriptive adequacy.

With this clarification in mind—how an interconnected group or system of data is managed becomes the subject of inquiry in this chapter.

The analysis of information network can be examined from the four main perspectives of (3.2) nature, (3.3) the mind, (3.4) culture and (3.5) society—respectively hereafter.

Network and Nature

Let's start first with the examination of information network from the perspective of nature.

The world of nature has made its distinctive marks on the construction of information network.

Three useful case studies can be provided here, namely, in relation to the domain of (3.2.1) chemistry, (3.2.2) micro-physics, and (3.2.3) macro-physics (or cosmology)—to be addressed in what follows, in that order (and summarized in *Table 4.3*).

Network and Chemistry

In chemistry, the study of network takes an exotic turn, since it can tell us something about different ways of manipulating energy.

And a good illustration concerns the study of "chemoton," or fluid (chemical) automaton.

Autocatalytic Chemical Reaction Networks

It is part of conventional wisdom that, for instance, humans have made much use of "mechanical" and "electric" means of manipulating energy—unlike the animal world, where much (though not all) of energy manipulation has been by way of "chemical" reactions in the state of nature. (T. Ganti 2007)

The "chemical" way of energy manipulations "occur in solutions, in the fluid state without using any solid construction. The essence of the design of these systems is provided by the organizational mode of various reaction networks. However, the results of these manipulations can be transformed into mechanical or electric energy changes by means of appropriate solid or semi-solid constructions (soft automata)." (T. Ganti 2007)

But scientists had proposed for many years the possibility for humans to use technology to create some "self-producing" fluid (or chemical) automata. For instance, "[h]alf a century ago, J. von Neumann proved that self-reproducing automata can be produced in principle, but no such automata have been produced since then by human technology. This is so, in spite of the fact that the phenomenon of self-reproduction has been known in chemistry already for a century (autocatalysis)," especially when we remember that "self-reproducing machineries can be actually realized in the realm of fluid (chemical) automata …by the tens of millions of living species in the state of nature." (T. Ganti 2007)

Yet, things started to change. In late 1960's, for instance, "Eigen and Gánti discovered independently of each other that autocatalysis is a self-reproducing chemical cycle. Neither of them published this as a separate chemical result, but Eigen published it in 1971, built it into his hypercycle theory, whereas Gánti in the same year used it as part of his chemoton theory. Later on, Gánti elaborated also the cycle stoichiometry of autocatalytic processes." (T. Ganti 2007)

However, the study of chemical networks was much limited at the time, since it was done primarily in a "qualitative" way (as in biochemistry), because "chemical stoichiometry could not handle chemical feed-backs, cycles or more complex reaction networks, as by using conventional stoichiometry, overall equations can be formed only from linearly coupled reactions." (T. Ganti 2007)

Later on, the use of "cycle stoichiometry" to study chemical reactions and the "mode of visualization of these networks developed in the chemoton theory (the separation of AND/OR branchings)" finally made "the quantitative design of these networks at a desk possible." (T. Ganti 2007)

These techniques now help scientists to understand and design "fluid automata"—and "self-reproducing, and even proliferating, spatially separated automata can be constructed. The simplest fluid automaton operating in a program-controlled way is called chemoton. The whole theory was named after this unit." (T. Ganti 2007)

Of course, much can be said about the research findings on chemoton theory in the last half century. But a few examples about some illuminating findings can illustrate their usefulness. Consider two of them below.

Firstly, there is a distinction between individually- and collectively-catalytic chemical reactions in fluid automata, with important implications for the understanding of species evolution and other issues.

In individually-catalytic chemical reactions, "an 'autocatalyst' is a molecular species which, in the presence of suitable reaction substrates, catalyses a reaction in which one or more molecules of that same catalyst molecular species are among the reaction products—over and above the original catalyst molecule itself. Note carefully the distinction here between the *original* catalyst molecule which—by definition—emerges unchanged from the catalysed reaction; and the one or more *additional* catalyst molecules which are among the reaction products." (B. McMullin 1999)

But in collectively-catalytic chemical reactions, something else happens, in that, as Stuart Kauffman (1993) once proposed, "while individually autocatalytic molecules might be rather unlikely to arise (or even sustain themselves) spontaneously, the same is *not* necessarily true for *sets* of molecular species which mutually catalyse each others production. The idea here is to consider sets of molecular species such that none of them need be individually autocatalytic (which may be an unfeasible requirement), but where production of every element of the set is effectively catalysed by at least one other member of the same set. In such a situation the whole set is said to be *collectively* autocatalytic." (B. McMullin 1999)

In this way, "we can imagine seeding a flow reactor with a collectively autocatalytic set of species (at least one molecule from each member of the set). Again, provided we maintain a flow of some basic substrate molecules (the 'exogenous food set' in Kauffman's terms) there should now be the possibility of an indefinitely sustained, self-reinforcing, reaction network, continuously producing more molecules of all the species in the set." (B. McMullin 1999)

Secondly, another amazing discovery concerning autocatalytic chemical networks in chemoton theory is that "[a]utocatalytic reaction displayed sensitivity to mixing; more rapid mixing corresponded to slower reaction rates." (C. Gerdts 2004)

Of course, it is "well-known that mixing affects the rates and even outcomes of autocatalytic reactions." But a new study found out that, for instance, "[e]fficient mixing reduces the rates of autocatalytic reactions by removing pockets of locally high concentration of autocatalyst.....[T]his autocatalytic reaction is sensitive to the rate of mixing; the reaction in the small channel (mixing time ~0.02 s) consistently occurred more slowly than the same reaction in the large channel (mixing time ~0.5 s)." (C. Gerdts 2004)

This understanding of how mixing affects the reaction rate (and of how individually-catalytic chemical networks differ from the collectively-catalytic ones) can help us improve our understanding of fluid automata and later, the technology to design them better—and, therefore, our comprehension of the nature of network at the chemical level.

Some Criticisms for Reflection

Yet, the promises of chemoton theory have a long way to go, indeed, especially in relation to the understanding of the nature of network at the chemical level. Consider two examples below.

Firstly, to master the manipulation of fluid automata is not easy. For instance, the "autocatalytic molecules...in modern organisms at least...are the nucleic acids. Note, however, that nucleic acids are themselves rather complex; and require complex substrates (nucleotides) and additional catalysts (replicases) in order to manifest their autocatalytic activity." (B. McMullin 1999)

And from here to the mastery of any future chemical manipulation of energy in relation to progressively more complex systems like "groups of co-evolving reactions, species, colonies, societies," cultures, or even larger entities in the cosmos has a very long way to go, indeed. (L. Steels 2005)

Secondly, when these more complex systems are factored in, the issue about mixing will be even more complicated, as many variables have to be taken into account, in choosing the right combination of autocatalysts, the right degree of concentration of them, and the like. Since time is important, the issue of mixing in cases like this will be an important hurdle to overcome.

So, once again, this brings us back to the ontological dilemmas concerning simpleness vs. complicatedness, and slowness vs. quickness in existential dialectics—although, this time, the inquiry is about understanding the nature of network (say, at the chemical level).

Network and Micro-Physics

A different illustration, though not less interesting, concerns the interrelationship between network and micro-physics, especially in relation to network topology in telecommunications.

To start, of course, the term "network topology" has to be defined. One formal definition of the term "network topology" refers to "the study of the arrangement or mapping of the elements (links, nodes, etc.) of a network, especially the physical (real) and logical (virtual) interconnections between nodes" in telecommunications. (WK 2007bb; D. Groth 2005)

Physical and Logical Network Topologies

With this definition in mind—a good example of a network topology is a "local area network (LAN)," which "exhibits both a physical and a logical topology. Any given node in the LAN will have one or more links to one or more other nodes in the network and the mapping of these links and nodes onto a graph results in a geometrical shape that determines the physical topology of the network." (WK 2007bb)

By the same logic, but in a different way, "the mapping of the flow of data between the nodes in the network determines the logical topology of the network. It is important to note that the physical and logical topologies might be identical in any particular network but they also may be different." (WK 2007bb)

In any event, a "particular network topology is determined only by the graphical mapping of the configuration of physical and/or logical connections between nodes....Distances between nodes, physical interconnections, transmission rates, and/or signal types may differ in two networks and yet their topologies may be identical." (WK 2007bb)

In this sense, "Network Topology is, therefore, technically a part of graph theory." (WK 2007bb)

Different Physical Network Topologies

Physical network topologies are interesting here, since there is a strong relationship between the impact of nature and their formation.

Traditionally, physical network topologies are constructed on the basis of imitating the shapes as discovered in nature (especially the physical world).

Good examples include the natural shapes of (a) a "point," (b) a "bus" or "backbone," (c) a "star," (d) a "ring" or a "circle," and (e) a "tree"—although there are other ones (be they on the basis of some other natural shapes or a hybrid of them).

In (a), the "point"-shaped network is "[t]he simplest topology" consisting of "a permanent link between two endpoints. Switched point-to-point topologies are the basic model of conventional telephony. The value of a permanent point-to-point network is the value of guaranteed, or nearly so, communications between the two endpoints. The value of an on-demand point-to-point connection is proportional to the number of potential pairs of subscribers, and has been expressed as Metcalfe's Law." (WK 2007bb)

Metcalfe's law was proposed by Robert Metcalfe for "the network effects of communication technologies and networks" like the Ethernet and the Internet. (WK 2007cc) It states that "the value of a telecommunications network is proportional to the square of the number of users of the system (n^2)....The law has often been illustrated using the example of fax machines: A single fax machine is useless, but the value of every fax machine increases with the total number of fax machines in the network, because the total number of people with whom each user may send and receive documents increases." (WK 2007cc)

In (b), the "bus"- or "backbone"-shaped network has a linear version, where "all of the nodes of the network are connected to a common transmission medium which has exactly two endpoints" and "all data that is transmitted between nodes in the network is transmitted over this common transmission medium and is able to be received by all nodes in the network virtually simultaneously (disregarding propagation delays)." (WK 2007cc)

In (c), the "star"-shaped network has "each of the nodes of the network...connected to a central node with a point-to-point link in a 'hub' and 'spoke' fashion, the central node being the 'hub' and the nodes that are attached to the central node being the 'spokes' (e.g., a collection of point-to-point links from the peripheral nodes that converge at a central node)." (WK 2007cc)

So, "all data that is transmitted between nodes in the network is transmitted to this central node, which is usually some type of device that then retransmits the data to some or all of the other nodes in the network, although the central node may also be a simple common connection point (such as a 'punch-down' block) without any active device to repeat the signals." (WK 2007cc)

In (d), the "ring"- or "circle"-shaped network is one "in which each of the nodes of the network is connected to two other nodes in the network and with the first and last nodes being connected to each other, forming a ring" (a circular shape), so that "all data that is transmitted between nodes in the network travels from one node to the next node in a circular manner and the data generally flows in a single direction only." (WK 2006cc)

In (e), the "tree"-shaped network is a type "of network topology in which a central 'root' node (the top level of the hierarchy) is connected to one or more other nodes that are one level lower in the hierarchy (i.e., the second level) with a point-to-point link between each of the second level nodes and the top level central 'root' node." (WK 2007cc)

By the same hierarchical logic, "each of the second level nodes that are connected to the top level central 'root' node will also have one or more other nodes that are one level lower in the hierarchy (i.e., the third level) connected to it, also with a point-to-point link, the top level central 'root' node being the only node that has no other node above it in the hierarchy." (WK 2007cc)

This is so, to the effect that "the hierarchy of the tree is symmetrical, each node in the network having a specific fixed number, f, of nodes connected to it at the next lower level in the hierarchy," with "the number, f, being referred to as the 'branching factor' of the hierarchical tree." (WK 2007cc)

Surely, there are other types too (like the ones with other natural shapes or a hybrid of them), but the examples here are illustrative, for the impact of nature on the construction of physical network topologies.

Advantages and Disadvantages of Each Network Topology

Yet, although the shapes of the network topologies are based on the geometry found in nature, they are not equal, with some better on the basis of some criteria and others better on the basis of something else.

Hereafter are some examples for illustration (as summarized in *Table 3.1*).

Firstly, in a "point"-shaped topology, the simplest topology may be easy and cheap to construct, but it is not very practical in the complicated mega-cities of our times.

Secondly, in a "ring"-shaped topology, the advantage is obvious, in that "the number of transmitters and receivers can be cut in half, since a message will eventually loop all of the way around....If the message is not accepted by any node on the network, it will travel around the entire ring and return to the sender." (WK 2007cc)

The disadvantage here is that a ring-shaped typology requires a message to travel around the entire ring, even when, on some occasions, this is not needed: "This potentially results in a doubling of travel time for data, but since it is traveling at a fairly insignificant multiple of the speed of light, the loss is usually negligible," especially in small circumstances. (WK 2007cc)

Thirdly, in a "star"-shaped network topology, the clear advantage is that "[t]he failure of a transmission line linking any peripheral node to the central node will result in the isolation of that peripheral node from all others, but the remaining peripheral nodes will be unaffected." (WK 2007cc)

The disadvantage, unfortunately, is that "the failure of the central node will cause the failure of all of the peripheral nodes also." (WK 2007cc)

And fourthly, in a "tree"-shaped network topology, the advantage is that "individual nodes may thus still be isolated from the network by a single-point failure of a transmission path to the node. If a link connecting a leaf fails, that leaf is isolated; if a connection to a non-leaf node fails, an entire section of the network becomes isolated from the rest." (WK 2007cc)

Conversely, the disadvantage is that it is both more expensive and time-consuming to build a complicated "tree"-shaped network topology than a simple, cheap point-to-point network topology.

In fact, in a more extreme form of "tree"-shaped network topologies, or a "fully connected network, complete topology or full mesh topology...there is a direct link between all pairs of nodes. In a fully connected network with n nodes, there are n(n-1)/2 direct links. Networks designed with this topology are usually very expensive to set up, but provide a high degree of reliability due to the multiple paths for data that are provided by the large number of redundant links between nodes. This topology is mostly seen in military applications." (WK 2007cc)

So, the dilemma remains, in that each network topology has its own advantages and disadvantages, to be sorted out in accordance to different criteria for a cost-benefit analysis.

And the outcome can reveal the final choice of different degrees of simpleness and complicatedness, slowness and quickness, or something else— so these ontological principles of existential dialectics become relevant once more here (at the micro-physical level).

Network and Macro-Physics (or Cosmology)

But the study of network takes a rather fascinating turn in macro-physics (or cosmology), not just in micro-physics (as discussed above).

Consider, say, a growing field of study in cosmology, especially, on spin networks, which first emerged several decades ago in the discipline of physics for the study of quantum geometry, as proposed by Roger Penrose, but it was not immediately accepted at the time.

Spin Networks

Roger Penrose proposed roughly three decades ago a unique way to understand quantum geometry, which has two novel properties, namely, (a) "discrete," such that the geometry is "built purely from combinatorial structures," and (b) "relational," such that "it makes reference to no background notions of space, time or geometry." (L. Smolin 1997)

Since then, the idea of self-spinning so understood has been influential in different fields like "quantum gauge theories, quantum gravity, topological quantum field theory and conformal field theory." (L. Smolin 1997)

More recently, the idea that networks can self-spin over time, with these two properties in mind, attracts some scholars who want to relate it to a friendly ally in evolutionary theory, yet with a different purpose in mind.

A good instance is Lee Smolin (2007), who in "What Is the Future of Cosmology?" thus explained why: "This is possible, because, since Darwin, we know that structure and complexity can be self-organized. We understand that there are natural processes, easily comprehensible, by which organization can arise naturally and spontaneously, without any need for a maker outside of the system. This requires, however, that we take a more historical view of fundamental physics and cosmology. We must be open to the possibility that the answers to many of the questions we have about why the elementary particles or the fundamental forces are as they are—and not otherwise—may have answers that are, at least in part, historical."

Thus, this "historical" perspective requires the inclusion of the two properties in Penrose's spin networks, in that, when applied to the challenging task "to understand why the universe we see around us emerged from the Big Bang with one set of laws rather than another," the answer may lie in treating the event of the Big Bang in terms of a cosmic network which is "relational" (in that all the elements in it are to be related to each other in a big system) and "discrete" (in that the system evolves over time into a self-organizational emergence, with all its laws, in the absence of any outside help). (L. Smolin 2007)

Smolin (2007) then further elaborated that "something like natural selection acts on the choice of the laws of physics….[W]e are discovering that…it may be that space is itself the result of spontaneous processes of self-organization. Processes of self-organization other than natural selection have been studied by people like Per Bak and Stuart Kauffman for some time, and they are known to occur in a variety of situations. It may very well be that mechanisms like self-organized criticality, which Bak and Kauffman describe, may play a role in the emergence of space itself, from a complex primordial network of interactions."

This discrete understanding of space geometry is important, since "those…studying the problem of combining general relativity with quantum theory have understood that the geometry of space must be discrete. Just like matter is made of atoms, space itself must be made of discrete bits." (L. Smolin 2007)

But why? The challenge is that, "we are faced with a new question: How do these discrete bits of space assemble themselves into a smooth structure that looks like the space we see around us? This turns out to be very much like asking why atoms often assemble themselves into solids, like plastics or metals, that look smooth when examined at scales larger than the atoms. It seems to be the case that without some special organization, the discrete bits of space—the networks—do not assemble themselves into big smooth structures that could describe the featureless space we observe. Instead, they typically form chaotic structures that do not resemble any previous notion of space. Thus, we are faced with the very real possibility that the fact that the world has any spatial extension at all is a contingent historical fact, that also requires explanation by some principle of self-organization." (L. Smolin 2007)

In fact, it turns out "that space and time should be self-organized. Systems which are self-organized turn out to be complex systems. What is a complex system? What is complexity? One approach to this question, which Julian Barbour and I have developed, is to define the complexity of a system in terms of the variety of the interactions of the parts of the system. Roughly speaking, the more variety a system has, the easier it is to distinguish the parts of the system from each other by describing each of their neighborhoods." (L. Smolin 2007)

In the context of the two properties in spin networks (as introduced above), this understanding means that (a) "space and time are to be defined solely in terms of relationships" and (b) "the world is a complex system whose structure is to be explained, in part, by its having undergone processes of self-organization. The first is the key idea behind general relativity, the second the idea behind modern biology. What joins them is that in the end both sets of ideas make sense as descriptions of systems, like the universe or life on earth, that must structure themselves from the inside, without being made or observed from the outside." (L. Smolin 2007)

Some Soul-Searching Questions

Of course, all this sounds nice and wonderful.

But does the theory of spin networks when used in the context of cosmology hold water? Consider, say, three critical examples for illustration.

Firstly, even Smolin (2007) himself admitted that it is one thing to speculate about something and another thing to prove it: "Of course, this does not mean that these ideas are right; only observation and experiment can, in the end, tell us that."

Secondly, the theory of spin networks also "goes against the expectation that the more fundamental an explanation is, the less historical it is. It also goes against the expectation that the ultimate answers to all questions about the elementary particles will be found with the discovery of a final, unified theory." (L. Smolin 2007) So, does the theory of spin networks sacrifice too much merely for a historical "quick fix" of understanding the reality in nature (or the Big Bang, in the present context)?

And finally, as I already wrote a few books on the subject like the ones titled *The Future of Complexity* (2007) and *The Future of Post-Human Consciousness* (2004) to explain the problem, there is a deep disagreement in the literature about the study of complexity, especially (though not exclusively) in relation to the recurrent fight between reductionism and emergencism (or alternatively, between connectionism and emergencism).

One serious problem here is that there lacks some fundamental explanatory adequacy in using the ideas of self-organization and emergence, besides others, to understand complexity.

After all, how much can "a contingent historical fact" like the one proposed here by Smolin and others on why the universe and its physical laws have evolved in the way (that they have) really explain?

But this is only to remind us all that the dilemma between simpleness and complicatedness in existential dialectics remains. The search for simplicity in understanding complex phenomena has its inherent risk of not doing justice to the complicatedness in question.

Network and the Mind

Information network can be explored from a different perspective.

An important perspective to consider here concerns the understanding of network in relation to the mind—or more specifically, in the domains of (3.3.1) psychology and (3.3.2) biology, to be addressed hereafter, in that order (and summarized in *Table 4.4*).

Network and Psychology

A fascinating illustration here can be had in regard to transformative grammar in cognitive psychology and its relation to language network—to be analyzed hereafter.

Language Network (in Cognitive Psychology)

In the second half of the 20th century, Noam Chomsky proposed something rather daring, in that the study of language acquisition should be treated as part of psychology, especially in relation to cognitive psychology.

His reason is that how the mind works in processing language information reveals some underlying syntactic structures which are hard-wired in the brain.

Deep Structure and Surface Structure

Chomsky's view has changed over the years about the underlying syntactic structures in the brain.

For instance, in his 1957 book *Syntactic Structures*, Chomsky made a name of himself in developing the idea of "transformative grammar," in that "each sentence in a language has two levels of representation—a deep structure and a surface structure." (WK 2007dd)

On the one hand, the "deep structure represented the core semantic relations of a sentence, and was mapped on to the surface structure (which followed the phonological form of the sentence very closely) via transformations. Chomsky believed that there would be considerable similarities between languages' deep structures, and that these structures would reveal properties, common to all languages, which were concealed by their surface structures." (WK 2007dd)

Logical Form and Phonetic Form

Later, however, Chomsky abandoned the distinction between deep structures and surface structures as too strong and introduced instead a weaker distinction, this time, the two alternative levels of representation known as LF (or "Logical Form") and PF ("Phonetic Form"). (WK 2007dd)

So, the study of these logical forms can enhance the understanding how information network is innately mapped out in the brain when language learning occurs—especially in relation to some universal syntactical rules.

Universal Syntactical rules

This language-learning innate ability, for Chomsky, can help us understand how "a baby can have a large body of prior knowledge about the structure of language in general, and need only actually learn the idiosyncratic features of the language(s) it is exposed to." (WK 2007dd)

In fact, "Chomsky goes so far as to suggest that a baby need not learn any actual rules specific to a particular language at all. Rather, all languages are presumed to follow the same set of rules, but the effects of these rules and the interactions between them can vary greatly depending on the values of certain universal linguistic parameters. This is a very strong assumption, and is one of the most subtle ways in which Chomsky's current theory of language differs from most others." (WK 2007dd)

But this difference in his theory from others also puts him in trouble. For instance, a critic can then ask: How exactly can one find out these universal syntactical rules in the brain?

Innate Mental Representations

One way to find out these universal syntactical rules is by way of discovering some mental representations which are innate in language acquisition.

With this goal in mind, Chomsky proposed, in the 1960's, two new distinctions.

The first distinction concerns "competence" and "performance." In performance, "Chomsky noted the obvious fact that people, when speaking in the real world, often make linguistic errors (e.g. starting a sentence and then abandoning it midway through). He argued that these errors in linguistic performance were irrelevant to the study of linguistic competence (the knowledge that allows people to construct and understand grammatical sentences). Consequently, the linguist can study an idealized version of language, greatly simplifying linguistic analysis." (WK 2007dd)

The second distinction concerns "descriptive adequacy" and "explanatory adequacy." (WK 2007dd) In descriptive adequacy, the task is to "define...the (infinite) set of grammatical sentences in that language; that is, it describes the language in its entirety." (WK 2007dd)

By contrast, in explanatory adequacy, the task goes further and "gives an insight into the underlying linguistic structures in the human mind; that is, it does not merely describe the grammar of a language, but makes predictions about how linguistic knowledge is mentally represented. For Chomsky, the nature of such mental representations is largely innate, so if a grammatical theory has explanatory adequacy it must be able to explain the various grammatical nuances of the languages of the world as relatively minor variations in the universal pattern of human language....In other words, real insight into the structure of individual languages could only be gained through the comparative study of a wide range of languages, on the assumption that they are all cut from the same cloth." (WK 2007dd)

The Minimalist Principles

But in his 1995 book titled *The Minimalist Program*, Chomsky refined further his views on innate mental representations, in two major ways.

Firstly, he also eliminated the LF-PF distinction altogether, not just the distinction between deep and surface structures.

Secondly, in their place, he proposed something which is more minimal for the universal syntactical rules, this time, in accordance to the two criteria, namely, (a) the principle of "economy of derivation" and (b) the principle of the "economy of representation." (WK 2007dd)

The first idea about the "[e]conomy of derivation" refers to "a principle stating that movements (i.e. transformations) only occur in order to match interpretable features with uninterpretable features. An example of an interpretable feature is the plural inflection on regular English nouns, e.g. dogs. The word *dogs* can only be used to refer to several dogs, not a single dog, and so this inflection contributes to meaning, making it interpretable. English verbs are inflected according to the grammatical number of their subject (e.g. 'Dogs bite' vs. 'A dog bites'), but in most sentences this inflection just duplicates the information about number that the subject noun already has, and it is therefore uninterpretable."

And the second idea about the "[e]conomy of representation is the principle that grammatical structures must exist for a purpose, i.e., the structure of a sentence should be no larger or more complex than required to satisfy constraints on grammaticalness (note that this does not rule out complex sentences in general, only sentences that have superfluous elements in a narrow syntactic sense)." (WK 2007dd)

Some Controversies

But the changes in Chomsky's project over the decades have raised some further controversies. Consider, say, five critical points for illustration.

Firstly, to what extent does the mind really have innate mental representations, to the extent that language network (like Chomsky's version of transformative grammar) is already mapped out, during the process of learning a particular language, in accordance to the two minimalist principles?

After all, how much does the human mind really prefer the economy of representation (for simplicity), as opposed to its contrary tendencies (e.g., for complicatedness, for chaos, etc.)?

It is interesting to contrast Chomsky's claim for order in the brain with the opposing recent research finding (as already addressed in *Sec.2.3.1* on "Neural Representational Instability in Info Processing"), where it was found that the brain can also impose chaos (not just order) in info processing.

And this issue on order and chaos was already already extensively analyzed in my book titled *The Future of Complexity*, or *FC*.

Secondly, even were the innate mental representations to exist, would the search for a context-free universal grammar (albeit in a weaker form in the minimalist program) be criticized as inadequate in understanding language, since it ignores the personal meaning and intentionality of information processing? For the critics, such "a context-free psychology [in cognitive psychology] is a contradiction in terms." (WK 2007dd)

Thirdly, the newly introduced minimalist principles (like the economy of derivation and the economy of representation) "are somewhat vague, and indeed the precise formulation of these principles is a major area of controversy in current research." (WK 2007dd)

Fourthly, it is also not clear how much, in the minimalist program, "the derivation of syntactic structures should be uniform; that is, rules should not be stipulated as applying at arbitrary points in a derivation, but instead apply throughout derivations....Recently, it has been suggested that derivations proceed in phases." (WK 2007dd)

Here again, the dilemmas in existential dialectics remain in regard to how much simple or complicated, orderly or chaotic, and precise or vague language network should be—even if put in the most recent round of the debate, this time, in relation to the minimalist program (with the previous two distinctions eliminated altogether, namely, the distinction between deep and surface structures and the distinction between LF and PF).

Network and Biology

In the case of biology, network formation takes a different beat, this time, in imitation of the original neural networks.

Artificial Neural Networks

The term "neural network" refers to a biological "group or groups of chemically connected or functionally associated neurons. A single neuron may be connected to many other neurons, and the total number of neurons and connections in a network may be extensive. Connections, called synapses, are usually formed from axons to dentrites....Apart from the electrical signaling, there are other forms of signaling that arise from neurotransmitter diffusion, which have an effect on electrical signaling. As such, neural networks are extremely complex." (WK 2007qq)

This "complex" characteristic of neural networks is very important, as this remains to this day one of the most difficult challenges for those working in the field of "artificial" neural networks to imitate the original biological ones.

In this sense, artificial intelligence for the study of artificial neural networks has yet to achieve a degree of complicated similarities when compared with the original biological model.

In fact, two questions in the literature which have been much debated concern "the degree of complexity and the properties that individual neural elements should be to reproduce something resembling animal intelligence." (WJ 2007qq)

For one thing, many would agree that neural networks are more complicated than the early research models of artificial intelligence, which were based primarily on "sequential processing," whereas biological neural networks can also use other ways of information processing (e.g., pattern recognition, parallel processing, etc.). (P. Baofu 2000)

The Use and Misuse of Neural Network Modeling

Over the years, however, artificial neural network modeling can have less and less to do with the original biological one.

On the one hand, something basic remains for any neural network modeling, and a good instance involves the use of such concepts as "simple nodes [which are] called variously 'neurons,' 'neurodes,' 'PEs' ('processing elements' or 'units') [and] are connected together to form a network of nodes— hence the term 'neural network.' While a neural network does not have to be adaptive per se, its practical use comes with algorithms designated to alter the strength (weights) of the connections in the network to produce a desired signal flow." (WK 2007qq)

On the other hand, artificial neural network modeling has come a long way to go beyond the original biological one. For instance, in "modern software implementation of artificial neural networks the approach inspired by biology has more or less been abandoned for a more practical approach based on statistics and signal processing. In some of these systems, neural networks, or parts of neural networks (such as artificial neurons), are used as components in larger systems that combine both adaptive and non-adaptive elements." (WK 2007qq)

Artificial neural network modeling can also come in all shapes and sizes. For instance, it ranges "from models of the short-term behavior of individual neurons, through models of how the dynamics of neural circuitry arise from interactions between individual neurons, to models of how behavior can arise from abstract neural modules that represent complete systems. These include models of the long-term and short-term plasticity of neural systems and its relation to learning and memory, from the individual neuron to the system level." (WK 2007qq)

Yet, the critics are quick to point out the pitfalls of artificial neural network modeling. For instance, A. K. Dewdney once wrote in 1997: "Although neural nets do solve a few toy problems, their powers of computation are so limited that I am surprised anyone takes them seriously as a general problem-solving tool." (WK 2007qq)

Others like Roger Bridgman went further and said: "Neural networks, for instance, are in the dock not only because they have been hyped to high heaven (what has not?) but also because you could create a successful net without understanding how it worked: the bunch of numbers that captures its behavior would in all probability be 'an opaque, unreadable table...valueless as a scientific resource.'" (WK 2007qq)

These two comments may be a bit too dismissive, for sure. Yet, a more concise way to put the criticisms together is that the dilemma concerning simpleness and complicatedness in existential dialectics, for example, still haunts artificial neural network modeling.

Network and Culture

Network can take a different turn, when examined from the perspective of culture—especially in the domains of (3.4.1) morality, (3.4.2) religion, (3.4.3) aesthetics, and (3.4.4) epistemology, to be hereafter analyzed, in that order (and summarized in *Table 4.5*).

Network and Morality

A good way to examine the impact of culture on interactive network formation is by way of the analysis of ethnocentrism, that is, through the vantage point of moral particularism.

Ethnocentrism and Interactive Network Innovation

The word "ethnocentrism" refers to "the belief that one's culture is superior to all others," to the point that one comes to love one's culture (in special relation to its values and beliefs) biasedly more so than others. (P. Herbig 1994; C. Maitland 1998)

There are two ways in which the relationship between the impact of culture and interactive network formation can be shown, by way of ethnocentrism, for illustration.

Firstly, P. A. Herbig (1994) argued in *The Innovation Matrix: Culture and Structure Prerequisites to Innovation,* as Carleen Maitland (1998) thus explained, that "cultures low on ethnocentrism will be able to accept ideas from other cultures, leading to a higher degree of innovativeness. This may also mean such cultures will more readily diffuse certain innovations, especially those developed in other cultures."

Secondly, another way is that "ethnocentrism may affect diffusion of communication technologies...through language. Low ethnocentrism implies a greater acceptance of ideas from other cultures. Ideas from other cultures will be shared in a variety of languages, which implies cultures low on ethnocentrism will support a greater number of languages. Language barriers have been shown to inhibit diffusion of communication technologies." (P. Herbig 1994; C. Maitland 1998)

For instance, a study on the diffusion of communication technologies (like the Internet) in Europe showed that "[l]anguage barriers are...seen as potential hurdle to expanding this market. On-line services would need to be translated to suit each local market." (C. Cunningham, 1995; C. Maitland 1998). Consequently, "cultures low in ethnocentrism should experience higher levels of demand and faster rates of diffusion of communication technologies." (C. Maitland 1998)

But the work on the diffusion of interactive network innovations requires some further conceptual refinement. For instance, as is the case of "uncertainty avoidance" in *Section 3.4.4* (as will be analyzed later)—the distinction between the "perceived" (as opposed to the "objective") attractiveness of an innovation is important.

With this in mind, some scholars like E. Rogers (1995) intorduced "an attribute labeled 'compatibility.' Compatibility in general is defined as the degree to which an innovation is perceived as consistent with the existing values, past experiences, and needs of potential adopters. Hence, three variables have been identified: value compatibility, compatibility with previously introduced ideas, and compatibility with needs. The focus here is on 'value compatibility.'" (C. Maitland 1998)

In this way, it can be predicted that "innovations compatible with local values" can increase "the overall number of positive attributes of an innovation" and thus "will be adopted more quickly." (C. Maitland 1998)

Consequently, "[i]n cultures with weak uncertainty avoidance, values include a tolerance for deviance and innovative ideas. What is different is seen as curious, as opposed to dangerous. Therefore, in cultures with low uncertainty avoidance, all innovations, not just interactive networks, will be looked upon more favorably than in cultures with high uncertainty avoidance." (C. Maitland 1998)

It is thus no wonder that, for Rogers (1995), "early adopters of communication technologies as being more cosmopolite than later adopters. Cosmopoliteness is the degree to which an individual is oriented outside the social system. Early adopters are also more directly in communication with scientific and technical sources of information about the new communication technologies." (C. Maitland 1998)

But this study on compatability has raised some challenging questions.

Some Persistent Problems

For instance, scholars in the field do not all agree with this compatibility business in relation to culture. For instance, E. Katz (1963) identified three major problems to consider.

Firstly, it is not easy to find "ways to characterize cultures in terms of their values." (E. Katz 1963; C. Maitland 1998) Here lies the dilemma concerning simpleness and complicatedness in existential dialectics. For instance, how simple or complicated should the characterization of a culture in terms of its values be?

Secondly, it is necessary to "specify...the concept of compatibility more clearly." (E. Katz 1963; C. Maitland 1998) Here is the dilemma concerning preciseness and vagueness in existential dialectics. For instance, how precise or vague should the concept of compatibility be defined and measured?

And thirdly, it is not clear "which elements of a culture are to be regarded as prominent in relation to the compatibility of a particular innovation with the adopting culture." (E. Katz 1963; C. Maitland 1998)

Here lie the two dilemmas at the same time, namely, concerning both preciseness and vagueness, on the one hand, and simpleness and complicatedness, on the other hand. For instance, how complicated should the analysis of the prominent characteristics of a culture be, in order to avoid being criticized as too simplistic in analysis? And how precise or vague should the prominent characteristics be defined?

Rogers (1995) was aware of this messy problem of compatability when he thus wrote: "Past diffusion research suggests that compatibility may be relatively less important in predicting rate of adoption than relative advantage. This finding may be in part an artifact of difficulties in measuring compatibility." (C. Maitland 1998)

In the end, in both cases concerning uncertainty avoidance and network diffusion, on the one hand, and ethnocentrism and network innovation, on the other hand—there is another dilemma in question, this time, concerning slowness and quickness in existential dialectics. For instance, how fast or slow should one measure the rate of diffusion and innovation in the analysis to make it more presentable?

The dilemmas do not disappear, even in the case of morality in relation to network formation.

Network and Religion

In the case of religion and its impact on network formation, an unusual account concerns how religion affects social networks in the age of globalization.

Transnational Religious Networks

Peggy Levitt of Wellesley College, in her book titled *God Needs No Passport* (2007), showed how religion has contributed to the spread of transnational networks in a global way that was not even thought possible before. (J. Lampman 2007)

Take the case of the American religious landscape as a good illustration. Globalization has brought different faiths together in unusual places than ever before, to the extent that people are put together in a kind of "transnational lives" crossing multiple traditional borders.

In her study, Peggy revealed the lives of immigrants to the U.S. from different parts of the world (e.g., Brazil in Latin America, Ireland in Europe, and India in Asia), to the extent that different faiths confront each other in a pluralistic way, be they about the Hindus, Muslims, Roman Catholics, or Protestants.

Hospitality and Hostility

The transnational lives are affected in different ways, both positive and negative.

On the positive side, different religious groups come and form new ties with those in their new homes. For instance, some "families from Valadares, Brazil, have set up home in Framingham, MA, helping that city renew its depressed downtown area even as Brazilian pastors lead the spread of Pentecostalism in New England." (J. Lampman 2007)

As Levitt put it, "[p]eople who know how to function across borders, who are bicultural and bilingual, have the best resume for today's world." (J. Lampman 2007) In fact, "they could be the best diplomats for moderating religious conflict," as Jane Lampman (2007) added.

When Levitt identified the groups that she studied, it was amazing to know that many "included views across the religious spectrum, from strict conservative to very liberal. They expressed similar ideas on what it means to be American and what constitutes a good society—including the opportunity to be oneself, to make choices, to live respectfully with those who are different." "(J. Lampman 2007)

On the negative side, however, things are not as nice as they may seem. To start, many immigrants maintain close ties with their old countries and their different values. Two immigrants in the study, like Dipa and Pratik Patel, for instance, "[e]ven as they pursue the American dream, they are still deeply connected to their community back in India's Gujarat state, with strong ties to their Hindu denomination (the International Swaminarayan Satsang Organization, ISSO)." (J. Lampman 2007)

Their distinct lifestyles and values are not often warmly received by their American neighbors. For instance, "Muslims especially have been looked upon with suspicion since 9/11 for maintaining such ties." (J. Lampman 2007) Other Americans question the degree of "loyalty" of these immigrants.

In the end, these religious networks, though formed together with the helping hand of globalization, reveal the dilemma (in existential dialectics) between order and chaos in networks, in that they contribute to the formation of new order in forging global networks and yet to the creation of new chaos in fermenting transnational conflicts—or, more metaphorically, the old fashioned love-and-hate relationships as often seen in human history so many times before.

Network and Aesthetics

When put in the context of aesthetics, networks can show a refreshing face unseen in other domains.

A good instance concerns aesthetic networks, or the use of aesthetics for shaping interactive networks.

Aesthetic Networks

M. K. Sterpka (2007) once asked a rather refreshing question: "[W]hat does aesthetics have to do with envisioning social networks and the Internet?"

The answer is straightforward enough, in that aesthetic sensibility can help us construct better social networks. Using the idea of "graphic referencing technique" by Carole MacKenzie and Kim James (2004)—Sterpka (2007) argued that this "visualization technique supplies a practical resource for envisioning the complex interconnections in social organization."

In the case of interactive social networks like the Internet, "aesthetics allows us to imagine the nature and disposition of the system, including a number of features such as accumulation, aggregations, acquisitions, borders, connection, constellation, dispossessions, dissipation, fission, fusion, formations, edges, margins, oscillations, spread, severance and new structural dynamics. By extension, aesthetics provides a means for examining social organization that is at once flat, and yet highly complex and multidimensional." (M. Sterpka 2007)

Disturbances and Reinforcements

To start, one must understand the nature of disturbances and reinforcements in interactive networks. (D. McNeil 2004; Castells 1996)

The importance of any network, especially (though not exclusively) when it is complicated, "lies not with its inventory of individuals, but rather how they assemble together. The connections affect the vitality of a network. The connections run on a recursive logic. Recursivity is an inherent feature of complex networks and refers to objects or actions that appear at intervals, overlap, reappear and come back again. Recursive systems often function on a cycle of feedback loops. When accumulated, the feedback in a recursive system may display an underlying chaotic trajectory because of the build up of disturbances in the feedback cycle." (M. Sterpka 2007)

In the case of the Internet, the network "is comprised of looping circuits that continually send feedback messages to each other. The distribution of feedback in a network may result from the connections between individuals. Or it may result from internal social disturbances, or changing external and environmental conditions within the network. Negative and positive feedback is central to the path a network takes." (M. Sterpka 2007)

On the one hand, in the case of negative feedback, its function is "to keep a system in check. It is associated with the maintenance and stability of a complex system. Negative feedback is also associated with a network's regulation."

This is important, since "[c]omplex networks like the Internet tend to swing between chaotic and anti–chaotic states with many indeterminate periods. Much of this variance has to do with the amount of feedback operating in the system. The manner in which the system changes over time displays nonlinear features and therefore, it rarely obtains any long–term equilibrium. Small changes may have radical effects on the system's functioning." (M. Sterpka 2007)

On the other hand, in the case of positive feedback, however, its function is to "lead toward a rich-gets-richer phenomenon. This feature of positive feedback is alternatively referred to as...'preferential attachment.' Positive feedback relates to an amplification of tendencies in a system because it reinforces the trajectory a system is taking." (G. Bateson 1987; M. Sterpka 2007)

Visualizing Techniques

Yet, to visualize the geometry of a network with both negative feedbacks (as "disturbances") and positive feedbacks (as "reinforcements") for aesthetic sensibility is not easy.

Steven Strogats (1998) and Duncan Watts, for instance, tried to do precisely that. With the work of Stanley Milgram (1967) on connecting small worlds in mind, Watts and Strogatz "approached the topic from a different perspective. They applied their backgrounds in physics to measure networks in terms of their order and randomness. They were also able to take advantage of faster computers." (M. Sterpka 2007)

They then "devised an experiment using the Internet. They used an e–mail version of a message sender which simulated the connectedness of a network. First, they designed an ordered example and then increasingly introduced randomness into it. They called the approach 'random rewiring.' The model aimed to replicate the connectivity of a friendship network. By taking a ring of nodes that connected neighboring edges to each other, the experiment sought to replace a few of the neighboring edges with randomly selected nodes." (M. Sterpka 2007)

Three intriguing results are worth mentioning here.

Firstly, "[o]f the 48,000 senders in their experiment, and among the 19 targets in 157 countries, the scientists discovered that the average number of separations was actually six—confirming Milgram's initial hypothesis." (M. Sterpka 2007)

Secondly, they also discovered that when "networks...were neither totally ordered nor random," they tend to interact in a "dynamic short-cut route....The authors chose to refer to the outcome as the 'small world network' because it exemplified the earlier experiment of the same name by Milgram. The network exhibited short cut global separations at the same time, as maintaining the density of clustering that is typified in the majority of social networks." (M. Sterpka 2007) And the network shapes often look like some "circles along a central ring which retained a necklace shape but was closed at the ends." (M. Sterpka 2007)

Thirdly, another result is that "a significant property of networks...form into clusters of connections. These clusters tend to form into triangles of relationships. Clusters, when illustrated on a low dimensional graph take the form of geodesic triangles (they look much like Buckminster Fuller's architectural creations). A network is likely to be made up of vertex A connected to vertex B and to vertex C and so on. The tendency indicates that there are a series of triangles in a network equaling the sum of three–set vertices. Yet, each vertex is likely connected to each of the others through the clustering of ties. In sociological literature, this form of local clustering illustrates the notion of 'network density.' Thus, the probability increases that vertex A will also be connected to vertex C." (M. Sterpka 2007)

Mark Newman (2003) once put it this way: "The friend of your friend is likely also to be your friend."

This kind of network research is appealing to some researchers on aesthetic network representations.

Aesthetic Network Representations

With these findings on small world networks in mind, some researchers become more interested in "employing aesthetics as a visualizing technique...to imagine a number of possibilities for rendering the network shape. The chains of relationships within a network may be orchestrated in any number of ways to indicate shape and connectivity." (M. Sterpka 2007)

Consider two aesthetic sensibilities in what follows.

Firstly, Sterpka (2007) proposed four "overlapping social circles" in the form of "a flower–like cluster representing the initial six separations between social groups. Multiplied by two the figure shows increased density that is reminiscent of images generated by a spirograph, a drawing toy for children. Multiplied even further by four, the composition resembles the dizzying optics of moiré patterns," and of course the multiplication can continue until it gets more and more complicated.

But the problem here is that "with...a circle however,...it is not possible for a number of circles to nest alongside one another without leaving diamond shaped gaps between them. Even if the circles are overlapped..., the diamond shaped gaps prevail." (M. Sterpka 2007) The aesthetic circles can become too simplistic, so to speak.

Secondly, for this reason, some others prefer hexagons, not circles, as the basis of constructing network aesthetics, because one way "of circumventing the problem of gaps is to use hexagons instead of circles to represent a given set of social acquaintances. The hexagons have the advantage of having six sides and are also stackable. Hexagons nested alongside one another in a honeycomb sequence form a geometrically efficient surface. They leave no gaps. This leaves the shape open to recursive possibilities. At the same time, all of the hexagon shapes may be combined into one large hexagon." (M. Sterpka 2007)

Yet, using hexagons is a handy (but unsatisfactory) solution, because it does not fix the entire problem: "One of the problems with the hexagon model is that the boundaries between shapes are more artificial than what would be encountered in the actual world. Rarely are the divisions between groups so neatly delineated. Social relations tend to overflow into each other blending one social network with the rest, and this shape shifting is exactly one of the most significant features of a social network worth exploring. In this sense, the hexagon model is incapable of indicating movement and association. The shapes identify geographic distinctions without representing the interchange between them." (M. Sterpka 2007)

In this sense, the hexagon model as an aesthetic construction does not do justice to the complexity and nuances in the real world. Things can look neatly delineated (and precisely drawn) for aesthetic visualization, but they may not have much to do with reality in interactive networks.

Heterogeneity and Complexity

In fact, this deeper problem has to do with the inherent features of interactive networks, in that they are (a) "complex" and (b) "heterogeneous." (M. Sterpka 2007)

Firstly, interactive networks are complex, because "[i]n a complex network, it is rare to observe simple cause and effect relationships between all of the elements. As in the Butterfly Effect, a small stimulus may have a great effect on the system. Another way to refer to the dynamic nature of a complex network is to invoke its history. The history of a complex network like the Internet explains its trajectory. Even small changes within this history may lead to large deviations which lead to more divergences in the future." (M. Sterpka 2007; E. Lorenz 1980)

Mark Newman (2003) spoke about the "phase transition" of complex networks, that is, "from a low–density,...in which there are few edges and all components are small, having an exponential size distribution and finite mean size, to a high–density,...in which an extensive...fraction of all vertices are joined together in a single giant component, the remainder of the vertices occupying smaller components with again an exponential size distribution and finite mean size."

Interactive networks thus "could be compared to a loose collectivity. Individuals connect to the medium autonomously, yet assemble into groups of their own accord. Combined, the actions represent an extraordinary level of complexity. This is a markedly different vision of behavioral communication than the hierarchic model, which dominates the literature on social organization. The Internet makes it possible to re–envision the way in which social organization is constituted; as an assembly of networks within networks— teeming, cellular and much like the varied human ecologies from whence they spring." (M. Sterpka 2007)

Secondly, interactive networks are also "heterogeneous," because there are "dissimilar elements that make up the composition of networks and the differences between networks. Heterogeneous networks do not assemble into hierarchies. Rather, they form into concentrations governed by the laws of preferential attachment. These concentration points can be considered the highly connected nodes in a network (think of Amsterdam's Schiphol Airport or the New York Stock Exchange). However, all around are billions of smaller networks that are also connected laterally. Small networks of low connectivity are not preferentially attached. However, they move information quite efficiently and are at low of a risk of disconnection and failure." (M. Sterkpa 2007)

In the case of the Internet, the property of heterogeneity can be revealed through its "evolving global network. It consists not only of the individual computers, routers, cables, but also a number of communication gadgets. Many technologies are connected to the Internet including but not limited to cell phones, palm devices, video equipment and text messengers; all of which expand the entire communicative architecture. Users are adept at simultaneity, data sharing and using open software." (M. Sterkpa 2007)

These properties of complexity and heterogeneity then makes things highly difficult to construct a highly appealing aesthetics of networks, because it has to accommodate them in different dimensions: "Ultimately, the aesthetics of networks allows for imaging the properties of structures that have an extra–dimensional constitutions—recursive weaves, Sierpinski nets, preferential knots, feedback spins, and chaotic divergences that comprise the irregularities of topographic emergence."

But this challenge only shows all the more the dilemmas concerning simpleness vs. complicatedness, order vs. chaos, preciseness vs. vagueness, slowness vs. quickness, and the like in existential dialectics.

For instance, to what extent is simplicity (or homogeneity) in constructing interactive networks valued, while they have to accommodate heterogeneity as an inherent property?

How much chaos (as in negative feedbacks) is allowed, while order (as in positive feedbacks) is strived for?

In what degree is quickness highly sought for in interactive networks, while slowness resulting from system breakdown is to be expected, because of complexity and heterogeneity?

And to what extent is preciseness in constructing interactive networks needed, while it should also allow new space (to be vaguely defined on purpose) for the inclusion of unexpected emergent behaviors and novel features?

Some of the problems in aesthetic visualization of interactive networks (as discussed below) reveal some of these dilemmas.

Network and Epistemology

The illustration of the interaction between network and epistemology in the domain of culture can be offered, by way of the analysis of the impact of uncertainty avoidance on interactive network diffusion.

Uncertainty Avoidance and Interactive Network Diffusion

In cultural studies, there is an interesting hypothesis concerning the degree of uncertainty avoidance in a culture and its impact on the diffusion of interactive networks (like the Internet).

To start, "uncertainty avoidance index…is interpreted as the extent to which the members of a culture feel threatened by uncertain or unknown situations." (C. Maitland 1998)

Therefore, "[i]n countries with low uncertainty avoidance (Jamaica, Denmark) it is common that motivation comes from achievement" and other values, so "there is a high tolerance for deviant or innovative ideas and behavior." (C. Maitland 1998)

By contrast, "[i]n strong uncertainty avoidance countries (Greece, Portugal) there is resistance to innovation," so "motivation for work comes from security" and other values. (C. Maitland 1998)

In this sense, the impact of culture on interactive network formation is quite straightforward: "The implications of uncertainty avoidance for diffusion of an innovation are clear. In low uncertainty avoidance cultures new ideas will be more readily accepted than in high uncertainty avoidance cultures. Thus, low uncertainty avoidance cultures should experience faster rates of diffusion of new technologies." (C. Maitland 1998)

A Critique of the Analysis

But a major critique of this analysis is two-fold, to be analyzed in what follows.

Firstly, "[i]t is widely recognized that the potential adopter's perceptions of the innovation, and not 'objective' characteristics of the innovation, are the determinants of an innovation's diffusion." (E. Rogers 1995; C. Maitland 1998)

Secondly, there is something deeper in the analysis of uncertainty avoidance index, in that it can also concern the implicit cultural preference for order (as in the yearning for certainty) or chaos (as in the opposite one for uncertainty).

Here then lies the dilemma concerning order and chaos in existential dialectics. For instance, how much uncertainty does a culture prefer to avoid, for a more predictable (orderly) future outcome—and, in the process, suffers from slower technological diffusion (or in this case, interactive network formation)?

Network and Society

Network can also shed light in a different way, when investigated from the perspective of society, especially in relation to the four main social categories, that is, (3.5.1) social organizations, (3.5.2) social institutions, (3.5.3) social structure, and (3.5.4) social systems—to be addressed below, respectively (and summarized in *Table 4.6*).

Network and Social Organizations

Network, when put in the context of social organizations, tells us something different about info processing, albeit from the organizational perspective.

A good illustration concerns organizational learning.

Organizational Learing

There are some educational relationships between networks and organizational learning, which can teach us something more about the nature of info processing.

Networks, for instance, take a specific form, when they are molded and shaped by organizational interests. Consider three illustrative case studies below, by scholars in the field over the years.

Firstly, the first case study concerns the "single-loop" and "double-loop" networks that organizations may face in their organizational learning. (WK 2007ii)

For instance, C. Argyris (1978) and D. Schon in *Organizational Learning: A Theory of Action Perspective* introduced this distinction, based on "Gregory Bateson's concepts of first and second order learning."

In the case of "single-loop learning, individuals, groups, or organizations modify their actions according to the difference between expected and obtained outcomes. In double-loop learning, the entities (individuals, groups or organizations) question the values, assumptions and policies that led to the actions in the first place; if they are able to view and modify those, then second-order or double-loop learning has taken place." (WK 2007ii)

In this sense, "[d]ouble loop learning is the learning about single-loop learning." (WK 2007ii)

Secondly, the second case study relates the "loop" of organizational learning in a different way, unlike the one by Argyris and Schon.

For instance, J. G. March (1975) and J. P. Olsen in "The Uncertainty of the Past; Organizational Ambiguous Learning" suggested instead that the loop has less to do with "the difference between expected and obtained outcomes" (as in the case study by Argyris and Schon) but more to do with the interactions between individuals and organizations.

In other words, they showed us how "to link up individual and organizational learning. In their model, individual beliefs lead to individual action, which in turn may lead to an organizational action and a response from the environment which may induce improved individual beliefs and the cycle then repeats over and over." (WK 2007ii)

In a different sense, instead of the axiom that "[d]ouble loop learning is the learning about single-loop learning" (as in the model by Argyris and Schon), the one proposed by March and Olsen is thus: "Learning occurs as better beliefs produce better actions." (WK 2007ii)

Thirdly, another case study shows something else, which differs from both the model by Argyris and Schon and the one by March and Olsen, in focusing instead on how and why all the loops (as mentioned in the previous case studies and others) can break down sometimes.

For instance, D. Kim (1993) in "The Link between Individual and Organizational Learning" argued precisely this. Kim attempted to "integrate... Argyris, March and Olsen and another model by Kofman into a single comprehensive model." (WK 2007ii)

In fact, Kim showed "all the possible breakdowns in the information flows in the model, leading to failures in organizational learning; for instance, what happens if an individual action is rejected by the organization for political or other reasons and therefore no organizational action takes place?" (WK 2007ii)

The loop in a network, in unfortunate cases like this, will look neither like the "single-loop" or "double-loop" in the model by Argyris and Schon nor like the loop between individuals and organizations in the model by March and Olsen.

In this sense, the loop simply breaks down, and the network collapses, until it is successfully repaired.

Learning Organization

But to repair the loop in the network successfully requires organizational learning, which any organization has to acquire over time.

So, what makes an organization learn better than others? This then brings us to a related concept, called "learning organization" and "feedback loops."

Peter Senge (1990) at M.I.T., for instance, in his book titled *The Fifth Discipline: The Art and Practice of the Learning Organization*, argued that a good learning organization learns better if it follows five disciplines, with the last integrating the first four, namely, (a) coming up with a shared vision in the organization, (b) constructing correct mental models (e.g., cognitive processes on how to understand the real world), (c) building good team work, (d) cultivating individual mastery (e.g., for personal discipline), and (e) creating an integrative system thinking—especially on the basis of the "feedback loops." (WK 2007jj; TNL 2007)

To successfully build a good learning organization for effective organizational learning is not easy. For instance, Senge identified some common mental blocks which are not conducive to organizatonal learning, and some good examples include simplistic thoughts like "I am my position," "The enemy is out there," "I am in charge," or "I can learn from experience." (WK 2007jj)

In their place, Senge proposed some rather thought-provoking ideas to make learning organizations learn better. Hereafter are 10 "laws" that he had proposed: (WK 2007jj)

- "Today's problems come from yesterday's 'solutions.'"
- "The harder you push, the harder the system pushes back."
- "Behavior will grow worse before it grows better."
- "The easy way out usually leads back in."
- "The cure can be worse than the disease."
- "Faster is slower."
- "Cause and effect are not closely related in time and space."
- "Small changes can produce big results...but the areas of highest leverage are often the least obvious."
- "Dividing an elephant in half does not produce two small elephants."
- "There is no blame."

Some Ideas for Reflection. Yet, Senge's ideas may sound nice, but do they hold water in real life?

Consider two main criticisms below, for illustration.

Firstly, Senge's idea on learning organization has been criticized as lacking depth and focus (since he tried to use different ideas from different cultures, especially from East and West—often superficially), with the consequence that the project of "the fifth discipline" can be overly simplistic in not accounting for the complicatedness of myriad factors working interactively in producing the outcomes, which are not as predictive as Senge would like.

Donald Clark (2007) was right when he wrote that "Senge is not without his critics. Thomas frank in *One Market Under God* says that Senge has embraced 'just about every bit of daft pop liberationism to cross the national consciousness since the sixties.'"

Secondly, this then brings us to a related problem, in that Senge follows the intellectual fad of our times, in championing the positive thinking that somehow we have control over our own destinies. And the fifth discipline is to contritute to this long-term realization for learning organizations.

Yet, this positive idea of our having control over our own destinies may well be an intellectual fad in our current business world. (TNL 2007) Perhaps Kim's more realistic assessment (1993) can be used as an earthly advice here, in that the real world may well be one in which organizational failures occures more often than what we would like to see.

But then, the dilemma between simplesness and complicatedness (in existential dialectics) haunts the analysis on network, even from the perspective of social orgnizations.

Network and Social Institutions

Network can also reveal something else on the nature of info processing, this time, in relation to its institutional interests—not solely on the basis of organizational concerns.

An excellent illustration here concerns the issue of network outage, on the nature of interruption in a system, especially when there exists some communication failure.

Network Outage

What is a network outage, more precisely? A network outage can be defined as "an interruption in availability of a system due to the communication failure of the network." (WK 2007ff)

What is interesting here for the understanding of network is that, from the institutional standpoint (especially in the context of doing business for money-making), "[n]etwork outages cost money directly to the organisation (for example, banks, airlines, online transaction companies); or cost money indirectly to customers...." (WK 2007ff)

In other words, "[c]orporations might lose business due to network outage or they may default on a contract, or might lose millions of dollars if an important application does not run for just an hour. It is the duty of the network designer to make sure that a network outage does not happen." (WK 2007ff)

Planned and Unplanned Network Outages

There are two types of network outages to distinguish one from the other.

In the first type known as the planned outage, it "is the result of a planned activity such as a change or an upgrade. It may be the result of a service provider's activities or the system owner, or the result of a predictable natural event, such as Sun outage." (WK 2007ff)

By contrast, in the second type known as the unplanned outage, it was often "not anticipated or announced and happened unexpectedly. This may be the result of a software bug, human error, equipment failure, malfunction, high bit error rate, power failure, or overload due to exceeding the channel capacity." (WK 2007ff)

But what difference does this distinction make on the issue concerning the institutional impact on network?

The Institutional Impact on Network

The consequence is not hard to understand, in that there is an institutional pressure on the proper maintenance of a network, to insure that the costs are minimized for the business in question. And this is true, especially in the case of an unplanned outage.

As an illustration, it was estimated that the average US$ cost per hour due to network outage for a business could range from $5.45 million (for brokerage operations) and $2.5 million (for credit card authorisations) to $14,000 (for ATM fees) and $69,000 (for tele ticket sales). (WK 2007ff)

A famous network outage is the incident involving AT&T which "lost its frame relay network for 26 hours on April 13 1998. This affected many thousands of customers, and bank transactions were one casualty. AT&T failed to meet the service level agreement on their contracts with customers and had to refund 6600 customer accounts, costing millions of dollars." (WK 2007ff)

Consequently, the behaviors of networks have been carefully monitored to reduce costs in case of network outages.

Process Architecture for Network Maintenance

Over the years, measures have been institutioned in some businesses to reduce and control potential damages (like the ones from a network outage, or something else).

These measures, in the form of process architecture, are to study the behavior and performance of a network, to identify any potential problems, and then to implement appropriate solutions for them. (WK 2007gg)

Good examples of these measures may include "a help desk, network engineer team. A network management system can be used to detect faulty or degrading components prior to customer complaints, with proactive fault rectification. Risk management techniques can be used to determine the impact of network outages on an organisaion and wat remediations may be required to minimise risk. Risk may be minimised by using reliable components, by performing maintenance, such as upgrades, by using redundant systems or by having a contingency plan or business continuity plan. Technical means can reduce errors with error correcting codes, retransmission, checksums, or diversity scheme." (WK 2007ff)

Some Skeptical Observations

It is one thing to say, of course, that some pro-active measures to monitor and control network behaviors are taken to prevent or minimize network outages or other problems, but it is another to guarantee their effectiveness.

Does the extent of the success (or failure) also depend on other factors, be they social, culture, natural, or mental?

If so, how precise (or vague), simple (or complicated), slow (or fast), orderly (or chaotic), or else (as suggested by the principles in existential dialectics) should these measures be understood, in relation to the multiple factors in question—in order to ensure or enhance their success rate?

Network and Social Structure

Network, when understood from the perspective of social structure, can show something which is not less important and illuminating about the nature of info processing.

A good illustration concerns the phenomenon of social network, especially in relation to its social structure.

Social Network

To start, social network analysis focuses more on "the importance of relationships among interacting units" in a group or system. (U. Gretzel 2001; S. Wasserman 1994)

Although the unit level of analysis in social network, by defnition, is not about a single individual, it can have different focuses, depending on the choice of a given researcher, and some examples may include "dyads (two actors and their ties), triads (three actors and their ties), or larger systems (subgroups of individuals, or entire networks." (U. Gretzel 2001; S. Wasserman 1994)

The relationships in each unit level of analysis can take multipe forms, be they about (a) the "interdependence" among actors and their actions, (b) the "transfer or 'flow' of resources (either material or nonmaterial)" among them, (c) the "environment as providing opportunities for or constraints on individual action," and (d) the "lasting patterns of relations" (e.g., economic, political, social) among them. (U. Gretzel 2001; S. Wasserman 1994)

The structure of social network analysis is especially, although not exclusively, concerned with (c) and (d).

Just consider two case studies for illustration, namely, (i) social comparison theory, as part of the larger category of homophily theory, and (ii) resource dependence theory. (U. Gretzel 2001; P. Monge 2007; WK 2007ll; J. Pfeffer 1982)

Social Comparison (in Network Theory)

There are several versions of understanding social comparison in social network analysis over the years.

Just consider three of them in what follows.

Firstly, in the early 1950's, social psychologist Leon Festinger (1954) proposed a rather intriguing thesis to explain "how individuals evaluate their own opinions and desires by comparing themselves to others." (WK 2007kk)

Festinger, as an illustration, hypothesized (a) that "humans have a drive to evaluate themselves by examining their opinions and abilities in comparison to others," (b) that "the tendency to compare oneself with some other specific person decreases as the difference between his opinion or ability and one's own become more divergent," and (c) that "there is an upward drive towards achieving greater abilities, but that there are non-social restraints which make it nearly impossible to change them" (viz., the abilities). (WK 2007kk)

Secondly, by the early 2000's, different versions have emerged to go beyond Festinger's work. Two good candidates concern the "Proxy Model" and the "Triadic Model." (J. Suls 2002; WK 2007kk)

In the Proxy model, the idea is that "if a person is successful or familiar to a similar task, then they would also be successful at a new task." And in the Triadic Model, a comparable idea is that "people with similar attributes and opinions will be relevant to each other and therefore influential to each other." (J. Suls 2002; WK 2007kk).

Thirdly, still other versions of understanding social comparison have been suggested, and a good candidate is the distinction between two types of social comparison: "upward" and "downward."

On the one hand, "[u]pward social comparison occurs when individuals compare themselves to others who are deemed socially better than [the rest of] us in some way. People intentionally compare themselves with others so that they can make their self views more positive. In this type of comparison, people want to believe themselves to be one of the elite, and make comparisons showing the similarities in themselves and the comparison group." (J. Suls 2002; WK 2007kk).

On the other hand, "[d]ownward social comparison acts in the opposite direction. Downward social comparison is a defensive tendency to evaluate oneself with a comparison group whose troubles are more serious than one's own. This tends to occur when threatened people look to others who are less fortunate than themselves. Downward comparison theory emphasizes the positive effects of comparisons, which people tend to make then when they feel happy rather than unhappy. For example, a breast cancer patient may have had a lumpectomy, but sees themselves as better off than another patient who lost their breast ." (J. Suls 2002; WK 2007kk).

Examples though these case studies are, one thing stands out quickly in an overall analysis, in that social comparison theory, as a field of research, has relied on multipe fields of study as diverse as "social communication, group dynamics, the autokinetic effect, compliant behavior, social groups and level of aspiration." (WK 2007kk; A. Kruglanski 1990)

And more, "it is imperative to understand that no one thought process created the theory, but rather, a compellation of experiments, historical evidence and philosophical thought" from diverse sources. (WK 2007kk)

But then, a major criticism of the theory is that, if its sources are so diverse on a subject matter which focuses on the complicatedness of the interdependency among myriad units, the outcome may not be as predictable as its researchers would like, since, for some scholars, network analysis in general "is sympathetic with systems theory and complexity theory," with emergent properties not entirely predictable, especially in relation to the interaction between order and chaos (which was already extensively analyzed in my book titled *The Future of Complexity*, or *FC*). (WK 2007kk)

So, social comparison theory is not immune from this constraint either.

Resource Dependence (in Network Theory)

But network analysis does not have to focus on individuals as the sole unit of analysis.

A different way to do network analysis from the standpoint of social structure concerns the larger unit of analysis, this time, on organizations from the structural perspective of social networks.

A good example is of course what is now known as the "resource dependency theory," which analysizes a social network and its structure with organizations as the unit of analysis.

In 1978, J. Pfeffer and G. Salancik published *The External Control of Organizations: A Resource Dependence Perspective*, in which they proposed the theory, with broad implications for "the optimal divisional structure of organizations, recruitment of board members and employees, production strategies, contract structure, external organizational links, and many other aspects of organizational strategy." (WK 2007ll)

The theory makes two main arguments, namely, (a) that "organizations will respond to demands made by external actors or organizations upon whose resources they are heavily dependent" and (b) "that organizations will try to minimize that dependence when possible." (WK 2007ll; J. Pfeffer 1982)

But how exactly do organizations minimize the dependence on others? To this question, W. Scott (2003) in *Organizations: Rational, Natural and Open Systems* provided an answer, in that "companies pursue a two-pronged approach to managing their resource dependence: buffering and bridging." (WK 2007ll)

In buffering strategies, the goal is "to increase a company's tolerance of external resource shortage over a limited period of time. They can consist of various methods, such as improving classification of inputs, increasing stock levels, adjusting workflow to minimize variation in the input and output requirements, forecasting resource needs and adjusting the scale of production." (WK 2007ll)

By contrast, in buffering strategies, the aim is "not to increase one's own tolerance to resource shortage, but to reduce the chances of a resource shortage, by strengthening the links between the organization and its suppliers. Bridging can consist of using bargaining to gain information and improve understanding between companies, contracts (standard or hierarchical) to ensure compliance, co-optation—the incorporation of suppliers in the decision making (for example by the way of board interlocks), the foundation of a mutually owned organization in the form of a joint venture, completely merging the ownership of the two firms, trade associations where links are nurtured and information is exchanged, and the use of government connections to ensure the availability of supplies." (WK 2007ll)

But the problems with resource dependence theory are several-fold. Consider, say, two examples below for illustration.

Firstly, unlike social comparison theory (which depends on myriad sources in many fields), resource dependency theory focuses primarily on organizational studies, this time, in relation to social (or more narrowly, business) structure. Its scale of relevance is therefore limited, as it is not broad enough in its scope of analysizing social networks.

Secondly, the focus of resource dependency theory is on a specific form of structure in social networks, this time, on dependency—but not on other forms (e.g., interdependency, chaos, or whatnot).

So, in the end, this analysis of network also confronts the dilemma (in existential dialectics) of how much simple (or conversely, complicated) it should be, in helping us understand the nature of social networks and their structure—especially in relation to the essential question of this book, Why do we process information about network (in this chapter) in the way that we do?

Network and Social Systems

Another most transformative way that society can have an impact on network formation is the role of technology in shaping social networks—which can shed further light on the nature of info processing.

Network Society

Something unusual is worth considering in the context of the Information Age and its aftermath—for example, of what Manuel Castells (1996) once called "the rise of the network society."

To start, the spread of telecommunication technologies like the Internet and mobile telephony, as scholars like Kazys Varnelis (2007) and others argue, has contributed to "the simultaneous superimposition of real and virtual space, the new participatory media," which "concerns about the virtues of mobilization versus deliberation in the networked public sphere and emerging debates over the nature of access."

The transforming power of this technological advance should not be underestimated, since "this shift in society is real and radical. During the space of a decade, the network has become the dominant cultural logic. Our economy, public sphere, culture, even our subjectivity are mutating rapidly and show little evidence of slowing down the pace of their evolution. When we buy our first cell phone we are unaware of how profoundly it will alter our lives. Soon, we find that shopping lists are hardly necessary when it is possible to call home from the store." (K. Varnelis 2007)

In our time, "networked connection replaces abstraction. Information is less the product of discrete processing units than the outcome of the networked relations between them, links between people, between machines, and between machines and people." (K. Varnelis 2007)

In fact, it is useful to compare and contrast the digital and network transformations: "Contrasting the physical sites in which the digital and the network operate illuminates the difference between the two. The site for the former is the desktop microcomputer, displaying information through a heavy CRT monitor, connected to the network via dial-up modem or perhaps through a high latency first generation broadband connection....To be sure, the Wi-Fi enabled laptop is now the most popular computing platform, but the mobile phone, Keitai, and smart phone compete with and complement it." (K. Varnelis 2007)

And "[w]hat unites these machines is their mobility and interconnectivity, making them more ubiquitous companions in our lives, key interfaces to global telecommunicational networks....A supercomputer, smart phone, laptop, iPod, wireless router, xBox game platform, Mars rover, video surveillance camera, television set-top box, and automobile computer are essentially the same device, running—or capable of running—operating systems derived from UNIX such as Linux or VxWorks and becoming specific only in terms of scale and their mechanisms for input and output, for sensing and acting upon the world." (K. Varnelis 2007)

More importantly, "the new technological grail for industry is a universal, converged network, capable of distributing audio, video, Internet transmissions, voice, text chat and any other conceivable networking task."

But are there any specific charactristics about this rapidly growing phenomenon of network society?

Five Characteristics of the Information Technology Paradigm

The rise of the network society, for Castells, has five main characteristics (as summarized in *Table 3.2*) which make it stand out, when compared with other previous technological revolutions in transforming society, especially the information foundation of society.

Firstly, in the network society, "information is the raw material," that is, "the fuel with which new information is generated, making it a unique occurrence in contrast to previous revolutions. As Castells summarizes it, 'these are technologies to act on information, not just information to act on technology.'" (B. Lake 2007)

Secondly, in the network society, the spread of these new technologies is pervasive. Of course, "technology does not determine the shape of society," but "it does define how we approach it, thus influencing our development." (B. Lake 2007)

Thirdly, in the network society, "the networking logic of any system or set of relationships" depends on "[t]he creative power of technological interaction and communication. The creative power and complex interactions amongst such large groups is now possible through the use of communications technology, providing a networking structure that was previously too cumbersome to implement." (B. Lake 2007)

Fourthly, in the network society, "increasing social cohesion is dependent on these technological dependent networks that provide structure while at the same time remaining sufficiently flexible for innovation to be considered possible....The information age has a great deal of flexibility available to it in that organization and institutions can be modified, as in the opinion of Castells, the material basis of the organization can be reprogrammed and retooled, although he does not specify how such an event would take place." (B. Lake 2007)

And finally, in the network society, there is "the convergence of specific technologies into an integrated system. Telecommunications has experienced a shift from being the only form of information processing to becoming one of many. Indeed, telecommunications has integrated other forms of information such as microprocessor and optoelectronic data transmission, in order to increase efficiency. This technological convergence is not particularly surprising in this instance, as the network through which technological developments occur would dictate that the experience gained in one field would almost inevitably overflow into a closely related field. Castells sums up nicely the information technology paradigm as a multi-edged network, which is comprehensive, and complex." (B. Lake 2007)

But to what extent is this analysis of network society plausible?

Some Tough Questions

Castells's idea of the pervasive networking logic in network society has provoked some tough criticisms.

Let's consider three majir criticisms for illustration, as shown hereafter.

Firstly, for Castells, "networks constitute the new social morphology of our societies," as opposed to the older social forms on the basis of individuals, groups, organizations, and communities.

But scholars do not go as far as Castells on this. For instance, Jan van Dijk in his 1991 book (*De Netwerkmaatschappij* in Dutch, or *The Network Society* in English in 1999) does not share Castells' extreme view and still considers the units like "individuals, groups, organizations and communities" as basic—even if they are also "increasingly linked by networks." (WK 2007ee)

Secondly, because "Castells puts great importance on the networks," he therefore "argues that the real power is to be found within the networks rather than confined in global cities." But his view "contrasts with other theorists who rank cities hierarchally." (WK 2007ee)

And lastly, it is also not clear how much Castells's account of the network society is complicated enough (e.g., in giving sufficient attention to other units of society)—or conversely, not simple enough (e.g., in refining his causal arguments more in terms of a few principles).

The dilemma in existential dialectics on simpleness and complicatedness, for instance, remains relevent here at the social-systemic level.

The Power of Network

The analysis of network from the four perspective of nature, the mind, culture, and society (as analyzed in this chapter) has the scholarly virtue to show us how and why info processing has been shaped in the way that it has, albeit this time in relation to network.

Network and Ontological Principles

This scholarly exercise has a deeper implication, in that the analysis of network also reveals something ontological in relation to some underlying principles, which impose some constraints on the formation of network, just as they do in relation to taxonomy (as shown in Chapter Two).

The conflicting requirements as embedded in the principles are to be negotiated among competing forces and interests in relation to the four perspectives of nature, the mind, culture, and society.

These principles, as is also true for the case study of taxonomy (in Chapter Two), refer to the three pairs, namely, preciseness and vagueness (like the debates on language network in *Sec. 3.3.1*, ethnocentrism and network innovation in *Sec. 3.4.1*, and network outage and network maintenance in *Sec. 3.5.2*), simpleness and complicatedness (like the debates on physical network topologies in *Sec. 3.2.2*, language network in *Sec. 3.3.1*, ethnocentrism and network innovation in *Sec. 3.4.1*, learning organization and organization learning in *Sec. 3.5.1*, network outage and network maintenance in *Sec. 3.5.2*, social comparison in *Sec. 3.5.3.1*, resource dependency in *Sec. 3.5.3.2*, and network society in *Sec. 3.5.4*), and slowness and quickness (like the debates on different physical network topologies in *Sec. 3.2.2*, uncertainty avoidance and network diffusion in *Sec. 3.4.4*, ethnocentrism and network innovation in *Sec. 3.4.1*, and network outage and network maintenance in *Sec. 3.5.2*).

Surely, there are other ontological pairs too, which, however, are not entirely new in this book, as they were already analyzed elsewhere in my previous ones.

And an excellent example concerns the one on order and chaos (in the context of the debates on language network in *Sec. 3.3.1*, uncertainty avoidance and network diffusion in *Sec. 3.4.4*, network outage and network maintenance in *Sec. 3.5.2*, and social comparison in *Sec. 3.5.3.1*).

Some Words for Thought

It is often tempting, indeed, to dismiss the case-studies and examples given in the chapter as not adequate, but, as already indicated in Chapter One, the case studies and examples are chosen with care, and the introduction of more of them will not necessarily make much of any difference to the conclusion.

Besides, it should be reminded too, that the case studies and examples are not mutually exclusive, as they can overlap on certain occasions. Things in the world are not so scholastically organized and neatly separated as some scholars would be tempted to see.

Anyway, what conclusion can we draw, now that we have analysized both taxonomy and network as a means to understand the nature of intelligent life in the context of information architecture?

This then is the last business that this book has to address, to which we now turn to the last chapter, namely, Chapter Four, on the conclusion in relation to the future of info architecture.

Table 3.1. Advantages and Disadvantages in Network:
The Case of Network Topologies

—In a "point"-shaped topology, the simplest topology may be easy and cheap to construct, but it is not very practical in the complicated mega-cities of our times.

—In a "ring"-shaped topology, the advantage is obvious, in that "the number of transmitters and receivers can be cut in half, since a message will eventually loop all of the way around....If the message is not accepted by any node on the network, it will travel around the entire ring and return to the sender." (WK 2007cc) The disadvantage here is that a ring-shaped typology requires a message to travel around the entire ring, even when, on some occasions, this is not needed: "This potentially results in a doubling of travel time for data, but since it is traveling at a fairly insignificant multiple of the speed of light, the loss is usually negligible," especially in small circumstances. (WK 2007cc)

—In a "star"-shaped network topology, the clear advantage is that "[t]he failure of a transmission line linking any peripheral node to the central node will result in the isolation of that peripheral node from all others, but the remaining peripheral nodes will be unaffected." (WK 2007cc) The disadvantage, unfortunately, is that "the failure of the central node will cause the failure of all of the peripheral nodes also." (WK 2007cc)

—In a "tree"-shaped network topology, the advantage is that "individual nodes may thus still be isolated from the network by a single-point failure of a transmission path to the node. If a link connecting a leaf fails, that leaf is isolated; if a connection to a non-leaf node fails, an entire section of the network becomes isolated from the rest." (WK 2007cc) Conversely, the disadvantage is that it is both more expensive and time-consuming to build a complicated "tree"-shaped network topology than a simple, cheap point-to-point network topology.

Source: Data from WK (2007cc). A summary of *Sec. 3.2.2* in *FIA*.

Table 3.2. Five Characteristics of Network Society
(Part I)

—Firstly, in the network society, "information is the raw material," that is, "the fuel with which new information is generated, making it a unique occurrence in contrast to previous revolutions. As Castells summarizes it, 'these are technologies to act on information, not just information to act on technology.'" (B. Lake 2007)

—Secondly, in the network society, the spread of these new technologies is pervasive. Of course, "technology does not determine the shape of society," but "it does define how we approach it, thus influencing our development." (B. Lake 2007)

—Thirdly, in the network society, "the networking logic of any system or set of relationships" depends on "[t]he creative power of technological interaction and communication. The creative power and complex interactions amongst such large groups is now possible through the use of communications technology, providing a networking structure that was previously too cumbersome to implement." (B. Lake 2007)

—Fourthly, in the network society, "increasing social cohesion is dependent on these technological dependent networks that provide structure while at the same time remaining sufficiently flexible for innovation to be considered possible....The information age has a great deal of flexibility available to it in that organization and institutions can be modified, as in the opinion of Castells, the material basis of the organization can be reprogrammed and retooled, although he does not specify how such an event would take place." (B. Lake 2007)

—And fifthly, in the network society, there is "the convergence of specific technologies into an integrated system. Telecommunications has experienced a shift from being the only form of information processing to becoming one of many. Indeed, telecommunications has integrated other forms of information such as microprocessor and optoelectronic data transmission, in order to increase efficiency. This technological convergence is not particularly surprising in this instance, as the network through which technological developments occur would dictate that the experience gained in one field would almost inevitably overflow into a closely related field. Castells sums up nicely the information technology paradigm as a multi-edged network, which is comprehensive, and complex." (B. Lake 2007)

(continued on next page)

Table 3.2. Five Characteristics of Network Society
(Part II)

Sources: From M. Castells's *The Rise of the Network Society* (1996) and B. Lake's "Manuel Castells and the Rise of the Network Society: An Overview" (2007). A summary of *Sec. 3.5.4* in *FIA*.

• PART FOUR •

Conclusion

CHAPTER 4
CONCLUSION—THE FUTURE OF INFORMATION ARCHITECTURE

Information is together with Matter and
Energy the building blocks of the Universe.
—WK (2007f)

The Information Answer

The question at the beginning of this book—Why is information managed, stored, and applied in the way that it has, since time immemorial?—now has an available answer, but in an unusual way.

Information processing is much affected, in the context of the four major perspectives, that is, in relation to nature, the mind, culture, and society.

None of the three theoretical paradigms as introduced in Chapter One—namely, the "reflective" argument, the "constructivist" argument, and the "representational" argument—is satisfactory, since each is limited in relation to its own parochialness.

For instance, firstly, the "reflective" argument is more concerned, relatively speaking, with the perspective of the mind.

Secondly, the "constructivist" argument is oppositely more interested, relatively speaking of course, in the societal and cultural perspectives.

Thirdly, the "representational" argument is more twisted, relatively speaking again, towards the perspective of nature, although in its less naïve version, it allows the veil of ignorance in any attempt to deal directly with the external world.

And fourthly, by contrast with the first three arguments as indicated, my "synthetic" argument is more holistic, in taking into account of the perspectives of nature, the mind, culture, and society, without favoring one over the others, although in practice, not all four of them are necessarily equal on the basis of relevant weight in a given case.

More specifically, my "synthetic" argument, or "the synthetic theory of information architecture," consists of six theses (and is summarized in *Table 4.2*), namely, (4.2) 1st thesis: the simpleness-complicatedness principle, (4.3) 2nd thesis: the preciseness-vagueness principle, (4.4) 3rd thesis: the slowness-quickness principle, (4.5) 4th thesis: the order-chaos principle, (4.6) 5th thesis: the symmetry-asymmetry principle, and (4.7) 6th thesis: the post-human stage— to be discussed and summarized hereafter.

The first two theses (for the simpleness-complicatedness principle and the preciseness-vagueness principle) are for the category in relation to "structure" in existential dialectics (as already summarized in *Sec. 1.5*).

The third and fourth theses (for the slowness-quickness principle and the order-chaos principle) are for the category in relation to "process" in existential dialectics.

And the fifth thesis (for the symmetry-asymmetry principle) is for the category in relation to "agency" in existential dialectics.

It should be stressed at the outset, however, that there are some other principles involved in understanding the nature of information processing, but they were already introduced and analyzed in my previous books, but they will be re-introduced hereafter and taken into account wherever relevant in the six theses as cited above.

For instance, the partiality-totality principle and the predictability-unpredictability principle (which are for the category in relation to "method" in existential dialectics) are already applied in this project (in accordance to my methodological holism).

The change-constancy principle (for the category in relation to "process" in existential dialectics) should be understood in relation to the order-chaos principle, since, for instance, even chaos needs the occurrence of change.

The transformation-evolution principle and the softness-hardness principle (for the category in relation to "agency" in existential dialectics) are also important to reveal, as an illustration, the vital role of technology and its seductive (soft) intoxication too—in relation to their opposites.

And the regression-progression principle and the same-difference principle (for the category in relation to "outcome" in existential dialectics) are also relevant here, in that there is no progress without progression, just as there is no similarity without difference—even in the context of the future of information architecture (as will be clear later).

This thus means that, if the other principles in existential dialectics are not explicitly listed in the six theses here, it is not because they are not important or relevant, but because they were already discussed elsewhere in my previous books (but will be re-introduced hereafter, whenever relevant).

1st Thesis:
The Simpleness-Complicatedness Principle

The first thesis concerns the simpleness-complicatedness principle, in that, as was analyzed in Chapter Two on taxonomy and Chapter Three on network, the conflicting requirements of different combinations of them reveal how much each is important in the way that information is handled, but a given requirement varies in the context of the four perspectives of nature, the mind, culture, and society—be the issue about taxonomy or network.

Firstly, in relation to taxonomy like the analysis of Linnaean classification in *Sec. 2.2.4.1*, the levels of species classification become more complicated, as knowledge about them becomes more advanced over time, and this is especially so in some fields like entomology.

So, simpleness has its heuristic usefulness, just as complicatedness has its realistic representation.

And secondly, in relation to network like the analysis of physical network topologies in *Sec. 3.2.2*, the more complicated a network is built, the more expensive it costs.

So, simpleness has its economical attractiveness, just as complicatedness has its practical reliability.

The simpleness-complicatedness principle reveals this conflicting dilemma without favoring one over the other, in that each is utilized, depending on the basis of the perspectives of nature, the mind, culture, and society. And even when a combination of them is preferred, the dilemma is only shifted to a combinational degree of concern.

The dilemma still remains, so does the dialectic for co-existence (or sometimes, for transcendence altogether in a different issue, as already summarized in *Sec.1.5*).

2nd Thesis:
The Preciseness-Vagueness Principle

The second thesis concerns the preciseness-vagueness principle, in that, as was illustrated in Chapter Two on taxonomy and Chapter Three on network, there is the essential tension between the two, to the extent that each is important for how information is managed, depending on the contextual circumstances from the four perspectives of nature, the mind, culture, and society, be the issue about taxonomy or network.

Firstly, in relation to taxonomy like the analysis of Dewey classification system in *Sec. 2.5.1*, the more precise (or less vague) a library classification system is, the less (or more) room it has for the addition of new subjects.

So, preciseness has its taxonomic clarity, just as vagueness has its classificatory flexibility.

And secondly, in relation to network like the analysis of the two minimalist principles in *Sec. 3.3.1*, the less vague the principles are constructed, the more restrictive they are in revealing the underlying universality of syntactic rules.

So, vagueness has its explorative liberty, just as preciseness has its conceptual definitiveness.

The preciseness-vagueness principle reveals this conflicting dilemma, not that one is better than the other, but that both are used, in different degrees of preference, in accordance to the contextual application from the perspectives of nature, the mind, culture, and society. Even when both are used in a combination, the dilemma is shifted instead to one of combinational concern.

In the end, the dilemma still exists, and the dialectic remains for co-existence, although this also opens up the horizon of transcendence (into a different issue).

3rd Thesis:
The Slowness-Quickness Principle

The third thesis concerns the slowness-quickness principle, in that, as was examined in Chapter Two on taxonomy and Chapter Three on network, the duality of slowness and quickness has its own internal rivalry, to the extent that each fights for its own relevance with the other, in accordance to the perspectives of nature, the mind, culture, and society, without one always being the victor or without the other always being the vanquished in the long haul—be the issue about taxonomy or network.

Firstly, in relation to taxonomy like the analysis of user-centered design principles in *Sec. 2.5.2*, the more quickly an information architecture is designed to run, the less it can offer in terms of emotional incorporation into the designs for aesthetic purpose.

So, quickness has its efficient usability, just as slowness has its aesthetic appeal.

And secondly, in relation to network like the analysis of ethnocentrism and interactive network innovation in *Sec. 3.4.1* (or, for that matter, uncertainty avoidance and interactive network diffusion in *Sec. 3.4.4*), the more ethnocentric (or, for that matter, uncertainty-avoiding) a culture is, the slower it welcomes interactive network innovation.

So, quickness has its adventurous readiness, just as slowness has its risk-adverse convenience.

The slowness-quickness principle reveals, once again, the conflicting requirements of both, to the extent that one is the favorite, on the basis of one logic, and the other becomes the favorite, on the different basis of another logic on some other occasions—in accordance to the perspectives of nature, the mind, culture, and society. Even when both are chosen in other cases, this delimma is only transferred into something else with a combinational character.

So, in the end, the dilemma still remains, and the dialectic continues its relevance, with the two co-existing in ever new ways, but the window of transcending into something else of interest is opened.

4th Thesis:
The Order-Chaos Principle

The fourth thesis concerns the order-chaos principle, which, however, is not new here, since this principle was already introduced and analyzed in previous books of mine, especially (though not exclusively) in relation to the one titled *The Future of Complexity* (or *FC* in short).

What makes this principle relevant in this book is that, however much some scholars may prefer order in the world of things, there is its opposite in action, which competes for legitimacy—in the context of the four perspectives of nature, the mind, culture, and society, be the issue about taxonomy or network.

In fact, this principle is related to another one, the change-constancy principle, since both are for the category in relation to "process" in existential dialectics. If there is change, there is also constancy. And if there is order, there is also chaos.

Firstly, in relation to taxonomy like the analysis of neural representational differences in info processing in *Sec. 2.3.1*, there are the dual roles of "teaching" (for order) and of "tinkering" (for chaos) in the human brain, to the effect that they both work together, albeit in opposite direction. The same opposite competition is seen in the analysis of political genetic differences in info process in *Sec. 2.3.2.2* (between the Conservative and the Liberal mindsets).

So, order has its conservative appeal, just as chaos has its liberal seduction.

And secondly, in relation to network like the analysis of network outage and network maintenance in *Sec. 3.5.2*, the more there is an institutional obsession with cost efficiency, the more order a social organization favors in its routine pro-active maintenance (to prevent network outage).

So, order has its institutional interest, just as chaos has its technical chance-occurrence.

The order-chaos principle shows, once more, the recurrent competition between the two, depending on the operational logic in relation to the four perspectives of nature, the mind, culture, and society. Even in the scenario that both are used simultaneously, the delimma is only shifted into something else with a combinational competition.

In the end, the dilemma does not diappear, and the dialectic continues its importance, with the two recurrently opting for attention, until a different window of opportunity shows up for a different issue altogether.

5th Thesis:
The Symmetry-Asymmetry Principle

The fifth thesis concerns the symmetry-asymmetry principle, which, however, was also already introduced in my previous books (as summarized in *Sec. 1.5*).

What makes the symmetry-asymmetry principle relevant here in that, if there is co-existence for the dual roles of opposing entities—be they about simpleness vs. complicatedness, preciseness vs. vagueness, slowness vs. vagueness, or order vs. chaos—they are not by all means necessarily equal (on the basis of relevance) in a given issue.

As an illustration, one can be regarded as more useful in accordance to a certain logic in relation to the four perspectives of nature, the mind, culture, and society in one era, whereas the other may in turn be welcome in a different light in a different era, be the subject in the context of taxonomy or network.

For instance, firstly, in relation to taxonomy like the analysis of phylogenetic taxonomy in *Sec. 2.2.4.2*, there is now a greater acceptance of a non-Linnaean taxonomy, especially with "evolution as the mechanism of biological diversity and species formation. It then became generally understood that classifications ought to reflect the phylogeny of organisms." (WK 2007j) But, in the older days, the Linnaean alternative was more popular. This is so, even if, from the historical standpoint, all have been mentioned, analyzed, and discussed.

So, asymmetry has its contingent triumph, just as symmetry has its historical relevance.

And secondly, in relation to network like the analysis of physical network topologies in *Sec. 3.2.2*, not everyone prefers a highly developed "tree"-shaped network, since "[n]etworks designed with this topology are usually very expensive to set up, but provide a high degree of reliability due to the multiple paths for data that are provided by the large number of redundant links between nodes. This topology is mostly seen in military applications." (WK 2007cc)

In this sense, some (like those in the military) prefer a "tree"-shaped network formation, although all topologies are routinely considered as part of the study of network topologies (including those which are not "tree"-shaped).

So, asymmetry has its discriminatory application, just as symmetry has its wider conceptual didactic.

The symmetry-asymmetry principle (for the category in relation to "agency" in existential dialectics) should be understood in relation to another principle, namely, the regression-progression principle (for the category in relation to "outcome" in existential dialectics), in that each of these shifts in acceptance and rejection— in different eras of history and also on the basis of different rationalities and interests embedded in the four perspectives of nature, the mind, culture, and society—has a dialectic character, in being both progressive and regressive, be the issue about taxonomy or network.

For instance, firstly, in relation to taxonomy like the analysis of phylogenetic taxonomy in *Sec. 2.2.4.2* above, if there is progress (like the more allowance of biological diversity in species classification), there is also regression (since "there are plenty of reasons for this false representation" in evolutionary tree, as already discussed in that sub-section).

Secondly, in relation to network like the analysis of physical network topologies in *Sec. 3.2.2* above, if there is progress (like the higher degree of reliability for military applications), there is also regression (like the higher costs involved).

In both cases (of taxonomy and network), consequently, progression has its euphoric promise, just as regression has its realistic persistence.

6th Thesis:
The Post-Human Stage

The sixth thesis concerns the future of information architecture, with the five theses in mind.

The future of information architecture can further be illuminated by another principle already introduced and analyzed in my previous books, namely, the predictability-unpredictability principle (for the category in relation to "method" in existential dialectics), in that any methodology can have the virtue of prediction, but the exact nature of the future is not entirely predictable, subject to the factor of uncertainty.

There have been plenty of volumes written on this subject, and some most famous examples are well illustrated in the literature concerning cybernetic theory in the 1960's, catastrophe theory in the 1970's, chaos theory in the 1980's, and complexity theory in the 1990's, as John Horgan (1995) once suggested—and I also already offered a detailed analysis of this topic in *FC*, and other books of mine. (B. Rosser 2003)

In the present context, a complicated factor about the future of information architecture concerns the role to play by the coming "post-humans"—a term that I originally coined in different books of mine over the years, be they *FHC, FCD, FPHC, BDPD, BCPC, BCIV, FPHST, BNN, BWT, FC, FAE,* and *RALD* (as already summarized in *Sec. 1.5*).

My post-human vision is holistic, in relation to the mind (e.g., "floating consciousness," "hyper-spatial consciousness," "thinking machines," "genetically altered superior beings"), nature (e.g., "post-human space-time"), society (e.g., "post-capitalism" and "post-democracy"), and culture (e.g., "post-civilization").

The future of information architecture, even with the analysis of taxonomy and network as the case studies here, will much depend on the future of these post-humans, be they here on the planet Earth or out there in deep space, unto multiverses—in accordance to different space-time frames of the future.

Firstly, in the foreseeable future, the Information Revolution and its aftermath will produce more revolutions to come, for sure, as already discussed in *FHC*, be they about Leisure Economy, Life Sciences Economy, Megamaterials Economy, Atomic Economy , Space Economy, or else, as Graham Molitor (1999) once suggested—and I also discussed the issue in *FCD*, together with some related ideas.

And secondly, in the farthest future, a most distant world may well be one in which there emerge the phenomena of different cosmic minds like "hyper-spatial consciousness" and "floating consciousness" to deal with taxonomy and network as analyzed in this book.

What then will taxonomy and network be like?

An Epilogue

No one in this relatively backward technological age knows for sure. But an educated prediction can be made, in that these most cosmic minds will not be immune from the constraints imposed by the principles in existential dialectics.

While the principles (12 so far) in existential dialectics are of course not exhaustive (but merely illustrative), they are sufficient to give a rough picture of the constraints in relation to "method," "structure," "process," "agency," and "outcome" in that most remote world to come that the human mind has never known.

A most sobering thought worthy to be considered here is that this very world to come will neither be utopian nor dystopian—however much information in that remote future can be processed in a way that the current human mind has never dreamed (or been capable) of.

For instance, the limits in that future post-human world can be revealed, in that if there is preciseness, there will likewise be vagueness—just as if there is simpleness, there will likewise be complicatedness. If there is progress, there will likewise be regression—just as if there is symmetry, there will likewise be asymmetry. And if....

So continues this existential dialectic logic.

Thus speak the principles in existential dialectics—for the future of info architecture in a special sense, or for the future of intelligent life in a general one.

Table 4.1. The Theoretical Debate on Information Architecture
(Part I)

• **The Reflective Approach**
  —An excellent example of *the reflective argument* is none other than Immanuel Kant's synthetic-a priori propositions in his "transcendental idealism," in that "[i]t is our mind...that processes...information about the world and gives it order, allowing us to comprehend it...." (WK 2007)
  —A good instance concerns elementary mathematics, which, "like arithmetic, is synthetic [i.e., true by revealing something about the world] a priori [i.e., true by nature of the meaning of the words involved]. Here Kant includes a priori and a posteriori concepts into his argument, and posits that it is in fact possible to have knowledge of the world that is not derived from empirical experience....He justifies this by arguing that experience depends on certain necessary conditions—which he calls a priori forms—and that these conditions hold true for the world." (WK 2007)
  —Thus, in accordance to his "'transcendental unity of apperception,' the concepts of the mind (Understanding) and the intuitions which garner information from phenomena (Sensibility) are synthesized by comprehension. Without the concepts, intuitions are nondescript; without the intuitions, concepts are meaningless." (WK 2007) So, Kant (1965) wrote in a classic passage: "Intuitions without concepts are blind; concepts without intuitions are empty." (WK 2007) In the end, for Kant, information about the world can therefore reflect the nature of the mind.
  —But Willard Quine in his influential article titled "The Two Dogmas of Empiricism" (1951) rejected Kant's synthetic-apriori propositions by questioning the very assumption in the latter's argument, that is, the synthetic-analytic distinction itself, which, upon closer examination, turns out to be untenable. (WK 2007d)

(continued on next page)

**Table 4.1. The Theoretical Debate on Information Architecture
(Part II)**

• **The Constructivist Approach**

—An opposing approach which stands in sharp contrast to Kant's transcendental idealism is a fashionable thesis in our time, that is, *the constructivist argument.*

—The constructivist argument regards all information about the world as a byproduct of the social institutions and values that contribute to their construction, based on different vested interests and power formations.

—Michel Foucault, for instance, had written different works on the multifaceted relationships between power and knowledge. As an illustration, he argued—in *The Order of Things* (1971) in English, or *L'Ordre des Choses* in French—that, "all periods of history possessed certain underlying conditions of truth that constituted what was acceptable....[And] these conditions of discourse changed over time, in major and relatively sudden shifts, from one period's episteme to another." (WK 2007c)

—But the critics are quick to point out that the attempt to treat information about the world as an epi-phenomenon of social construction based on power formations and vested interests is too reductionistic indeed.

—As an illustration, Noam Chomsky showed in *Logical Structure of Linguistic Theory* (1955) the structure of transformational grammars, in that "utterances (sequences of words)...have a syntax which can be (largely) characterized by a formal grammar; in particular, a context-free grammar extended with transformational rules. Children are hypothesized to have an innate knowledge of the basic grammatical structure common to all human languages (i.e. they assume that any language which they encounter is of a certain restricted kind). This innate knowledge is often referred to as universal grammar." (WK 2007e)

—However, Chomsky changed a bit of his position in a later work titled *Minimalist Program* (1995), in which he revised his original version of universal grammar by giving it a weaker form, that is, keeping only the "barest necessary elements, while advocating a general approach to the architecture of the human language faculty that emphasizes principles of economy and optimal design." (WK 2007e)

(continued on next page)

Table 4.1. The Theoretical Debate on Information Architecture
(Part III)

- **The Representational Approach**
  —One good instance of *the representational argument* is Realism in epistemology, which treats information as representing some reality in the world. There are different versions of realism, however, and two main examples are "direct realism" and "indirect realism."
  —In "direct realism" (also known as "naïve realism" or "common sense realism"), the world of information is treated "pretty much as common sense would have it," because "when we look at and touch things we see and feel those things directly, and so perceive them as they really are...whether or not there is anyone present to observe them...." (WK 2007a) A problem here is that the same information may be perceived differently by different people. Yet, someone like Myles Burnyeat's in "Conflicting Appearances" argued that this problem is really no problem at all, and his reasoning is that "[t]o say that something cannot really possess a property if it appears different at different times, from different perspectives and under different conditions, is logically equivalent to saying that something cannot really possess a property unless it always appears to possess that property." (WK 2007a)
  —In "indirect realism," however, direct realism is attacked in a different way, in that "we do not (and can not) perceive the external world directly; instead we know only our ideas or interpretations of objects in the world. Thus, a barrier or a veil of perception prevents first-hand knowledge of anything beyond it. The 'veil' exists between the mind and the existing world." (WK 2007b) Aristotle, for instance, in "On the Soul," showed "how the eye must be affected by changes in an intervening medium rather than by objects themselves. He then speculates on how these sense impressions can form our experience of seeing and reasons that an endless regress would occur unless the sense itself were self-aware. He concludes by proposing that the mind is the things it thinks. He calls the images in the mind 'ideas.'" (WK 2007b) But indirect realism poses some serious problems: "How well do sense-data represent external objects, properties, and events? Indirect realism creates deep epistemological problems, such as solipsism and the problem of the external world," but this does not prevent indirect realism from being influential among scholars like Bertrand Russell, Spinoza, René Descartes, and John Locke." (WK 2007b)

(continued on next page)

Table 4.1. The Theoretical Debate on Information Architecture
(Part IV)

• **The Synthetic Approach**

—My *synthetic argument* learns from the weaknesses and strengths of the previous three approaches—without, however, siding with any of them (or even integrating them in a harmonious whole, since they can be incompatible). For instance, none of the three theoretical paradigms is satisfactory, since each is limited in relation to its own parochialness.

—As an illustration, the "reflective" argument is more concerned with the perspective of the mind. Conversely, the "constructivist" argument is oppositely more interested in the societal and cultural perspectives. And the "representational" argument is more twisted towards the perspective of nature, although in its less naïve version, it allows the veil of ignorance in any attempt for direct representation of the external world.

—By contrast, my synthetic argument is more holistic, in taking into account of the perspectives of nature, the mind, culture, and society, without favoring one over the others, although in practice, not all four of them are necessarily of equal relevant weight in a given case.

—My *synthetic argument,* when put in the context of the information question, can be more precisely called *the synthetic theory of information architecture,* since it treats the processing, storage, and application of information into taxonomy and network from the four main perspectives of the mind, nature, society, and culture.

—This theory of mine contains six major theses, namely, (a) the simpleness-complicadness principle, (b) the exactness-vagueness principle, (c) the slowness-quickness principle, (d) the order-chaos principle, (e) the symmetry-asymmetry principle, and (f) the post-human stage—to be analyzed in the rest of the book and summarized in Chapter Four (the concluding chapter).

Source: From Ch.1 of *FIA*. See also the table on the six theses in the synthesizing theory of information architecture.

Table 4.2. Six Theses in the Synthetic Theory
of Information Architecture
(Part I)

• **1ˢᵗ Thesis: The Simpleness-Complicatedness Principle**

—The first thesis concerns the simpleness-complicatedness principle, in that, as was analyzed in Chapter Two on taxonomy and Chapter Three on network, the conflicting requirements of different combinations of them reveal how much each is important in the way that information is handled, but a given requirement varies in the context of the four perspectives of nature, the mind, culture, and society—be the issue about taxonomy or network.

—Firstly, in relation to taxonomy like the analysis of Linnaean classification in *Sec. 2.2.4.1*, the levels of species classification become more complicated, as knowledge about them becomes more advanced over time, and this is especially so in some fields like entomology. So, simpleness has its heuristic usefulness, just as complicatedness has its realistic representation.

—And secondly, in relation to network like the analysis of physical network topologies in *Sec. 3.2.2*, the more complicated a network is built, the more expensive it costs. So, simpleness has its economical attractiveness, just as complicatedness has its practical reliability.

—The simpleness-complicatedness principle reveals this conflicting dilemma without favoring one over the other, in that each is utilized, depending on the basis of the perspectives of nature, the mind, culture, and society. And even when a combination of them is preferred, the dilemma is only shifted to a combinational degree of concern.

—The dilemma still remains, so does the dialectic for co-existence (or sometimes, for transcendence altogether in a different issue).

(continued on next page)

Table 4.2. Six Theses in the Synthetic Theory
of Information Architecture
(Part II)

• **2nd Thesis: The Preciseness-Vagueness Principle**

—The second thesis concerns the preciseness-vagueness principle, in that, as was illustrated in Chapter Two on taxonomy and Chapter Three on network, there is the essential tension between the two, to the extent that each is important for how information is managed, depending on the contextual circumstances from the four perspectives of nature, the mind, culture, and society, be the issue about taxonomy or network.

—Firstly, in relation to taxonomy like the analysis of Dewey classification system in *Sec. 2.5.1*, the more precise (or less vague) a library classification system is, the less (or more) room it has for the addition of new subjects. So, preciseness has its taxonomic clarity, just as vagueness has its classificatory flexibility.

—And secondly, in relation to network like the analysis of the two minimalist principles in *Sec. 3.3.1*, the less vague the principles are constructed, the more restrictive they are in revealing the underlying universality of language. So, vagueness has its explorative liberty, just as preciseness has its conceptual definitiveness.

—The preciseness-vagueness principle reveals this conflicting dilemma, not that one is better than the other, but that both are used, in different degrees of preference, in accordance to the contextual application from the perspectives of nature, the mind, culture, and society. Even when both are used in a combination, the dilemma is shifted instead to one of combinational concern.

—In the end, the dilemma still exists, and the dialectic remains for co-existence, although this also opens up the horizon of transcendence (into a different issue).

(continued on next page)

Table 4.2. Six Theses in the Synthetic Theory
of Information Architecture
(Part III)

- **3rd Thesis: The Slowness-Quickness Principle**
  - —The third thesis concerns the slowness-quickness principle, in that, as was examined in Chapter Two on taxonomy and Chapter Three on network, the duality of slowness and quickness has its own internal tension, to the extent that each fights for its own relevance with the other, in accordance to the perspectives of nature, the mind, culture, and society, without one being the victor and the other being the vanquished in the long haul—be the issue about taxonomy or network.
  - —Firstly, in relation to taxonomy like the analysis of user-centered design principles in *Sec. 2.5.2*, the more quickly an information architecture is designed to run, the less it can offer in terms of emotional incorporation into the designs. So, quickness has its efficient usability, just as slowness has its aesthetic appeal.
  - —And secondly, in relation to network like the analysis of ethnocentrism and interactive network innovation in *Sec. 3.4.1* (or, for that matter, uncertainty avoidance and interactive network diffusion in *Sec. 3.4.4*), the more ethnocentric (or, for that matter, uncertainty-avoiding) a culture is, the slower it welcomes interactive network innovation. So, quickness has its adventurous readiness, just as slowness has its risk-adverse convenience.
  - —The slowness-quickness principle reveals, once again, the conflicting requirements of both, to the extent that one is the favorite, on the basis of one logic, and the other becomes the favorite, on the different basis of another logic on some other occasions—in accordance to the perspectives of nature, the mind, culture, and society. Even when both are chosen in other cases, this delimma is only transferred into something else with a combinational character.
  - —So, in the end, the dilemma still remains, and the dialectic continues its relevance, with the two co-existing in ever new ways, but the window of transcending into something else of interest is opened.

(continued on next page)

Table 4.2. Six Theses in the Synthetic Theory
of Information Architecture
(Part IV)

• 4th Thesis: The Order-Chaos Principle

—The fourth thesis concerns the order-chaos principle, which was already introduced and analyzed in my previous books like *The Future of Complexity* (or *FC* in short) and others.

—What makes this principle relevant in this book is that, however much some scholars may prefer order in the world of things, there is its opposite in action, which competes for legitimacy—in the context of the four perspectives of nature, the mind, culture, and society, be the issue about taxonomy or network.

—In fact, this principle is related to another one, the change-constancy principle, since both are for the category in relation to "process" in existential dialectics. If there is change, there is also constancy. And if there is order, there is also chaos.

—Firstly, in relation to taxonomy like the analysis of neural representational differences in info processing in *Sec. 2.3.1*, there are the dual roles of "teaching" (for order) and of "tinkering" (for chaos) in the human brain, to the effect that they both work together, albeit in opposite direction. The same opposite competition is seen in the analysis of political genetic differences in info process in *Sec. 2.3.2.2* (between the Conservative and the Liberal mindsets). So, order has its conservative appeal, just as chaos has its liberal seduction.

—And secondly, in relation to network like the analysis of network outage and network maintenance in *Sec. 3.5.2*, the more an institutional obsession with cost efficiency is, the more order a social organization favors in its routine pro-active maintenance (to prevent network outage). So, order has its institutional interest, just as chaos has its technical chance-occurrence.

—The order-chaos principle shows, once more, the recurrent competition between the two, depending on the operational logic in relation to the four perspectives of nature, the mind, culture, and society. Even in the scenario that both are used simultaneously, the delimma is only shifted into something else with a combinational competition.

—In the end, the dilemma does not diappear, and the dialectic continues its importance, with the two recurrently opting for attention, until a different window of opportunity shows up for a different issue altogether.

(continued on next page)

Table 4.2. Six Theses in the Synthetic Theory
of Information Architecture
(Part V)

• **5th Thesis: The Symmetry-Asymmetry Principle**
  —The fifth thesis concerns the symmetry-asymmetry principle, which was also already introduced in my previous books (as summarized in *Sec. 1.5*).
  —As an illustration, any one of the opposite entities can be regarded as more useful in accordance to a certain logic in relation to the four perspectives of nature, the mind, culture, and society in one era, whereas the other may in turn be welcome in a different light in a different era, be the subject in the context of taxonomy or network.
  —Firstly, in relation to taxonomy like the analysis of phylogenetic taxonomy in *Sec. 2.2.4.2*, there is now a greater acceptance of a non-Linnaean taxonomy, especially with "evolution as the mechanism of biological diversity and species formation. It then became generally understood that classifications ought to reflect the phylogeny of organisms." (WK 2007j) But, in the older days, the Linnaean alternative was more popular. This is so, even if, from the historical standpoint, all have been mentioned, analyzed, and discussed. So, asymmetry has its contingent triumph, just as symmetry has its historical discussion.
  —And secondly, in relation to network like the analysis of physical network topologies in *Sec. 3.2.2*, not everyone prefers a highly developed "tree"-shaped network, since "[n]etworks designed with this topology are usually very expensive to set up, but provide a high degree of reliability due to the multiple paths for data that are provided by the large number of redundant links between nodes. This topology is mostly seen in military applications." (WK 2007cc) In this sense, some (like those in the military) prefer a "tree"-shaped network formation, although all topologies are routinely considered as part of the study of network topologies (including those which are not "tree"-shaped). So, asymmetry has its discriminatory application, just as symmetry has its wider conceptual didactic.

(continued on next page)

**Table 4.2. Six Theses in the Synthetic Theory
of Information Architecture
(Part VI)**

• **5ᵗʰ Thesis: The Symmetry-Asymmetry Principle (*cont'd*)**

—The symmetry-asymmetry principle (for the category in relation to "agency" in existential dialectics) is related to another principle, namely, the regression-progression principle (for the category in relation to "outcome" in existential dialectics), in that each of these shifts in acceptance and rejection— in different eras of history and also on the basis of different rationalities and interests embedded in the four perspectives of nature, the mind, culture, and society—has a dialectic character, in being both progressive and regressive, be the issue about taxonomy or network.

—Firstly, in relation to taxonomy like the analysis of phylogenetic taxonomy in *Sec. 2.2.4.2* above, if there is progress (like the more allowance of biological diversity in species classification), there is also regression (since "there are plenty of reasons for this false representation" in evolutionary tree, as already discussed in *Sec. 2.2.2*).

—Secondly, in relation to network like the analysis of physical network topologies in *Sec. 3.2.2* above, if there is progress (like the higher degree of reliability for military applications), there is also regression (like the higher costs involved).

—In both cases (of taxonomy and network), consequently, progression has its euphoric promise, just as regression has its realistic persistence.

(continued on next page)

**Table 4.2. Six Theses in the Synthetic Theory
of Information Architecture
(Part VII)**

• **6th Thesis: The Post-Human Stage**

—The sixth thesis concerns the future of information architecture, with the five theses in mind.

—The future of information architecture can further be illuminated by another principle already introduced and analyzed in my previous books, namely, the predictability-unpredictability principle (for the category in relation to "method" in existential dialectics), in that any methodology can have the virtue of prediction, but the exact nature of the future is not entirely predictable, subject to the factor of uncertainty.

—In the present context, a complicated factor about the future of information architecture concerns the role to play by the coming "post-humans"—a term that I originally coined in different books of mine over the years, be they *FHC, FCD, FPHC, BDPD, BCPC, BCIV, FPHST, BNN, BWT, FC, FAE,* and *RALD* (as already summarized in *Sec. 1.5*).

—My post-human vision is holistic, in relation to the mind (e.g., "floating consciousness," "hyper-spatial consciousness," "thinking machines," "genetically altered superior beings"), nature (e.g., "post-human space-time"), society (e.g., "post-capitalism" and "post-democracy"), and culture (e.g., "post-civilization").

—The future of information architecture, even with the analysis of taxonomy and network as the case studies here, will much depend on the future of these post-humans, be they here on the planet Earth or out there in deep space, unto multiverses—in accordance to different time frames of the future.

—Firstly, in the foreseeable future, the Information Revolution and its aftermath will produce more revolutions to come, for sure, as already discussed in *FHC*, be they about Leisure Economy, Life Sciences Economy, Megamaterials Economy, Atomic Economy, Space Economy, or else, as Graham Molitor (1999) once suggested—and I also already discussed the topic in *FCD*, together with some related ideas.

—And secondly, in the farthest future, a most distant world may well be one in which there emerge the phenomena of different cosmic minds like "hyper-spatial consciousness" and "floating consciousness" to deal with taxonomy and network as analyzed in this book.

(continued on next page)

Table 4.2. Six Theses in the Synthetic Theory
of Information Architecture
(Part VIII)

- **6th Thesis: The Post-Human Stage (*cont'd*)**

  —What then will taxonomy and network be like then? No one in this relatively backward technological age knows for sure. But an educated prediction can be made, in that these most cosmic minds will not be immune from the constraints imposed by the principles in existential dialectics.

  —While the principles (12 so far) in existential dialectics are of course not exhaustive (but merely illustrative), they are sufficient to give a rough picture of the constraints in relation to "method," "structure," "process," "agency," and "outcome" in that most remote world to come that the human mind has never known.

  —A most sobering thought worthy to be considered here is that this very world to come will neither be utopian nor dystopian—however much information in that remote future can be processed in a way that the current human mind has never dreamed of.

  —For instance, the limits in that future post-human world can be revealed, in that if there is preciseness, there will likewise be vagueness—just as if there is simpleness, there will likewise be complicatedness. If there is progress, there will likewise be regression—just as if there is symmetry, there will likewise be asymmetry. And if....

  —So the existential dialectic logic continues.

  —Thus speak the principles in existential dialectics—for the future of info architecture in a special sense, or for the future of intelligent life in a general one.

Source: From Ch.4 of *FIA*

Table 4.3. Information Architecture and Nature

• **Taxonomy and Nature**
　—*in Chemistry*
　　▪ Ex: Chemotaxonomy
　—*in Micro-Physics*
　　▪ Ex: Particle Taxonomy
　—*in Macro-Physics (Cosmology)*
　　▪ Ex: Cosmological Taxonomy
　—*in Biology (Animal)*
　　▪ Ex: Linnaean taxonomy
　　▪ Ex: Phylogenetic taxonomy

• **Network and and Nature**
　—*in Chemistry*
　　▪ Ex: Autocatalytic Chemical Reaction Networks
　—*in Micro-Physics*
　　▪ Ex: Network Topology (in Telecommunications)
　—*in Macro-Physics (Cosmology)*
　　▪ Ex: Spin Networks

Notes: The examples in the categories are solely illustrative (not exhaustive), and the comparison is relative (not absolute), nor are they necessarily mutually exclusive. And some can be easily re-classified elsewhere. As generalities, they allow exceptions.

Source: A partial summary of Ch.2 and Ch.3 of *FIA*

Table 4.4. Information Architecture and the Mind

• **Taxonomy and the Mind**
  —*in Psychology*
    ▪ Ex: Gender Differences in Info Processing
    ▪ Ex: Political Differences in Info Processing
  —*in Biology (Human)*
    ▪ Ex: Neural Representational Differences in Info Processing

• **Network and and the Mind**
  —*in Psychology*
    ▪ Ex: Language Network (in Cognitive Psychology)
  —*in Biology*
    ▪ Ex: Artificial Neural Networks

Notes: The examples in the categories are solely illustrative (not exhaustive), and the comparison is relative (not absolute), nor are they necessarily mutually exclusive. And some can be easily re-classified elsewhere. As generalities, they allow exceptions.
Source: A partial summary of Ch.2 and Ch.3 of *FIA*

Table 4.5. Information Architecture and Culture

• **Taxonomy and Culture**
  —*in Morality*
    ▪ Ex: The Genealogy of Moral Taxonomy
  —*in Religion*
    ▪ Ex: Taxonomy and Religious Cults
  —*in Epistemology*
    ▪ Ex: Taxonomy and the Epistemic Orders
  —*in Aesthetics*
    ▪ Ex: The Taxonomy of the Arts

• **Network and and Culture**
  —*in Morality*
    ▪ Ex: Ethnocentrism and Interactive Network Innovation
  —*in Religion*
    ▪ Ex: Transnational Religious Networks
  —*in Epistemology*
    ▪ Ex: Uncertainty Avoidance and Interactive Network Diffusion
  —*in Aesthetics*
    ▪ Ex: Aesthetic Networks

Notes: The examples in the categories are solely illustrative (not exhaustive), and the comparison is relative (not absolute), nor are they necessarily mutually exclusive. And some can be easily re-classified elsewhere. As generalities, they allow exceptions.

Source: A partial summary of Ch.2 and Ch.3 of *FIA*

Table 4.6. Information Architecture and Society

• **Taxonomy and Society**
  —*in Social Organizations*
      ▪ Ex: Traditional Library Science Classification
      ▪ Ex: Faceted Classification
  —*in Social Institutions*
      ▪ Ex: Info Designing Principles
  —*in Social Structure*
      ▪ Ex: The Primitive Forms of Classification
      ▪ Ex: The Marxist Classification of Social Class
  —*in Social Systems*
      ▪ Ex: The Role of Technology on Taxonomy

• **Network and and Society**
  —*in Social Organizations*
      ▪ Ex: Organizational Learning
      ▪ Ex: Learning Organization
  —*in Social Institutions*
      ▪ Ex: Network Outage
      ▪ Ex: Process Architecture (for Network Maintenance)
  —*in Social Structure*
      ▪ Ex: Social Comparison (in Network Theory)
      ▪ Ex: Resource Dependence (in Network Theory)
  —*in Social Systems*
      ▪ Ex: Network Society

Notes: The examples in the categories are solely illustrative (not exhaustive), and the comparison is relative (not absolute), nor are they necessarily mutually exclusive. And some can be easily re-classified elsewhere. As generalities, they allow exceptions.
Source: A partial summary of Ch.2 and Ch.3 of *FIA*

Table 4.7. The Conceptual Dimensions of Consciousness (and Other Mental States)

• **On Heredity and Time**
—Heredity and the Environment
—The Past and the Present

• **On Layers of Mental States and Abnormality**
—Consciousness, Unconsciousness, and Preconsciousness
—Normality and Paranormality

• **On Organicity and Motivation**
—Mechanicity and Organicity
—Primary Motivations and Multiple Motivations

• **On Other (Mostly Epistemic) Considerations**
—Synthesis and Analysis
—Situation and the Subject
—Process and Outcome
—Reasoning and Other Modes of Thinking
—Meta-Conceptual Nominalism and Realism

Notes:: These examples are solely illustrative (not exhaustive), and some of the items can be reclassified somewhere else. Nor are they always mutually exclusive. Since they are generalities, exceptions are expected.
Sources: From *FPHC*. A re-construction, but with my own contribution, originally from G.Lindzey & C.Hall, *Introduction to Theories of Personality* (NY: John Wiley & Sons, 1985).

Table 4.8. The Theoretical Levels of Consciousness
(and Other Mental States)
(Part I)

• **At the Micro-Physical Theoretical Level**
   —Quantum-Mechanics
   —Electromagnetism

• **At the Chemical Theoretical Level**
   —Biochemistry

• **At the Biological Theoretical Level**
   —Evolutionary Biology
   —Neuroscience
   —Artificial Intelligence

• **At the Psychological Theoretical Level**
   —Psychodynamic Psychology
      • Psychoanalytical Psychology
      • Analytical Psychology
      • Socially Oriented Psychology
   —Experimental (Behavioral) Psychology
      • Operant Reinforcement Theory
      • Stimulus-Response Theory
      • Social Learning Theory
   —Cognitive (Gestalt) Psychology
      • Humanist Psychology
      • Existential Psychology
      • Field Theory
   —Psychometric Psychology
      • Idiographics
      • Constitutional Psychology
   —Social Psychology
      • Symbolic Interactive Theory
      • Social Exchange Theory

(continued on next page)

Table 4.8. The Theoretical Levels of Consciousness
(and Other Mental States)
(Part II)

• **At the Organizational Theoretical Level**
—Managerial-Bureaucratic Theory
—Oligarchic Theory
—Network Theory

• **At the Institutional Theoretical Level**
—Functionalist Theory
—Anomic Theory

• **At the Structural Theoretical Level**
—Conflict Theory
• Marxian Theory
• Critical Theory
• Weberian Theory
—Games Theory (in Formal Theory)
—Feminist Theory
• Feminist Concerns
• Feminist Hopes

• **At the Systemic Theoretical Level**
—Equilibrium Theory
—System Theory
—Chaos Theory

• **At the Cosmological Theoretical Level**
—Superluminal Model
—The Theory of Floating Consciousness

(continued on next page)

**Table 4.8. The Theoretical Levels of Consciousness
(and Other Mental States)
(Part III)**

- **At the Cultural Theoretical Level**
    —Substantive Theories
      - Structuralist Theory
      - Post-Structuralist Theory (in Postmodernism)
    —Meta-Theories
      - Epistemic Objectivism vs. Epistemic Historicism
      - Epistemic Subjectivism vs. Epistemic Non-Subjectivism
        –Phenomenology
        –Ethnomethodology
        –Hermeneutics
      - Epistemic Relativism vs. Epistemic Absolutism
      - Epistemic Reductionism vs. Epistemic Emergencism

- **At Other Levels**
    —Structuration Theory
    —Reflexive Socioanalysis

Notes: These examples are solely illustrative (not exhaustive), and some of the items can be reclassified somewhere else. Nor are they always mutually exclusive. Since they are generalities, exceptions are expected.
Source: From many different sources as indicated in *FPHC*

Table 4.9. The Theoretical Debate on Nature vs. Nurture
(Part I)

• **The Environmental Approach**

—*Thesis*: It focuses, relatively speaking, more on the environment (culture and society) in explaining the achievement gap among individuals and for that matter, countries or regions, when contrasted with the natural factors.

—*Discourse*: Examples include Jose Ortega y Gasset ("Man has no nature; what he has is history"), Ashley Montagu ("Man is man because he has no instincts, because everything he is and has become he has learned from his culture, from the man-made part of the environment, from other human beings"), Stephen Jay Gould ("[The] brain [is] capable of a full range of behaviors and predisposed to none"), and Jesse Jackson (who blames white racism for the failure of blacks to close the achievement gap between whites and blacks in America). The works on dependency theory in international political economy (with a Marxian influence) and on the Protestant work ethic (by Max Weber) also point to this environmental direction.

• **The Genetic Approach**

—*Thesis*: It focuses instead, relatively speaking again, on hereditory factors (e.g., genes and evolution) in explaining the achievement gap among individuals and for that matter, countries or regions, when contrasted with the envrionmental factors.

—*Discourse*: Examples are Hans Eysenck and William Sheldon (in constitutional psychology), Konrad Lorenz (in his work on innate aggressive human nature), Gary Marcus (on the complexities of human thought by a tiny number of genes) and Robert Plomin, together with Michael Owen and Peter McGuffin (on the genetic basis of complex human behaviors).

(continued on next page)

**Table 4.9. The Theoretical Debate on Nature vs. Nurture
(Part II)**

• **The Compromise Approach**
   —*Thesis*: It seeks the middle-of-the-road argument in regard to nature and nurture and regards all differences among individuals and groups as the result of the mixture of both nature and nurture, more or less equally.
   —*Discourse*: Examples include C. Murray and R. Herrnstein ("It seems highly likely to us that both genes and environment have something to do with this issue") and Dan Dennett ("Surely 'everyone knows' that the nature-nurture debate was resolved long ago, and neither side wins since everything-is-a-mixture-of-both-and-it's-all-very-complicated....")

• **The Transcendent Approach**
   —*Thesis*: It goes beyond both nature and nurture (without, however, committing the compromise fallacy) in showing their closely intertwined interactions in producing the behavioral differences as often seen in individual human endeavors on the micro scale, and for that matter, in country (or regional) endeavors on the macro one—in the context of my five theses, namely, (a) the compromise fallacy, (b) no oppression without self-oppression, (c) no success without failure, (d) the factor of randomness, and (e) the post-human vision, to be elaborated in Chapter Six.
   —*Discourse*: Peter Baofu proposed this approach on the basis of his "theory of contrastive advantages" (as an original theoretical contribution to the debate, which was first proposed and analyzed in *The Future of Capitalism and Democracy*). In the end, the human genes will not last, to be eventually superseded by post-human life forms, so the debate between genes and memes has obscured something profoundly important about the future that the world has never known. And the debate is also misleading and faulty in its dichotomy.

Source: From *BNN*. See the book for citations and details.

Table 4.10. Physical Challenges to Hyper-Spatial Consciousness

• **The Understanding of a Higher-Dimensional World of Space-Time**
—Ex: 4 for traditional aspects of space-time (e.g., length, width, breadth and time) plus 6 more new dimensions in theory of hyper-space, with profound implications for practical applications to new forms of consciousness.

• **The Mastering of Dark Matter and Dark Energy**
—Ex: "ordinary matter" (e.g., atoms, molecules) as a mere 4.4% of the universe, with 23% made of "cold dark matter" and the rest (about 73%) of mysterious "dark energy," with fundamental significance to questions about the limit of the speed of energy (or info), the availability of energy for use, and the nature of space-time, just to cite some examples.

• **The Exploration of Multiverses**
—Ex: theoretical speculation of other universes (e.g., "baby universes," "gateways" in black holes, "wave function of the universe," "many worlds," "brane worlds"), with potentially seminary discoveries of different physical laws in relation to matter-energy and space-time, and vital differences to the future of post-human conquest of other universes (for the emergence of new forms of consciousness).

Notes: These examples are solely illustrative (not exhaustive), and some of the items can be reclassified somewhere else. Nor are they always mutually exclusive. Since they are generalities, exceptions are expected. The point here is to give a rough picture of the evolution of consciousness to the hyper-spatial consciousness and others totally unknown to current earthlings. As a note of clarification, it makes no difference to my argument as to whether or not the hyper-spatial consciousness may emerge before, during, and after floating consciousness.
Source: From *Table 4.5* of *FPHC*

Table 4.11. The Theory of Floating Consciousness
(Part I)

• **At the Micro-Physical Level**
　—Ex: intelligent life without the human physical-chemical system

• **At the Chemical Level**
　—Ex: space radiation and toxins

• **At the Bio-Psychological Level**
　—Ex: exo-biological evolution in deep space
　—Ex: genetic engineering of new beings

• **At the Institutional Level**
　—Ex: post-capitalism
　—Ex: post-democracy

• **At the Organizational Level**
　—Ex: less legal-formalistic routines

• **At the Structural Level**
　—Ex: alien forms of violence

• **At the Cultural Level**
　—Ex: transcending freedom
　—Ex: transcending equality

(continued on next page)

Table 4.11. The Theory of Floating Consciousness
(Part II)

• **At the Cosmological Level**
 —Ex: parallel universes
 —Ex: pocket universes

• **At the Systemic Level**
 —Ex: space habitats (in zero-gravity)

Notes: Each example draws from the works of different scholars in the field. For instance, at the cosmological level, the idea of parallel universes is from the theoretical speculation in quantum cosmology by Stephen Hawking and others, while the one of pocket universes comes from the theoretical work of Allan Guth at MIT. And at the institutional level, I proposed post-capitalism and post-democracy in *FCD* (and later, from *BDPD* and *BCPC*). In addition, the examples are solely illustrative (not exhaustive), and some of the items can be reclassified somewhere else. Nor are they always mutually exclusive. Since they are generalities, exceptions are expected.

Sources: From *FPHC*—and, originally, from *FCD*

Table 4.12. The Theory of Post-Democracy I:
The Priority of Freedom over Equality
(Part I)

• **Differences**
　—*For the aggressive Lions (the strong Elitists)*
　　•Setting up　rank distinctions among unequals (e.g., between inferior humans and superior post-humans, or later among inferior post-humans and superior ones, relatively speaking)
　　•Yearning for being　not only distinguished from unequals, but also the first among equals (the best of the very best)
　　•Soul-searching for a　high　spiritual culture (not the trashy one for the masses). Mass culture is a dirty joke for them.
　—*For the manipulative Foxes (the weak Counter-Elitists)*
　　•Seeking a gentle hegemony by way of more communitarian concerns (for inferior humans and, later, inferior post-humans)
　　•Being more　sympathetic　to less　formal-legalistic institutions and values

• **Similarities**
　—*For both Lions and Foxes*
　　•Exploring different spheres of non-human consciousness in the cosmos (something vastly superior than the human one)
　　•Recognizing the democratic illusions (e.g., no freedom without unfreedom, no equality without inequality, or simply no justice without injustice, and vice versa)

(continued on next page)

Table 4.12. The Theory of Post-Democracy I:
The Priority of Freedom over Equality
(Part II)

Notes: The two callings and examples in each category are solely illustrative (not exhaustive), since there will be many different post-human value ideals in the distant future of post-human civilization. The comparison is also relative (not absolute) towards post-democracy, so this is not just a version of free-market democracy (nor Fascism/Nazism, as shown in the table later on democracy, non-democracy, and post-democracy). Nor are they mutually exclusive. As generalities, they allow exceptions. And the specific forms of post-human post-democratic ideals need to be further developed in future after-postmodern history, as they will be different from the ones we now know. The point here is to solely give an extremely rough picture of a small part of the world to come that we have never known.

Source: From Ch.10 of *FCD*. Refer to text for more info and references.

Table 4.13. The Theory of Post-Democracy II:
The Priority of Equality over Freedom

• **Hybrid Versions of**
—Ex: the Trans-Feminine Calling
—Ex: the Trans-Sinitic Calling
—Ex: the Trans-Islamic Calling
—Ex: the Trans-Outerspace Calling

• **Qualifications**
—These four versions of post-capitalist value ideals need not automatically be post-democratic, just as capitalism does not necessarily mean democracy. They are two different entities—though closely related.
—But up to a certain threshold of elevating equality at the farther expense of freedom, the democratic ideals will be overcome and cease to exist.
—The overcome will not be socialist or communist, but post-democratic with no freedom without unfreedom and no equality without inequality, subject to the constraints of existential dialectics.

Notes: The callings are solely illustrative (not exhaustive), since there will be many different post-human value ideals in the distant future of post-human lifeforms. The comparison is also relative (not absolute), nor are they mutually exclusive. As generalities, they allow exceptions. And the specific forms of post-human post-democratic ideals need to be further developed in future after-postmodern history, as they will be different from the ones we now know. The point here is to solely give an extremely rough picture of a small part of the world to come that we have never known.
Source: From Ch.10 of *FCD*. Refer to text for more info and references.

**Table 4.14. The Theory of Post-Democracy III:
The Transcendence of Freedom and Equality
(Part I)**

• **Transcending Freedom in Floating Existence**
  —*Freedom*: seeking an ultimate elimination of the body. Being without the body. The aim is to transcend freedom in the end into a metaphysical state (i.e., beyond the physique).
  —*Unfreedom*: yet facing difficult trade-offs. The sacrifice of bodily existence and its joyfulness. An eternal boredom in floating existence in dark deep space, though with alternative pleasures. There is no free lunch even in the state of transcending freedom.

• **Transcending Equality in the Rivalry of Cosmic Hegemony**
  —*Inequality*: competing to outlast other lifeforms in floating existence, or just marginalizing them for one's hegemonic expansiveness in the rest of the cosmos (and even beyond). Universalism is only for the mediocre.
  —*Equality*: accepting only those of one's rank as equal partners in the vast spacetime for cosmic supremacy. Even here, the aim is to transcend equality into a metaphysical state.

(continued on next page)

Table 4.14. The Theory of Post-Democracy III:
The Transcendence of Freedom and Equality
(Part II)

Notes: Do not confuse this transcendence of freedom and equality (as one version of post-democracy) with the naïve temptation to transcend the freedom/unfreedom and equality/inequality dialectics. Existential dialectics hold true for freedom and equality in all cultures and societies—past, present, or future (i.e., democracy, non-democracy, and post-democracy), regardless of whether freedom and equality are conventionally understood as "negative" or "positive."

Also, the two features and examples in each are solely illustrative (not exhaustive), since there will be many different post-human value ideals in the distant future of post-human lifeforms. The comparison is also relative (not absolute), nor are they mutually exclusive. As generalities, they allow exceptions. And the specific forms of post-human ideals even for these radically alien floating lifeforms (and others unknown to us) need to be further developed in future after-postmodern history, as they will likely be different from the ones herein illustrated. The point here is to solely give a very rough picture of a small part of the extremely alien world to come that we have never known.

Source: From Ch.10 of *FCD*. Refer to text for more info and references.

Table 4.15. Democracy, Non-Democracy, and Post-Democracy
(Part I)

• **Democracy**
  —*Theoretical Constructs*
  • The pursuit of freedom and equality (in various degrees), regardless of whether freedom and equality can be understood as "negative" or "positive"
    (1) more equality than freedom: The relative priority of the good over the right
    (2) more freedom than equality: The relative priority of the right over the good
  —*Types*
  • Only (1): Different versions of communitarian moral universalism
  • Only (2): Different versions of liberal moral universalism
  • (1) or (2): Different versions of anarchic (non-nation-state) moral universalism
  • (1) or (2): Different versions of postmodern moral localism

• **Non-Democracy**
  —*Theoretical Constructs*
  • The focus on (1') equality or (2') freedom, but not both, regardless of whether freedom and equality can be understood as "negative" or "positive"
  —*Types*
  • Only (1'): Different versions on the Far Left (e.g., Stalinism, Robespierrianism)
  • Only (2'): Different versions on the Far Right (e.g., Nazism, absolute monarchism)

(continued on next page)

Table 4.15. Democracy, Non-Democracy, and Post-Democracy
(Part II)

• **Post-Democracy**

—*Theoretical Constructs*

• The priority of (1'') equality over freedom, or (2'') freedom over equality, or (3'') the transcendence of freedom and equality, regardless of whether freedom and equality are "negative" or "positive." In degree, (1'') or (2'') is less than (1') or (2') but more than (1) or (2)—respectively.

• Like democracy and non-democracy, post-democracy is also subject to the freedom/unfreedom and equality/inequality dialectics (or existential dialectics in general). Unlike them, post-democracy acknowledges the constraints of existential dialectics and no longer value freedom and equality as sacred virtues. There is no utopia, in the end; even were there one, dystopia would exist within it.

—*Types*

• (1''): Different versions of trans-Sinitic value ideals

• (1''): Different versions of trans-feminine value ideals

• (1''): Different versions of trans-Islamic value ideals

• (1''): Different versions of trans-outerspace value ideals

• (2''): Different versions of post-human elitist value ideals

• (3''): Different versions of the value ideals of floating consciousness (etc.)

(continued on next page)

Table 4.15. Democracy, Non-Democracy, and Post-Democracy
(Part III)

Notes: The examples are solely illustrative (not exhaustive), nor are they mutually exclusive. As generalities, they allow exceptions. "Negative" freedom is freedom "from" (e.g., freedom from poverty), whereas "positive" freedom is freedom "to" (e.g., freedom to the state of enlightenment). "Negative" equality is "procedural" equality (e.g., equality of opportunity), while "positive" equality is "substantive" equality (e.g., equality of outcome). Existential dialectics impose constraints on freedom and equality in democracy, non-democracy, and post-democracy, regardless of whether freedom and equality can be understood as "negative" or "positive" in conventional discourse. Therefore, do not confuse the transcendence of freedom and equality in (3'') with the naïve temptation to transcend existential dialectics. There is no utopia, in the end; even should there be one, it would not exist without dystopia embedded within it.

Sources: A summary, based on my previous works, especially Ch.5 of *FHC*, Chs.5-10 of *FCD*, Chs.2-4 of *FPHC*, and Chs.1 & 7 of *BDPD*. The reader should consult the books for more analysis, as this is only a summary here.

Table 4.16. Multiple Causes of the Emergence of Post-Democracy
(Part I)

• **At the Micro-Physical Level**
—Ex: intelligent life without the human physical-chemical system
—Sources: Ch.7 of *FHC*; Chs.9-10 of *FCD*; Ch.1 of *FPHC*

• **At the Chemical Level**
—Ex: space radiation and toxins
—Sources: Ch.7 of *FHC*; Chs.9-10 of *FCD*

• **At the Bio-Psychological Level**
—Ex: exo-biological evolution in deep space
—Ex: genetic engineering of new beings
—Ex: limits of cognitive partiality
—Ex: illusions of emotional neutrality
—Ex: human biological inequality
—Sources: Ch.2 & Chs.9-10 of *FCD*; Ch.7 of *FHC*; Ch.4 of *BCPC*

• **At the Institutional Level**
—Ex: the flawed logic of equality
—Ex: the conflicting nature of governance
—Sources: Ch.5 of *FHC*; Chs.6 & 10 of *FCD*; Ch.3 of *FPHC*; Chs.2-5 of *BDPD*

• **At the Organizational Level**
—Ex: e-civic alienation
—Ex: the dark sides of formal-legalistic routines
—Sources: Ch.3 of *FHC*; Ch.7 of *FCD*; Ch.3 of *FPHC*

• **At the Structural Level**
—Ex: ever new forms of inequities, at home and abroad
—Ex: the emergence of China, women, and Islam as major actors
—Sources: Chs.5-6 of *FHC*; Chs.7, 9 & 10 of *FCD*; Chs.4-5 of *BDPD*

(continued on next page)

Table 4.16. Multiple Causes of the Emergence of Post-Democracy
(Part II)

• **At the Cultural Level**
  —Ex: freedom/unfreedom dialectics
  —Ex: equality/inequality dialectics
  —Ex: system fragmentation and integration
  —Sources: Ch.5 of *FHC*; Chs.3, 9 & 10 of *FCD*; Ch.4 of *FPHC*; Ch.1 of *BDPD*; Ch.4 of *BCPC*

• **At the Systemic Level**
  —Ex: space habitats (in zero-gravity) and colonization
  —Ex: ultra advanced future info systems
  —Ex: qualitative demography
  —Sources: Ch.7 of *FHC*; Chs.9 &10 of *FCD*

• **At the Cosmological Level**
  —Ex: the colonization of multiverses
  —Ex: the expansion of floating consciousness
  —Ex: the spread of hyper-spatial consciousness
  —Sources: Ch.7 of *FHC*; Chs.9 &10 of *FCD*; Ch.4 of *FPHC*

Notes: The examples in each category are solely illustrative (not exhaustive), and some of the items can be reclassified somewhere else. Nor are they always mutually exclusive. Since they are generalities, exceptions are expected.
Sources: From *FHC*, *FCD*, *FPHC*, *BCPC*, and *BDPD*. See also tables on my perspectives on civilizational holism.

Table 4.17. Some Clarifications
about Post-Capitalism and Post-Democracy
(Part I)

• The prefix "trans-" in the first category of post-capitalism (with its four versions) refers to something "going beyond" (not "uniting" or "combining"). Ex: *Sec.10.3.3* of *FCD*; *Sec.2.4* & *Sec.4.4* of *FPHC*; *Sec.7.2* of *BCPC*

• Such terms like "post-democracy," "post-capitalism," "post-human elitist," "trans-feminine calling," and the like as used in my works are more for our current intellectual convenience than to the liking of future humans and post-humans, who will surely invent more tasteful neologisms to call their own eras, entities, and everything else, for that matter. But the didactic point here is to use the terms to foretell what the future might be like, not that its eras and entities must be called so exactly and permanently.
Ex*:* *Sec.11.1* of *FCD*; *Sec.7.2* of *BCPC*

• The four versions in the first category of post-capitalist value ideals need not automatically be post-democratic, just as capitalism does not necessarily mean democracy. They are two different entities—though closely related. But up to a certain threshold of elevating equality at the farther expense of freedom, the democratic ideals will be overcome and cease to exist. The same is true for the post-human elitist calling in the second category of post-capitalism in relation to post-democracy, depending on the extent to which freedom is elevated at the expense of equality.
Ex: *Sec.10.4.3.3* of *FCD*; *Table 3.9* of *FPHC*; *Table 7.6* of *BDPD*

• The comparison in each of the three realms of existence in all forms of post-capitalism is not absolute, but relative. Examples include "communal" vs. "individualistic," and the like.
Ex: Notes in *Table 10.8, Table 10.9, Table 10.10, & Table 10.11* of *FCD*; Chs.2-4 of *FPHC*; *Sec.7.2* of *BCPC*

• The emergence of post-capitalism (and post-democracy, for that matter) has multiple causes (to not be reduced to one or only a few).
Ex: Ch.10 of *FCD*, Chs.2-4 of *FPHC*; *Sec.1.3* & *Sec.7.2* of *BCPC* (or *Table 1.8* & *Table 7.11*)

(continued on next page)

Table 4.17. Some Clarifications
about Post-Capitalism and Post-Democracy
(Part II)

• The specific forms of post-capitalism (and post-democracy, for that matter) need to be further developed in future after-postmodern history, as they will be different from the ones we now know. The point here is to solely give an extremely rough sketch of a world to come that we have never known.
Ex: *Sec.10.3.3 & Sec.10.4.3.3* of *FCD*; *Table 10.14 & Table 10.15* of *FCD*; *Sec.7.2* of *BCPC*

• All forms of post-capitalism are not part of a "teleological law," but of "historical trends" only. The same is also true for all forms of post-democracy.
Ex: *Sec.7.1* of *FHC*; *Sec.9.5.3.2 & Sec.10.3.4.2* of *FCD*; *Sec.7.2* of *BCPC*

• Post-capitalism is not better than capitalism in an "absolute" sense but only fits in better, on the basis of the historical contingency of culture, society, nature, and the mind in some future eras. The same is true for post-democracy in relation to democracy. The term "better" is historically relative.
Ex: *Sec.10.3.3* of *FCD*; *Sec.1.7* of *BDPD*; *Sec.1.5* of *BCPC*

• All forms of post-capitalism and post-democracy are subject to the constraints of existential dialectics. In the process, the dialectic direction is to go beyond the conventional "either-or" dichotomies (e.g., freedom vs. unfreedom, equality vs. inequality, freedom vs. equality, individuality vs. communality, spirituality vs. materiality, formal legalism vs. informal legalism, etc.). As is true in post-civilization, to go beyond the dichotomies is to acknowledge the co-existence of both in each dichotomy, although the degree of scaling one over the over varies from case to case (e.g., the theory of post-capitalism I, the theory of post-capitalism II, the theory of post-democracy I, the theory of post-democracy II, etc.)—but is not to be extreme in largely favoring one over the other, *on average* (all things considered). There is no utopia to be had in the end; even should there be one, dystopia would exist within it.
Ex: *Ch.5* of *FHC*; *Sec.10.4.4.2* of *FCD*; *Sec.1.5* of *BDPD*; *Sec.1.3* of *BCPC*; *BCIV*

(continued on next page)

Table 4.17. Some Clarifications
about Post-Capitalism and Post-Democracy
(Part III)

• All forms of post-capitalism, however different from each other though they are, share one common feature, in that they all inspire for a higher spiritual culture. The same is also true for post-democracy.
Ex: *Sec.10.3, Sec.10.4 & Sec.10.5 of FCD; Chs.2-4 of FPHC; Sec.7.2 of BCPC*

• All forms of post-capitalism try to avoid the excess in capitalist consumerism by favoring more basic than artificial needs in having, but the quality and quantity of these "basic" needs will be measured by future standards, not by our current ones. Standards are historically relative.
Ex: *Sec.10.3, Sec.10.4 & Sec.10.5 of FCD; Ch.2 of FPHC; Sec.7.2 of BCPC*

• All forms of post-capitalism make use of a different degree of political authority with advanced info systems in future history and strives for higher spiritual cultures (especially in the post-human age), while acknowledging the constraints of existential dialectics and no longer valuing free market (as in capitalism) and economic control (as in non-capitalism) as sacred virtues.
Ex: *Sec.10.3.4.2, Sec.10.3, Sec.10.4 & Sec.10.5 of FCD; Chs.2-4 of FPHC; Sec.1.5 of BDPD; Sec.7.2 of BCPC*

Notes:: The main points here are solely illustrative (not exhaustive) nor necessarily mutually exclusive, and the comparison is relative (not absolute). As generalities, they allow exceptions. The sections as cited are only illustrative (not exhaustive).
Sources: From *FHC, FCD, FPHC,* and *BDPD*

Table 4.18. The Theory of Post-Capitalism I.1:
By Group—
Ex: Spiritual/Communal in the Trans-Feminine Calling

• **More Communal Than Individual**
—*Sharing*: learning from others, as different ideas mutually enrich
—*Cooperative*: encouraging a sense of shared leadership and teamwork

• **More Informal-Legalistic Than Formal-Legalistic**
—*Specific*: listening more from the heart than from the head, to know a person as a concrete, not as an abstract, unit
—*Affective*: thinking and acting with others on a more affective tone. Business can mix with an emotional touch.
—*Ascriptive*: hiring (or firing) can be done on the basis of merit (or lack of it), but deep solidarity (sisterhood) is important too.
—*Particularistic*: making decisions on the basis of cost-benefit analysis, but a given group relationship is vital

• **More Spiritual Than Secular**
—*Long-Term Looking*: sharing for a long-term relationship (e.g., love, friendship), not just for a short-term gain
—*Loving/Caring*: showing compassion for the sufferings of others, without quickly blaming and pre-judging
—*Respectful*: showing acceptance about others' feelings (and thoughts)

Notes: The categories and examples are solely illustrative, since there can be different versions, and the comparison is relative (not absolute), nor are they mutually exclusive. As generalities, they allow exceptions. The specific forms of the trans-feminine version need to be further developed in future after-postmodern history, as they will be different from the ones we now know, since the prefix "trans-" here means going beyond or deconstructing the feminine values, while using them as the inspirational point at the beginning.
Source: From Ch.10 of *FCD*. Refer to text for more info and references.

Table 4.19. The Theory of Post-Capitalism I.2:
By Nation-State—
Ex: Spiritual/Communal in the Trans-Sinitic Calling

• **More Communal Than Individualistic**
  —*Centralized*: being more top-down in management
  —*Collective*: encouraging more group cooperation
  —*Social*: investing in trust and connection

• **More Informal-Legalistic Than Formal-Legalistic**
  —*Specific*: knowing more of those related or connected
  —*Affective*: behaving in a paternalistic, hierarchical way
  —*Ascriptive*: favoring family members and those related
  —*Particularistic*: building connection (guanxi) as imperative

• **More Spiritual Than Secular**
  —*Expansionist*: diffusing civilizational values (e.g., the superiority complex of civilizationalism)
  —*Holistic*: synthesizing things into a panoramic horizon
  —*Historical*: learning from the lessons of the ancient past
  —*Respectful*: deferential to elders and superiors

Notes: The categories and examples are solely illustrative, since there can be different versions, and the comparison is relative (not absolute), nor are they mutually exclusive. As generalities, they allow exceptions. The specific forms of the trans-Sinitic version need to be further developed in future after-postmodern history, as they will be different from the ones we now know, since the prefix "trans-" here means going beyond or deconstructing the Sinitic values, while using them as the inspirational point at the beginning.
Source: From Ch.10 of *FCD*. Refer to text for more info and references.

Table 4.20. The Theory of Post-Capitalism I.3:
By Region—
Ex: Spiritual/Communal in the Trans-Islamic Calling

• **More Communal Than Individualistic**
  —*Collective*: building the webs of relationships to bind individuals
  —*Sharing*: cultivating the established "wisdom" through common experience
  —*Cooperative*: stressing harmony, solidarity, and commonality

• **More Informal-Legalistic Than Formal-Legalistic**
  —*Specific*: making efforts to know well the participants (family and larger community) in matters of common concern
  —*Affective*: mixing work with language and ritual on explicit religious (Islamic) ideals, texts, stories, and examples
  —*Ascriptive*: privileging local history and custom on relationships among kinship groups
  —*Particularistic*: preferring an unbiased insider with ongoing connections to all parties

• **More Spiritual Than Secular**
  —*Historical*: learning from the lessons of the past as a source of stability and guidance
  —*Deferential*: showing respect for age, experience, status, and leadership in communal affairs
  —*Honorable*: emphasizing face, dignity, prestige, and fairness
  —*Compassionate*: giving mercy and charity ("Zahah") to others

Notes: The categories and examples are solely illustrative (not exhaustive), and the comparison is relative (not absolute), nor are they mutually exclusive. As generalities, they allow exceptions. The specific forms of the trans-Islamic version need to be further developed in future after-postmodern history, as they will be different from the ones we now know, since the prefix "trans-" here means going beyond or deconstructing the Islamic values, while using them as the inspirational point at the beginning.

Sources: From Ch.10 of *FCD*. Refer to text for more info and references, especially from the works by George Irani (2000) and C. Murphy (September 19, 2001).

Table 4.21. The Theory of Post-Capitalism I.4:
By Universe—
Ex: Spiritual/Communal in the Trans-Outerspace Calling

• **More Communal Than Individual**
  —*Cooperative*: requiring teamwork in small space habitats
  —*Sharing*: learning from, and enjoying being with, each other in a small group in outer space

• **More Informal-Legalistic Than Formal-Legalistic**
  —*Specific*: knowing more about each other to facilitate living and working together in space, both as fellow astronauts and space-mates
  —*Affective*: being friendly and social to each other as vital to working and living in small space quarters
  —*Ascriptive*: nurturing comaraderie among fellow astronauts as if they are family members over time
  —*Particularistic*: building work relationship with enduring memory in a space mission

• **More Spiritual Than Secular**
  —*Long-Term*: looking beyond selfish materialistic concerns in a precarious space environment with potential life or death
  —*Loving/Caring*: cultivating deep bondage for the success of a long term space mission
  —*Transcendent*: searching for life meaning in outer space

Notes: The calling and examples in each category are solely illustrative (not exhaustive), since there will be many different outer-space value ideals in the distant future of space colonization. The comparison is also relative (not absolute), nor are they mutually exclusive. As generalities, they allow exceptions. And the specific forms of trans-outer-space calling need to be further developed in future after-postmodern history, as they will be different from the ones we now know, since the prefix "trans-" here means going beyond or deconstructing the current outer-space values, while using them as the inspirational point at the beginning. The point here is to solely give an extremely rough picture of a small part of the world to come that we still do not know much about.

Source: From Ch.10 of *FCD*. Refer to text for more info and references.

Table 4.22. The Theory of Post-Capitalism II:
Spiritual/Individualistic in the Post-Human Elitist Calling
(Part I)

• **More Individualistic Than Communal**
 —Setting up rank distinctions among unequals (e.g., between inferior humans and superior post-humans, or later among inferior post-humans and superior ones, relatively speaking)
 —Yearning for being not only distinguished from unequals, but also the first among equals (the best of the very best)
 —Recognizing the constraints of equality/inequality dialectics (or existential dialectics in general)

• **More Spiritual Than Secular**
 —Soul-searching for a high spiritual culture (not the trashy one for the masses). Mass culture is a dirty joke for them.
 —Exploring different spheres of non-human consciousness in the cosmos (something vastly superior than the human one)
 —Recognizing the constraints of freedom/unfreedom dialectics (or existential dialectics in general)

• **Qualifications**
 —Although post-human elitist post-democracy is comparable to post-human elitist post-capitalism in some respects, the former does not necessarily imply the latter (post-human elitist post-capitalism), just as democracy does not have to entail capitalism. They are two different (though related) entities.
 —But up to a certain threshold of incorporating government intervention with advanced info systems in future civilizations for higher spiritual concerns at the expense of the free market and materialist pursuit, the capitalist ideal will be overcome.
 —The overcome will not be Fascist or feudalistic, but post-capitalist, subject to the constraints of existential dialectics.

(continued on next page)

Table 4.22. The Theory of Post-Capitalism II:
Spiritual/Individualistic in the Post-Human Elitist Calling
(Part II)

Notes: The calling and examples in each category are solely illustrative (not exhaustive). The comparison is also relative (not absolute), nor are they mutually exclusive. As generalities, they allow exceptions. And the specific forms of post-human elitist post-capitalism need to be further developed in future after-postmodern history, as they will be different from the ones we now know, while using them as the inspirational point at the beginning. The point here is to solely give an extremely rough picture of a small part of the world to come that we still do not know much about.

Sources: From Ch.10 of *FCD* (and also *FPHC*, *BDPD*, and *BCPC*). Refer to the text for more info and references.

Table 4.23. Capitalism, Non-Capitalism, and Post-Capitalism (Part I)

• **Capitalism**
—*Theoretical Constructs*
  •Allocation of scarce resources among alternative wants largely by free market for competition (whose characteristics in its ideal form include, for instance, no barrier to entry or exit, homogeneity, perfect information, a large number of buyers/sellers, and perfect factor mobility)
  •More formal-legalistic than informal-legalistic, more individualistic than communal, and more material (secular) than spiritual
  •Either (1) minimal government or (2) relatively active government
—*Types*
  •Only (1): Different versions of market capitalism (e.g., the U.S.)
  •Only (2): Different versions of welfare capitalism (e.g., Sweden)

• **Non-Capitalism**
—*Theoretical Constructs*
  •Allocation of scarce resources among alternative wants mainly by political authority for policies (which can be regulative, redistributive, symbolic, and participatory)
  •More informal-legalistic than formal-legalistic
  •Either (1') more individualistic (for the elites), often (though not always) for material (secular) concerns, or (2') more communal (for the masses), often (though not always) for spiritual concerns
—*Types*
  •Only (1'): Different versions on the Right (e.g., Fascist corporate-state economy for the glory of the new Rome, medieval lord-vassal-serf economy for the power of the feudalistic order)
  •Only (2'): Different versions on the Left (e.g., Soviet command economy for the creation of the New Socialist Man)

(continued on next page)

Table 4.23. Capitalism, Non-Capitalism, and Post-Capitalism (Part II)

• **Post-Capitalism**

—*Theoretical Constructs*

• Allocation of scarce resources among alternative wants largely by political authority with advanced info systems in future civilizations, subject to existential dialectics. In degree of allocating by authority, post-capitalism is more than capitalism but less than non-capitalism.

• More spiritual than secular (material)

• Either (1'') more individualistic or (2'') more communal

• Like capitalism and non-capitalism, post-capitalism is also subject to the freedom/unfreedom and equality/inequality dialectics (or existential dialectics in general). There is no utopia, in the end; even were there one, dystopia would exist within it.

• Unlike capitalism and non-capitalism, post-capitalism makes use of a different degree of political authority with advanced info systems in future civilizations and strives for higher-spiritual cultures (especially in the post-human age), while acknowledging the constraints of existential dialectics and no longer valuing free market (as in capitalism) and economic control (as in non-capitalism) as sacred virtues.

—*Types*

• Only (1''): Different versions of post-human elitist value ideals

• Only (2''): Different versions of trans-Sinitic value ideals

• Only (2''): Different versions of trans-feminine value ideals

• Only (2''): Different versions of trans-Islamic value ideals

• Only (2''): Different versions of trans-outerspace value ideals

(continued on next page)

Table 4.23. Capitalism, Non-Capitalism, and Post-Capitalism
(Part III)

Notes: The calling and examples in each category are solely illustrative (not exhaustive). The comparison is also relative (not absolute), nor are they mutually exclusive. As generalities, they allow exceptions. And the specific forms of each calling need to be further developed in future after-postmodern history, as they will be different from the ones we now know, while using them as the inspirational point at the beginning. The point here is to solely give an extremely rough picture of a small part of the world to come that we still do not know much about.

Source: From Ch.10 of *FCD*. Refer to the text for more info and references.

**Table 4.24. Multiple Causes of the Emergence of Post-Capitalism
(Part I)**

• **At the Micro-Physical Level**
—Ex: intelligent life without the human physical-chemical system
—Ex: mastering of quantum mechanics, electromagnetism, and other fields
for the understanding of a broad range of anomalous experiences and the
application for artificial intelligence for spiritual quest
—Sources: Ch.7 of *FHC*; Chs.9-10 of *FCD*; Ch.1 of *FPHC*

• **At the Chemical Level**
—Ex: space radiation and toxins
—Sources: Ch.7 of *FHC*; Chs.9-10 of *FCD*

• **At the Bio-Psychological Level**
—Ex: exo-biological evolution in deep space
—Ex: genetic engineering of new beings
—Ex: limits of human cognition
—Sources: Ch.2 & Chs.9-10 of *FCD*; Ch.7 of *FHC*

• **At the Institutional Level**
—Ex: the flawed logic of the free market
—Ex: the need of a post-autistic economics
—Sources: Ch.10 of *FCD*

• **At the Organizational Level**
—Ex: the dark sides of formal-legalistic routines
—Sources: Ch.3 of *FHC*; Ch.7 of *FCD*; Ch.3 of *FPHC*

• **At the Structural Level**
—Ex: ever new forms of inequities, at home and abroad
—Ex: the emergence of China, women, and Islam as major actors
—Sources: Chs.5-6 of *FHC*; Chs.7, 9 & 10 of *FCD*; Chs.4-5 of *BDPD*

(continued on next page)

Table 4.24. Multiple Causes of the Emergence of Post-Capitalism
(Part II)

• **At the Cultural Level**
  —Ex: freedom/unfreedom dialectics
  —Ex: equality/inequality dialectics
  —Sources: Ch.5 of *FHC*; Chs.3 & 10 of *FCD*; Ch.4 of *FPHC*; Ch.1 of *BDPD*

• **At the Systemic Level**
  —Ex: space habitats (in zero-gravity) and colonization
  —Ex: ultra advanced future info systems
  —Ex: qualitative demography
  —Sources: Ch.7 of *FHC*; Chs. 9 & 10 of *FCD*

• **At the Cosmological Level**
  —Ex: multiverses
  —Sources: Ch.7 of *FHC*; Chs. 9 & 10 of *FCD*; Ch.4 of *FPHC*

Notes: The examples in each category are solely illustrative (not exhaustive), and some of the items can be reclassified somewhere else. Nor are they always mutually exclusive. Since they are generalities, exceptions are expected.
Sources: From *FHC, FCD, FPHC, BCPC*, and *BDPD*. See also tables on my perspective on civilizational holism.

Table 4.25. The Theoretical Debate on Civilization

- **The Progressive Theory of Civilization**
  —*Thesis*: The "civilizing" process is "good," as opposed to the "barbarizing" process as something "bad," relatively speaking.
  —*Discourse*: Especially, though not exclusively, in the Enlightenment era and a bit before. Example: Thomas Hobbes—in that the tribes in primitive societies were "savages."

- **The Romantic Theory of Barbarity**
  —*Thesis*: The "civilizing" process is "bad," as opposed to the "barbarizing" process as something "good," relatively speaking.
  —*Discourse*: Especially, though not exclusively, in the Counter-Enlightenment circle. Example: Jean-Jacques Rousseau—in that civilization "corrupts" men, and the "savages" are in fact "noble."

- **The Moderate Theory of Civilization**
  —*Thesis*: The "civilizing" process is "good," but there is a price to pay, especially in systematic (compulsive) self-control.
  —*Discourse*: Especially, though not exclusively, in some late modern and postmodern circles. Example: Norbert Elias—in that social manners become more refined in the civilizing process, but self-control also becomes more systematic.

- **The Theory of Post-Civilization**
  —*Thesis*: The civilizing process is as evil and good as barbarity, and each cannot exist without the other, to be eventually superseded by post-civilization unto the post-human age.
  —*Discourse*: Proposed by Peter Baofu. See the rest of *BCIV* for more analysis.

Source: From *BCIV* on the theoretical debate

Table 4.26. No Freedom Without Unfreedom in the Civilizing Processes
(Part I)

- **The Rationalizing Process (at the Level of Culture)**
  —if freer from the dominance of unreason (as in barbarism) in the civilizing process, then less free from the rationalizing process (be it in the form of the principle of either transcendence or immanence)
  —if freer from the principle of immanence in the rationalizing process, then less free from the inclination to commit terror in the name of reason and the relative underdevelopment of non-reason (e.g., in relation to yoga and meditation)
  —if freer from the principle of transcendence in the rationalizing process, then less free from the relative underdevelopment of reason (e.g., in relation to systematic methodology) and the occurrence of oppression in the name of non-reason

- **The Pacifying Process (at the Level of Society)**
  —if freer from the dominance of pillage (as in savagery) in the civilizing process, then less free from the pacifying process (be it in the form of external control or self-control)
  —if freer from self-control in the pacifying process, then less free from the temptation of expansionist oppression and rebellious mindset in external control
  —if freer from external control in the pacifying process, then less free from the gruesome psychological self-torture and conformism in self-control

(continued on next page)

Table 4.26. No Freedom Without Unfreedom in the Civilizing Processes (Part II)

• **The Stewardizing Process (at the Level of Nature)**
—if freer from the dominance of nature (as in the state of nature) in the civilizing process, then less free from the stewardizing process (be it in the form of the stewardship of creation or the covenant with nature)
—if freer from the stewardship of creation in the stewardizing process, then less free from material underdevelopment, relatively speaking, and spiritual exclusion in the covenant with nature
—if freer from the covenant with nature in the stewardizing process, then less free from ecological degradation and spiritual disconnection from nature in the stewardship of creation

• **The Subliming Process (at the Level of the Mind)**
—if freer from the dominance of spontaneity (as in the wild state of the mind) in the civilizing process, then less free from the subliming process, be it in the form of (cyclical-centric) self-refinement or (linear-centric) self-discipline
—if freer from (cyclical-centric) self-refinement in the subliming process, then less free from the (linear-centric) self-regimen (as a form of neurosis)
—if freer from (linear-centric) self-discipline in the subliming process, then less free from the (cyclical-centric) self-torture (equally as a form of neurosis)

Notes: The examples in each category are solely illustrative (not exhaustive), and the comparison is relative (not absolute), nor are they necessarily mutually exclusive. And some can be easily re-classified elsewhere. As generalities, they allow exceptions.
Sources: From *BCIV*. See also *FHC, FCD, FPHC, BDPD, BCPC, ALD*, and other books of mine.

Table 4.27. No Equality Without Inequality in the Civilizing Processes (Part I)

• **The Rationalizing Process (at the Level of Culture)**
 —if more equal for the role of rationalization in the rationalizing process (of civilizational making), then less equal for that of mythicization (as in barbarism)
 —if more equal for the principle of transcendence in (linear-centric) rationalizing process, then less equal for the principle of immanence
 —if more equal for the principle of immanence in (cyclical-centric) rationalizing process, then less equal for the principle of transcendence

• **The Pacifying Process (at the Level of Society)**
 —if more equal for pacification in civilizational making, then less equal for the institution of pillaging and others (as in savagery)
 —if more equal for external control, relatively speaking, in pacifying process, then less equal for self-control
 —if more equal for self-control, relatively speaking, in pacifying process, then less equal for external-control

• **The Stewardizing Process (at the Level of Nature)**
 —if more equal for stewardship in the stewardizing process (of civilizational making), then less equal for reverent (submissive) existence (as in barbarism)
 —if more equal for the stewardship of creation in (linear- centric) stewardizing process, then less equal for the (cyclical-centric) covenant with nature for harmonious co-existence
 —if more equal for the (cyclical-centric) covenant with nature in the stewardizing process, then less equal for the (linear-centric) stewardship of nature for domination

(continued on next page)

Table 4.27. No Equality Without Inequality in the Civilizing Processes (Part II)

• **The Subliming Process (at the Level of the Mind)**
  —if more equal for the role of reason in the subliming process, then less equal for that of unreason (as in the natural state of wildness)
  —if more equal for the primacy of reason in (linear-centric) subliming process, then less equal for other faculties (e.g., intuition, existential feelings, and analogous thinking) in cyclical-centric one
  —if more equal for the exercise of other faculties (e.g., intuition, existential feelings, and analogous thinking) in cyclical-centric subliming process, then less equal for the role of reason in linear-centric counterpart

Notes: The examples in each category are solely illustrative (not exhaustive), and the comparison is relative (not absolute), nor are they mutually exclusive. And some can be easily reclassified else-where. As generalities, they allow exceptions.
Sources: From *BCIV*. See also *FHC*, *FCD*, *FPHC*, *BDPD*, *BCPC*, *ALD*, and other books of mine.

Table 4.28. Five Theses on Post-Civilization

• Post-civilization no longer treats civilization as good and barbarity as evil (relatively speaking), nor does it nostalgically regard barbarity as good and civilization as evil (relatively speaking again). Civilization is as evil and good as barbarity.

• Post-civilization also no longer accepts the dichotomy between civilization and barbarity. Civilization cannot exist without barbarity. It is no longer necessary to preserve civilization, any more than it is imperative to destroy barbarity. To go beyond civilization and barbarity is to acknowledge the co-existence of both, although the degree of scaling one over the over varies from case to case—but is not to be extreme in largely favoring one over the other, *on average* (subject to the constraints of existential dialectics).

• Post-civilization is thus subject to the constraints of existential dialectics. There is no freedom without unfreedom, and no equality without inequality, for instance. There will be no utopia; even should there be one, there would be dystopia embedded within it.

• Post-civilization will eventually replace civilization (as a form of life settlement), to be dominated by post-capitalist and post-democratic lifeforms here on earth and in deep space (besides other alien lifeforms that we have never known), unto the post-human age in multiverses. Those few post-humans who keep civilization will live in a "post-human civilization," while the rest (the majority), who choose post-civilization, will evolve towards the state of "post-human post-civilization." One therefore should not confuse "post-human civilization" with "post-human post-civilization," as the two are not the same.

• Post-civilization will confront psychosis as a primary problem in the culture of virtuality unto the post-human age, just as civilization has neurosis as a primary one of its own (although both neurosis and psychosis are major problems in both).

Notes: The comparison in each category is relative (not absolute), nor are they necessarily mutually exclusive. And some can be easily re-classified elsewhere. As generalities, they allow exceptions.
Sources: From *BCIV*. See also *FHC, FCD, FPHC, BDPD, BCPC, ALD*, and other books of mine.

Table 4.29. Barbarity, Civilization, and Post-Civilization

• **The Rationalizing Process (at the Level of Culture)**
—*Barbarity*
  • More mythicizing than rationalizing, relatively speaking
—*Civilization*
  • More rationalizing than mythicizing, relatively speaking
—*Post-Civilization*
  • Beyond the dichotomy, subject to existential dialectics

• **The Pacifying Process (at the Level of Society)**
—*Barbarity*
  • More pillaging than pacifying, relatively speaking
—*Civilization*
  • More pacifying than pillaging, relatively speaking
—*Post-Civilization*
  • Beyond the dichotomy, subject to existential dialectics

• **The Stewardizing Process (at the Level of Nature)**
—*Barbarity*
  • More revering than stewardizing, relatively speaking
—*Civilization*
  • More stewardizing than revering, relatively speaking
—*Post-Civilization*
  • Beyond the dichotomy, subject to existential dialectics

• **The Subliming Process (at the Level of the Mind)**
—*Barbarity*
  • More impulsing than subliming, relatively speaking
—*Civilization*
  • More subliming than impulsing, relatively speaking
—*Post-Civilization*
  • Beyond the dichotomy, subject to existential dialectics

Notes: The comparison in each category is relative (not absolute), nor are they necessarily mutually exclusive. And some can be easily re-classified elsewhere. As generalities, they allow exceptions.
Sources: From *BCIV*. See also *FHC, FCD, FPHC, BDPD, BCPC, ALD*, and other books of mine.

Table 4.30. Types of Super Civilization in the Cosmos
(Part I)

• **Type I**

—a civilization which gains control of and uses the total energy output "falling on its planet from its sun for interstellar communication" (or, in general, space colonization). For N. Kardashev, who proposed the first three types, human civilization is currently Type Zero (Type O), which is below even Type I, since its present energy consumption for all purposes, let alone for interstellar communication, is still 10,000 times less.

• **Type II**

—a civilization which gains control of and uses directly the total energy output of its sun for interstellar communication (or, in general, space colonization).

• **Type III**

—a civilization which gains control of and uses the total energy output of its galaxy for interstellar communication (or, in general, space colonization).

• **Type IV**

—a civilization which gains control of and uses the total energy output of its cluster of galaxies for interstellar communication (or, in general, space colonization).

• **Type V**

—a civilization which gains control of and uses the total energy output of its supercluster of galaxies for interstellar communica-tion (or, in general, space colonization).

(continued on next page)

Table 4.30. Types of Super Civilization in the Cosmos
(Part II)

• **Type...n**
  —So continues the series in what I call the cyclical progression of hegemony in the cosmos and beyond.

Notes: The Russian astrophysicist Nikolai Kardashev proposed the first three types of super civilization in terms of total energy out-put for interstellar communication. (CSM 1979) I extend his argument further to propose Type IV, Type V, Type VI, and Type...n, in the context of my claim about the cyclical progression of he-gemony in the cosmos and beyond.
Sources: From *Table 9.4* of *FCD*. See *FHC, FCD, FPHC*, for more info—and of course other books of mine.

**Table 4.31. The Civilizational Project
from Pre-Modernity to After-Postmodernity
(Part I)**

	Pre-Modern	*Modern*	*Postmodern*	*After-Postmodern*
Main narratives	•Sacralness •Courtliness •Vitalism •Animism	•Freedom •Equality •Fraternity	•Multiplicity •Hybridization	•Naked contingency •Cyclical progression of hegemony
Main institutions	•Monarchy •Aristocracy •Feudalism •Holy order •Primitivism	•Capitalism •Liberalism •Socialism •Nazism •Fascism	•Capitalism •Liberalism •Postmodern politics of difference	•Post-Capitalism •Post-Democracy •Others
Main technological and economic revolutions	•Agricultural	•Service •Industrial	•Informational	•Biological •Material •Energy •Space •Others

(continued on next page)

**Table 4.31. The Civilizational Project
from Pre-Modernity to After-Postmodernity
(Part II)**

	Pre-Modern	*Modern*	*Postmodern*	*After-Postmodern*
Main agents	•Males •Upper strata •Mini-states	•Males •Upper strata •Whites •Empires	•Males •Upper strata •Whites •Others •Supra-states •IO's	•Post-humans •Humans •Others
Main impacts	•Local	•Inter-national	•Global	•Outer-space •Multiverse
Main outcomes	•Towards moderntiy •Rise of linear- & cyclical-centric civiliza-tions	•Towards post-modernity •Dominance of linear-centric civilization	•Towards after-post-moderntiy •Linear-centric civiliza-tion in crisis	•Towards human (& maybe post-human) extinction •Rise of post-civiliza-tion, especially in post-human forms of space-time

Notes: The examples in each category are solely illustrative (not exhaustive) nor necessarily mutually exclusive, and the comparison is relative (not absolute). As generalities, they allow exceptions.

Sources: From *Table 10.16* of *FCD*—and also from *BCIV* on post-civilization (and *FPHST*)

Table 4.32. Civilizational Holism
(Part I)

• **At the Micro-Physical Theoretical Level**
  —Ex: Mastering of quantum mechanics, electromagnetism, and other fields for the understanding of a broad range of anomalous experiences and theapplication for artificial intelligence (*Sec.1.4.1* of *FPHC*)

• **At the Chemical Theoretical Level**
  —Ex: Unprecedented expansion of (and violence to) the mind through ever new forms of drugs (and virtual technologies, for that matter) (Ch.9 of *FCD*)

• **At the Biological Theoretical Level**
  —Ex: Humans are not biologically equal, on the basis of race, gender, ethnicity, age, and whatnot. (*Sec.2.6* & Ch.10 of *FCD*; *BNN*) And post-humans will experience the same fate, in an even more amazing way.

• **At the Psychological Theoretical Level**
  —Ex: Human cognitive impartiality and emotional neutrality are quite limited. (*Secs.2.4-2.5* of *FCD*)
  —Ex: Rise of Floating Consciousness (Ch.10 of *FCD*; Chs.1 & 4 of *FPHC*)

• **At the Organizational Theoretical Level**
  —Ex: Administrative colonization of deep space, with less legal-formalism in some corners. (Chs.9-10 of *FCD*)

• **At the Institutional Theoretical Level**
  —Ex: Both capitalism and democracy will not last, to be superseded by different versions of post-capitalism and post-democracy in after-postmodernity. (Ch.10 of *FCD*)

• **At the Structural Theoretical Level**
  —Ex: Social stratification reappears in ever new forms, also with new causes and new players in the cyclical progression of hegemony. (Chs.8-10 of *FCD*)
  —Ex: The world of hyper-empires, and the union of the unions (*BWT*)

(continued on next page)

Table 4.32. Civilizational Holism
(Part II)

• **At the Systemic Theoretical Level**
  —Ex: Outerspace expansion: local → regional → global → solar → galactic → clustery → multiversal (Ch.9 of *FCD*)
  —Ex: Demographic transition: human extinction, and the rise of post-humans (e.g., cyborgs, thinking machines, thinking robots, genetically altered superior beings, floating consciousness, hyper-spatial consciousness) (Ch.4 of *FPHC*; Ch.10 of *FCD*; & Ch.7 of *FHC*)
  —Ex: New technological forces in material sciences, electronic and communication sciences, energy sciences, biosciences, manufacturing and engineering sciences, and space sciences (Ch.10 of *FCD* & Ch.7 of *FHC*)
  —Ex: Systematic dominance towards nature for space colonization (Chs.9-10 of *FCD*; Chs.2 & 7 of *FHC*)

• **At the Cultural Theoretical Level**
  —Ex: The post-human transcendence of freedom and equality (Ch.10 of *FCD*)
  —Ex: Methodological   Holism (Ch.1 of *FCD*; Ch.1 of *FPHC*; *Sec.2.1* & *Sec.2.5* of *BCPC*)
  —Ex: The Evolution from Barbarity to Post-Civilization (*BCIV*)

• **At the Cosmological Theoretical Level**
  —Ex: Mastering of dark matter and dark energy, and the exploration of multiverses (Ch.4 of *FPHC*; Ch.10 of *FCD*; & Ch.7 of *FHC*)
  —Ex: Alternation of space-time (*FPHST*)
  —Ex: The emergence of hyper-spatial consciousness (*FPHC*)

• **At Other Levels**
  —Ex: Historical: pre-modernity → modernity → postmodernity → after-postmodernity (human distinction, and the rise of post-humans, including floating consciousness) (Ch.7 of *FHC* & Ch.10 of *FCD*)

Notes: These examples are solely illustrative (not exhaustive), and some of the items can be reclassified somewhere else. Nor are they always mutually exclusive. Since they are generalities, exceptions are expected. And the comparison is relative, not absolute.
Sources: From *Table 5.1* of *FPHC*—with details from *FHC*, *FCD*, and the rest

Table 4.33. Theories on Civilizational Holism
(Part I)

I. Theories in Relation to Nature
—At the Macro-Physical (Cosmological) Theoretical Level
- 25. Theory of Hyper-Spatial Consciousness (Peter Baofu)
  (Ch.4 of *FPHC*)
- (• 23). Perspectival Theory of Space-Time (Peter Baofu)
  (*FPHST*)
- (• 22). Dialectic Theory of Complexity (Peter Baofu)
  (*FC*)
- (• 20). Theory of Floating Consciousness (Peter Baofu)
  (Ch.10 of *FCD*; Chs.1 & 4 of *FPHC*)
- 24. Theory of the Geopower of Nature (Peter Baofu)
  (Ch.4 of *ALD*)

—At the Micro-Physical Theoretical Level
- 23. Perspectival Theory of Space-Time (Peter Baofu)
  (*FPHST*)
- 22. Dialectic Theory of Complexity (Peter Baofu)
  (*FC*)

II. Theories in Relation to the Mind
—At the Biological Theoretical Level
- 21. Theory of Contrastive Advantages (Peter Baofu)
  (*Sec.2.6* & Ch.10 of *FCD; BNN*)

—At the Psychological Theoretical Level
- 20. Theory of Floating Consciousness (Peter Baofu)
  (Ch.10 of *FCD*; Chs.1 & 4 of *FPHC*)
- 19. Theory of Cognitive Partiality (Peter Baofu)
  (*Sec.2.4* of *FCD*; *Sec.4.5.1.1* of *BCPC*)
- 18. Theory of Emotional Non-Neutrality (Peter Baofu)
  (*Sec.2.5* of *FCD*; *Sec.4.5.2* of of *BCPC*)
- 17. Theory of Behavioral Alteration (Peter Baofu)
  (*Sec.4.5.3* of *BCPC*)

(continued on next page)

Table 4.33. Theories on Civilizational Holism
(Part II)

III. Theories in Relation to Society
—At the Organizational Theoretical Level
- 16. Theory of E-Civic Alienation (Peter Baofu)
  (Ch.7 of *FCD*)
- 15. Combinational Theory of Organizational Behavior (Peter Baofu)
  (Ch.6 of *ALD*)

—At the Institutional Theoretical Level
- 14. Theory of Post-Capitalism (Peter Baofu)
  (Ch.10 of *FCD*; Chs.2 & 4 of *FPHC*; *BCPC*)
- 13. Theory of Post-Democracy (Peter Baofu)
  (Ch.10 of *FCD*; Chs.3 & 4 of *FPHC*; *BDPD*)
- 12. Dynamic Theory of Comparative Political Systems (Peter Baofu)
  (*ALD*)

—At the Structural Theoretical Level
- 11. Theory of the Cyclical Progression of Hegemony (Peter Baofu)
  (Chs.9-10 of *FCD*; Chs.1, 3 & 4 of *FPHC*; *BDPD*)
- 10. Theory of the Cyclical Progression of Empire-Building
  (Peter Baofu)
  (*BWT*)

—At the Systemic Theoretical Level
- 9. Theory of Post-Humanity (Peter Baofu)
  (Ch.7 of *FHC*; Chs.3, & 10 of *FCD*; Chs.1, 3 & 4 of *FPHC*; and
  other books of mine)
- 8. Theory of the Cyclical Progression of System Integration
  and Fragmentation (Peter Baofu)
  (Chs.9-10 of *FCD*)
- 7. Synthetic Theory of Information Architecture (Peter Baofu)
  (*FIA*)

(continued on next page)

Table 4.33. Theories on Civilizational Holism
(Part III)

IV. Theories in Relation to Culture
 —At the Cultural Theoretical Level
 • 6. Theory of Post-Civilization (Peter Baofu)
   (*BCIV*)
 • 5. Theory of the Trinity of Modernity to Its After-Postmodern Counterpart (Peter Baofu)
   (*FHC*; Ch.10 of *FCD*)
 • 4. Transformative Theory of Aesthetic Experience (Peter Baofu)
   (*FAE*)

V. Theories in Relation to the Rest
 —At Other Levels (Historical)
 • 3. Theory of the Evolution from Pre-Modernity to After-Postmodernity (Peter Baofu)
   (*FHC*; Ch.9-10 of *FCD*; *FPHC*)

VI. Meta-Theories (in Relation to Theories)
 —At the Methodological Meta-Theoretical Level
 • 2. Theory of Existential Dialectics (Peter Baofu)
   (*FHC*; *FCD*; *FPHC*; *BDPD*; *FC*; *FAE*; *ALD; FIA*)
 —At the Ontological Meta-Theoretical Level
 • 1. Theory of Methodological Holism (Peter Baofu)
   (Ch.1 of *FCD*; Ch.1 of *FPHC*; *Sec.2.1* & *Sec.2.5* of *BCPC*; *FC*)

Notes: All these theories are my constructions, as some of the main contributions of my grant project on civilization and its future. These examples are solely illustrative (not exhaustive), and some of the items can be reclassified somewhere else. Nor are they always mutually exclusive. Since they are generalities, exceptions are expected.
Sources: From *FHC, FCD, FPHC, BDPD, BCPC, BCIV, FPHST, BNN, BWT, FC, FAE, ALD*, and *FIA*

BIBLIOGRAPHY

Argyris, C. & D. Schon. 1978. *Organizational Learning: A Theory of Action Perspective.* Reading MA: Addison-Wesley.

Atkatz, D. & H. Pagels. 1982. "Origin of the Universe as a Quantum Tunneling Event." *Phys. Rev.*, D25: 2065-2072.

_____.1981. *The Creation.* Oxford: W. H. Freeman.

Bailey, Mark. 2002. "Education and Values: Interface on the Internet: Reconceptualizing Teaching and Learning in a Technocracy." *Berglund Center for Internet Studies.* Forest Grove, Oregon: Pacific University. <http://education.ed.pacificu.edu/ aacu/workshop/reconcept2B.html>.

Baofu, Peter. 2007. *The Rise of Authoritarian Liberal Democracy: A Preface to a New Theory of Comparative Political Systems.* Cambridge, England: Cambridge Scholars Publishing.

_____.2007a. *The Future of Aesthetic Experience: Conceiving a Better Way to Beauty, Ugliness, and the Rest.* Cambridge, England: Cambridge Scholars Publishing.

_____.2007b. *The Future of Complexity: Conceiving a Better Way to Understand Order and Chaos.* London, United Kingdom: World Scientific Publishing Co.

_____.2007c. *Beyond the World of Titans, and the Remaking of World Order: A Preface to a New Logic of Empire-Building.* Cambridge, England: Cambridge Scholars Publishing.

_____.2006. *Beyond Nature and Nurture: Conceiving a Better Way to Understand Genes and Memes.* Cambridge, England: Cambridge Scholars Publishing.

_____.2006a. *The Future of Post-Human Space-Time: Conceiving a Better Way to Understand Space and Time.* New York: Peter Lang Publishing, Inc.

_____.2006b. *Beyond Civilization to Post-Civilization: Conceiving a Better Model of Life Settlement to Supersede Civilization.* New York: Peter Lang Publishing, Inc.

_____.2005. *Beyond Capitalism to Post-Capitalism: Conceiving a Better Model of Wealth Acquisition to Supersede Capitalism.* New York: The Edwin Mellen Press.

_____.2004. *The Future of Post-Human Consciousness.* New York: The Edwin Mellen Press.

_____.2004a. *Beyond Democracy to Post-Democracy: Conceiving a Better Model of Governance to Supersede Democracy* (2 volumes). New York: The Edwin Mellen Press.

_____.2002. *The Future of Capitalism and Democracy*. Maryland: The University Press of America.

_____.2000. *The Future of Human Civilization* (2 volumes). New York: The Edwin Mellen Press.

Barrett, J. A. 1999. *The Quantum Mechanics of Minds and Worlds*. Oxford: Oxford University Press.

Bateson, Gregory & Mary Bateson. 1987. *Angels Fear: Toward an Epistemology of the Sacred*. New York: Macmillan.

Beichler, Jim, ed. 1998. "The Emergence of Paraphysics during the Scientific Era: 1970 to Present." *YGGDRASIL: The Journal of Paraphysics*. <http://members.aol.com/jebco1st/Paraphysics/search3.htm>.

Blome, H. J. & W. Priester. 1991. "Big Bounce in the Very Early Universe." *Astron. Astrophys*, 250: 43-49.

Bloom, Benjamin, & Krathwohl, D.R. 1956. *Taxonomy of Educational Objectives: The Classification of Educational Goals: Handbook I, Cognitive Domain*. New York: Longmans, Green.

Boivin-Jahns, V.; A. bianchi; R. Ruimy; J. Garcin; S. Daumas; & R. Christen. 1995. "Comparison of Phenotypical and Molecular Methods for the Identification of Bacterial Strains Isolated from a Deep Subsurface Environment." *Applied and Environmental Microbiology*, vol. 61, no. 9 (Sept. 1995): 3400–3406.

Borneo Marine Research Institute (BMRI). 2007. "Harnessing the Ocean: Marine Research in Borneo." <http://www.bic.org.my/BICalert/0705/p4.html>.

Brewer, Jess. 1994. "Where Will It End?" <http://musr.physics.ubc.ca/~jess/p200/hep/node20.html#SECTION00050000000000000000>.

Brout, R., F. Englert, F. & E. Gunzig. 1978. "The Creation of the Universe as a Quantum Phenomenon." *Annals of Physics*, 115: 78-106.

Carlson, Roger. 1989. "Are Universalistic Psychological Explanations Across Cultures Possible?" Paper presented at the XXII Interamerican Congress of Psychology, Buenos Aries (June). <http://rufy.com/roger/universalistic.html>.

Castells, Manuel. 1996. *The Rise of the Network Society*. Cambridge, MA: Blackwell Publishers.

Chomsky, Noam. 1995. *The Minimalist Program*. Cambridge, MA: The MIT Press.

_____.1957. *Syntactic Structures*. The Hague/Paris: Mouton.

_____.1955. *Logical Structure of Linguistic Theory*.

Clark, Donald. 2007. "Book Review: The Fifth Discipline." *Epic: Partners in Learning*. <http:// www. epic. co. uk/ content/ resources/ book_ reviews/senge_ 5th_discipline. htm>.

Cunningham, C. 1995. "Europe Not Ready for Multimedia." *Computerworld*: 29, 76.

DeLue, Steven. 2002. *Political Thinking, Political Theory, and Civil Society*. New York: Longman.

Derrida, Jacques. 1984. *The Ear of the Other: Otobiography, Transference, Translation*.

Claude Levesque & Christie McDonald, eds. Peggy Kamuf, tr. NY: Schocker Books.

Dewdney, A. K. 1997. *Yes, We Have No Neutrons: An Eye-Opening Tour through the Twists and Turns of Bad Science.* NY: Wiley.

DeWitt, B. S.; N. Graham, eds. 1973. The *Many-Worlds Interpretation of Quantum Mechanics.* Princeton: Princeton University Press.

Dictionary of the History of Ideas (DHI). 2007. "Classification of the Arts" (September 27). <http://etext.lib.virginia.edu/egi-local/DHI/dhi.cgi?id=dv1-56>.

Diggs, George; Barney Lipscomb; & Bob O'Kennon. 1999. "Taxonomy, Classification, and the Debate about Cladistics." An appendix from *Shinners, & Mahler's Illustrated Flora of North Central Texas.* Texas: The Botanical Research Institute of Texas. <http://artemis.austincollege.edu/acad/bio/gdiggs/taxonomy.html>.

Dogan, Mattei. 2004. "From Social Class and Religious Identity to Status Incongruence in Post-Industrial Societies." *Comparative Sociology.*

Durkheim, Emile & M. Mauss. 1903. [1963]. *Primitive Classification.* Chicago: University of Chicago Press.

Economist, the (ET). 2007. "Evolutionary psychology: Sex, Shopping and Thinking Pink—The Brains of Men and Women Are, Indeed, Different" (August 23). <http://www.economist.com/science/displaystory.cfm?story_id= 9682588>.

Eddington, A. S. 1930. "On the Instability of Einstein's Spherical World." *M. N. R. A. S.* 19: 668-678.

Einstein, A. 1917. Kosmologische Betrachtungen zur allgemeinen Relativitätstheorie. Königlich Preußische Akademie der Wissenschaften (Berlin). Sitzungsberichte, 142-152. Reprinted in *The Collected Papers of Albert Einstein.* A. Knox, M. Klein, & R. Schulmann, eds. Princeton: Princeton University Press, vol. 6 (1996): 541-552.

Encyclopædia Britannica (EB). 2007. "Chemotaxonomy" (September 22). <http://concise.britannica.com/ebc/article-9360476/chemotaxonomy>.

Festinger, Leon. 1954. "A Theory of Social Comparison Processes." *Human Relations,* 7(2): 117-140.

Foucault, Michel. 1971. *The Order of Things.* New York: Pantheon Books.

Ganti, Tibor. 2007. *Chemoton Theory. Volume 1: Theoretical Foundation of Fluid Machineries.* A commentary by James Griesermer & Eors Szathmary. <http://www.chemoton.com/eng3.html>.

Gauthier, Jacques. 1986. "Saurischian Monophyly and the Origin of Birds," in *The Origin of Birds and the Evolution of Flight,* Kevin Padian, ed. Memoirs California Academy of Sciences 8: 1–55.

Gell-Mann, M., Hartle, J. 1993. "Time Symmetry and Asymmetry in Quantum Mechanics and Quantum Cosmology." *Physical Origins of Time Asymmetry.* J. Halliwell, J. Perez-Mercader, and W. Zurek, eds. Cambridge: Cambridge University Press: 311-345. <http://arXiv.org/abs/gr-qc/9304023>.

_____.1990: "Quantum Mechanics in the Light of Quantum Cosmology." *Complexity, Entropy, and the Physics of Information.* W. Zurek, ed. Redwood City: Addison-Wesley: 425-458.

Gerdts, Cory; David Sharoyan; Rustem Ismagilov. 2004. "A Synthetic Reaction Network: Chemical Amplification Using Nonequilibrium Autocatalytic Reactions Coupled in Time." *J. Am. Chem. Soc.*, vol.126, n.20. <http://ismagilovlab.uchicago.edu/Ismagilov_J_Am_Chem_Soc_2004_126_6327_ Gerdts_Synthetic_Rxn_Ntwk_Amplification_Time.pdf>.

Giddens, Anthony. 1985. *Capitalism and Modern Theory: An Analysis of the Writings of Marx, Durkheim and Max Weber.* Cambridge: Cambridge University Press.

Gödel, K. 1949. "An Example of a New Type of Cosmological Solutions of Einstein's Field Equations." *Rev. Mod. Phys.*, 21: 447-450.

Goodrich, Edwin. 1916. "On the Classification of the Reptilia." *Proceedings of the Royal Society*, Series B, 89: 261–276.

Gott III, J. R.. & L. Li. 1998. "Can the Universe Create Itself?" *Phys. Rev.*, D58. <http://arxiv.org/abs/astroph/9712344>.

_____. 1982. "Creation of Open Universes from de Sitter Space." *Nature*, 295: 304-307.

Gould, Stephen Jay. 1996. "Taxonomy as Politics." Lectures on Thinking about Thinking, with Robert Nozick and Allan Dershowik. Cambridge, MA: Harvard University (spring semester).

_____.1990. "Taxonomy as Politics." *Dissent* (winter):73-8.

Gretzel, Ulrike. 2001. "Social Network Analysis: Introduction and Resources" (November). <http://lrs.ed.uiuc.edu/tse-portal/analysis/social-network-analysis/>.

Groth, David; Toby Skandier. 2005. *Network + Study Guide.* Sybex, Inc.

Harris, Pamela. 2006. "Active Learning: Non-Traditional Teaching & Learning Strategies." <http://www.montana.edu/teachlearn/PageFrames/ActLearn2.html>.

Hartle, J. & S. Hawking. 1983. "The Wave Function of the Universe." *Phys. Rev.*, D28: 2960-2975.

Hawking, S. W. 1988. *A Brief History of Time.* New York: Bantam.

Hein, Laura. 2002. "How Objects End up in Museums (or Craft vs. Art)" (December 13). <http://grove.ufl.edu/~naea/NAEAstuff/artvscraft.pdf>.

Herbig, P. A. 1994. *The Innovation Matrix: Culture and Structure Prerequisites to Innovation.* Westport, CT: Quorum Books.

Hilbert, D. 1964. "On the Infinite." *Philosophy of Mathematics.* P. Benacerraf & H. Putnam, eds. Englewood Cliff: Prentice Hall.

Hood, Marlowe. 2007. "Homo Politicus: Brain Function of Liberals, Conservatives Differs" (September 09). <http://news.yahoo.com/s/afp/20070909/hl_afp/ scienceneuroscience_070909173324>.

Horgan, John. 1995. "From Complexity to Perplexity", *Scientific American*, 272(6): 104-109.

Howard Hughes Medical Institute (HHMI). 2007. "Brain Uses both Neural 'Teacher' and 'Tinkerer' Networks in Learning" (June 04). *M.I.T. News.* <http://web.mit.edu/ newsoffice/2007/noisy-brain-0604.html>.

James, Kim & Carole McKenzie. 2004. "Aesthetics as an Aid to Understanding Complex Systems and Decision Judgment in Operating Complex Systems." *Emergence Complexity and Organization*, vol. 6, n. 1–2: 32–39. <http://emergence.org/ ECO_site/ECO_Archive/Issue_6_1-2/McKenzie_James.pdf, accessed 2 September

2007>.

Jonassen, D.; K. Peck, K. & B. Wilson. 2000. *Learning With Technology: A Constructivist Perspective*. Upper Saddle, NJ: Merrill.

Jordan, Patrick W. 2000. *Designing Pleasurable Products: An Introduction to the New Human Factors*. New York: Taylor & Francis.

Israelit, M. 2002. "Primary Matter Creation in a Weyl-Dirac." *Cosmological Model. Foundations of Physics*, 32: 295-321.

Kant, Immanuel. 1965. *The Critique of Pure Reason*. Norman Kemp Smith, Tr. New York: St. Martins.

Katz, E. 1963. "The Characteristics of Innovations and the Concept of Compatibility." Conference paper at the Rehovoth Conference on Comprehensive Planning of Agriculture in Developing Countries (Rehovoth, Israel: August 19-29).

Kauffman, S. A. 1993. *The Origins of Order: Self-Organization and Selection in Evolution*. Oxford: Oxford University Press.

Kim, D. 1993. "The Link between Individual and Organizational Learning." *Sloan Management Review*, Fall: 37-50.

KMconnection.com (KMC) 2007. "Faceted Classification of Information." <http://www.kmconnection.com/DOC100100.htm>.

Korf, Richard. 2005. "Reinventing Taxonomy: A Curmudgeon's View of 250 years of Fungal
Taxonomy, the Crisis in Biodiversity, and the Pitfalls of the Phylogenetic age." Mycotaxon, vol. 93 (July-September): 407–415. <http://www.mycotaxon.com/407korf324.pdf>.

Kruglanski, A. & O. Mayseless. 1990. "Classic and Current Social Comparison Research: Expanding the Perspective." *Psychological Bulletin*, 108(2): 195-208.

Lake, Brian. 2007. "Manuel Castells and the Rise of the Network Society: An Overview." <http://www.ucs.mun.ca/~brianl/academic/ma/Manuel_Castells_Rise_of_Network_Society.pdf>.

Lampman, Jane. 2007. "How Religion Forges Global Networks: Immigrants with Religious Ties Are Cheating 'Transnational' Communities in the United States" (September 07). *The Christian Science Monitor*. <http://www.publicbroadcasting.net/wypr/.artsmain/article/5/1032/1139622/Books/How.religion.forges.global.netwo rks/>.

Lane, Michael. 1970. "Introduction." *Introduction to Structuralism*. Michael Lane, ed. Also cited in a shorter piece as "Durkheim and Mauss on Primitive Classification." <http://instruct.uwo.ca/anthro/333/durkpc.htm>.

Lemaître, G. 1933. "L'Univers en Expansion." *Ann. Soc. Sci. Bruxelles*, A53: 51-85.

_____.1927. "Un Univers Homogène de Masse Constante et de Rayon Croissant, Rendant Compte de la Vitesse Radiale des Nébuleuses Extragalactiques." *Ann. Soc. Sci. Bruxelles*, A47: 49-59.

Levitt, Peggy. 2007. *God Needs No Passport: Immigrants and the Changing American Religious Landscape*. New York: New Press.

Linde, A. 1983. "Chaotic Inflation." *Phys. Lett.*, B129: 177-181.

Lorenz, Edward. 1980. "Noisy Periodicity and Reverse Bifurcation." International Conference on Nonlinear Dynamics: Nonlinear dynamics. Robert H.G. Helleman, ed. *Annals of the New York Academy of Sciences*, vol. 357: 282–291.

Maitland, Carleen. 1998. "Global Diffusion of Interactive Networks: The Impact of Culture." *Proceedings Cultural Attitudes Towards Communication and Technology '98*. C. Ess and F. Sudweeks, eds. Australia: University of Sydney: 268-286. <http://www.it.murdoch.edu.au/~sudweeks/catac98/pdf/24_maitland.pdf>.

March, J. G. & Olsen, J. P. 1975. "The Uncertainty of the Past; Organizational Ambiguous Learning." *European Journal of Political Research*, vol. 3: 147-171.

McMullin, Barry. 1999. "Some Remarks on Autocatalysis and Autopoiesis." Presented at the workshop, *Closure: Emergent Organizations and their Dynamics* (May 3-5, 1999). Belgium: University of Ghent. <http://www.eeng.dcu.ie/~alife/bmcm9901/html-single/>.

McNeil, Donald. 2004. "What's Going on with the Topography of Recursion?" (September 2). <http://www.library.utoronto.ca/see/SEED/Vol4-1/McNeil.htm>.

Merriam-Webster's Collegiate Dictionary Online (MWD). 2007. "Clade." (September 08). <http://www.m-w.com/dictionary/clade>.

_____.2007a. "Network." (September 16). <http://www.m-w.com/dictionary/network>.

Milgram, Stanley. 1967. "The Small World Problem." *Psychology Today* (May): 60–67.

Molitor, Graham. 1999. "The Next 1,000 Years: The 'Big Five' Engines of Economic Growth" (December). *The Futurist*.

Monge, P. R., & N. S. Contractor. 2007. "Emergence of Communication Networks." *New handbook of Organizational Communication*. L. Putnam and F. Jablin, eds. Newbury Park, CA: Sage. <http://www.spcomm.uiuc.edu:1000/contractor/HOCNets.html>.

Newman, Mark. 2003. "The Structure and Function of Complex Networks." *SIAM Review*, vol. 45, n. 2: 167–256. <http://aps.arxiv.org/abs/cond-mat/0303516>.

Nielsen, Donald. 2007. "Durkheim, Emile." *Encyclopedia of Religion and* Society. William Swatos, Jr., ed. Altamira Press. <http://hirr.hartsem.edu/ency/durkheim.htm>.

Nietzsche, Friedrich. 1969. "On the Genealogy of Morals." *The Birth of Tragedy and the Genealogy of Morals*. W. Kaufmann, et al., tr. NY: Vintage Books.

Norman, Donald A. 1986. *The Psychology of Everyday Things*. New York: Doubleday.

Nozick, R. 1981. "Why is there something rather than nothing?" *Philosophical Explanations*. Oxford: Clarendon.

Paul, Richard. 1992. *Critical thinking: What Every Person Needs to Survive in a Rapidly Changing World*. A.J.A. Binker, ed. Rohnert Park, CA: Foundation for Critical Thinking.

Pfeffer, J. 1982. *Organizations and Organization Theory*. Marshfield, MA: Pitman.

_____.& G. Salancik. 1978. *The External Control of Organizations: A Resource Dependence Perspective*. New York, Ny: Harper and Row.

Quine, W. V. O. 1951. "Two Dogmas of Empiricism." *The Philosophical Review*, 60:

20-43. Republished in *From a Logical Point of View* (Harvard University Press, 1953).

Rebhan, E. 2000. "'Soft Bang' instead of 'Big Bang': Model of an Inflationary Universe without Singularities and with Eternal Physical Past Time." *Astron. Astrophys*, 353: 1-9.

Rogers, E. M. 1995. *Diffusion of Innovations.* New York: The Free Press.

Rosen, N. & M. Israelit. 1989. "A Singularity-Free Cosmological Model in General Relativity." *Astrophys, J.*, 342: 627-634.

Rosser, J. Barkley, ed. 2003. *Complexity in Economics.* <http://cob.jmu.edu/rosserjb/COMPLEXITY%20IN%20ECONOMICS.doc>.

Saliba, John. 2003. *Understanding New Religious Movements.* Altamira Press.

Schmaus, Warren. 2007. "Durkheim and the Social Character of the Categories." *Rethinking Durkheim and His Tradition.* Cambridge, England: Cambridge University Press.

Scott, W. R. 2003. *Organizations: Rational, Natural and Open Systems.* NY: Prentice Hall.

Senge, P. M. 1990. *The Fifth Discipline: The Art and Practice of the Learning Organization.* New York: Doubleday.

Sitter, W. de. 1917 "On the Relativity of Intertia." Koninglijke Nederlandse Akademie van Wetenschappen Amsterdam. *Proceedings of the Section of Science* 19: 1217-1225.

Smolin, L. 2007. "What Is the Future of Cosmology?" *Stephen Hawking's Universe* <http://www.pbs.org/wnet/hawking/mysteries/html/smolin-1.html>.

_____.1997. "The Future of Spin Networks" (January 26). <http://www.arxiv.org/abs/gr-qc/9702030>.

_____.1992. "Did the Universe Evolve?" *Class. Quant. Grav.*, 9: 173-191.

Spitzer, R. J. 2000. "Definitions of Real Time and Ultimate Reality." *Ultimate Rality and Meaning*, 23 (3): 260-276.

Steels, Luc. 2005. "Evolving Complex Adaptive Systems." <http://arti.vub.ac.be/~steels/origin/subsection3_3_1.html>.

Sterpka, M. K. 2007. "The Aesthetics of Networks: A Conceptual Approach toward Visualizing the Composition of the Internet" (September 27). *First Monday: Peer-Reviewed Journal of the Internet.* <http://www.firstmonday.org/issues/issue12_9/sterpka/index.html>.

Stoeger, W. R.; G. Ellis; U. Kirchner. 2004. "Multiverses and Cosmology: Philosophical Issues." <http://arxiv.org/abs/astro-ph/0407329>.

Strogats, Steven & Duncan Watts. 1998. "Collective Dynamics of 'Small–World' Networks." *Nature*, vol. 393, n. 6684 (4 June): 440–442.

Suls, J.; R. Martin & L. Wheeler. 2002. "Social Comparison: Why, With Whom and With What Effect?" *Current Directions in Psychological Science*, 11(5): 159-163.

Tamil Nation Library (TNL). 2007. "Peter M.Senge—The Fifth Discipline: The Art and Practice of the Learning Organization, 1990." <http://www.tamilnation.org/books/Leadership/senge.htm>.

Tegmark, M. 2004. "Parallel Universes." *Science and Ultimate Reality.* J. Barrow, P.

Davies, and C. Harper, eds. Cambridge: Cambridge University Press. <http://arXiv.org/abs/astro-ph/0302131>.

Tolman, R. C. 1934. *Relativity, Thermodynamics and Cosmology*. Clarendon Press: Oxford.

Turok, N. & P. Steinhardt. 2002. "The Cyclic Universe: An Informal Introduction." <http://arxiv.org/abs/astro-ph/0204479>.

Turok, N. & S. Hawking. 1998. "Open Inflation, the Four Form and the Cosmological Constant." *Phys. Lett.*, B432: 271-278. <http://arxiv.org/abs/hep-th/9803156>.

Udovic, D.; D. Morris; A. Dickman; J. Postlethwait & P. Wetherwax. 2002. *Workshop Biology: Demonstrating the Effectiveness of Active Learning in an Introductory Biology Course. BioScience*, 52 (3): 272-282.

Vaas, Rudiger, 2003. "Time before Time: Classifications of Universes in Contemporary Cosmology, and How to Avoid the Antinomy of the Beginning and Eternity of the World." <http://philsci-archive.pitt.edu/archive/00001910/01/VAASTIME.PDF>.

_____.2001. "Why Quantum Correlates of Consciousness Are Fine, But Not Enough." *Information and Cognition.*   <http://www.marilia.unesp.br/atividades/extensao/revista/v3/artigo4.html>.

van Dijk, Jan. 1991. *De Netwerkmaatschappij* (in Dutch), or *The Network Society: Social Aspects of New Media* (in English in 1999).

Varnelis, Kazys. 2007. "Network Culture." <http://varnelis.net/blog/admin/introducing_network_culture>.

Vilenkin, A. 1982. *Creation of Universes from Nothing. Phys. Lett.*, B117: 25-28.

Wasserman, S. & K. Faust. 1994. *Social Network Analysis*. Cambridge, England: Cambridge University Press.

Wedgwood, Ralph. 1998. "What is the Best Way to Live? Lecture on Friedrich Nietzsche" (website version).

Wheeler, J. A.; W. Zurek (eds.). 1983. *Quantum Theory and Measurement*. Princeton: Princeton University.

Wikipedia (WK). 2007. "Kant's Theory of Perception" (August 31). <http://en.wikipedia.org/wiki/Kant#Kant.27s_theory_of_perception>.

_____. 2007a. "Naïve Realism" (September 01). <http://en.wikipedia.org/wiki/Na%C3%AFve_realism>.

_____. 2007b. "Representative Realism" (September 01). <http://en.wikipedia.org/wiki/Indirect_realism>.

_____. 2007c. "Michel Foucault" (September 01). <http://en.wikipedia.org/wiki/Michel_Foucault>.

_____. 2007d. "Willard Quine" (September 01). <http://en.wikipedia.org/wiki/Willard_Van_Orman_Quine>.

_____. 2007e. "Noam Chomsky" (September 01). <http://en.wikipedia.org/wiki/Noam_chomsky>.

_____. 2007f. "Information Revolution" (September 02). <http://en.wikipedia.org/wiki/Information_revolution>.

_____. 2007g. "Taxonomy" (September 07). <http://en.wikipedia.org/wiki/Taxonomy>.

_____. 2007h. "Alpha Taxonomy" (September 07). <http://en.wikipedia.org/wiki/Alpha_taxonomy>.

_____. 2007i. "Evolutionary Tree" (September 07). <http://en.wikipedia.org/wiki/Evolutionary_tree>.

_____. 2007j. "Linnaean Taxonomy" (September 07). <http://en.wikipedia.org/wiki/Linnaean_taxonomy>.

_____. 2007k. "Carl Linnaeus" (September 07). <http://en.wikipedia.org/wiki/Carl_Linnaeus>.

_____. 2007l. "Species" (September 08). <http://en.wikipedia.org/wiki/Species>.

_____. 2007m. "Phylocode" (September 08). <http://en.wikipedia.org/wiki/Phylocode>.

_____. 2007n. "Phylogentic Nomenclature" (September 08). <http://en.wikipedia.org/wiki/Phylogenetic_nomenclature>.

_____. 2007o. "Phylogenetics" (September 08). <http://en.wikipedia.org/wiki/Phylogeny>.

_____. 2007p. "Cladistics" (September 08). <http://en.wikipedia.org/wiki/Cladistics#Definitions>.

_____. 2007q. "Episteme" (September 11). <http://en.wikipedia.org/wiki/Episteme>.

_____.2007r. "Classifications of Cults and New Religious Movements" (September 11). <http://en.wikipedia.org/wiki/Classifications_of_cults_and_new_religious_moveme nts>.

_____.2007s. "Enumeration" (September 13). <http://en.wikipedia.org/wiki/Enumeration>.

_____.2007t. "Dewey Decimal Classification" (September 13). <http://en.wikipedia.org/wiki/Dewey_Decimal_Classification>.

_____.2007u. "Library of Congress Classification" (September 13). <http://en.wikipedia.org/wiki/Library_of_Congress_Classification>.

_____.2007v. "Information Architecture" (September 13). <http://en.wikipedia.org/wiki/Information_architecture>.

_____.2007w. "User-Centered Design" (September 14). <http://en.wikipedia.org/wiki/User-centered_design>.

_____.2007x. "Techniques for Creating a User-Centered Design" (September 14). <http://en.wikipedia.org/wiki/Techniques_for_creating_a_User_Centered_Design>.

_____.2007y. "Social Class" (September 14). <http://en.wikipedia.org/wiki/Social_class#Objective_and_subjective_factors_in_class_in_Marxism>.

_____.2007z. "Taxonomy of Educational Objectives" (September 15). <http://en.wikipedia.org/wiki/Taxonomy_of_Educational_Objectives>.

_____.2007aa. "Faceted Classification" (September 15). <http://en.wikipedia.org/wiki/Faceted_classification>.

_____.2007bb. "Network Topology" (September 16). <http://en.wikipedia.org/wiki/Network_topology>.

_____.2007cc. "Metcalfe's Law" (September 16). <http://en.wikipedia.org/wiki/Metcalfe%27s_Law>.

_____.2007dd. "Transformational Grammar" (September 16). <http://en.wikipedia.org/wiki/Transformational_grammar>.

_____.2007ee. "Network Society" (September 16). <http://en.wikipedia.org/wiki/Network_society>.

_____.2007ff. "Network Outage" (September 16). <http://en.wikipedia.org/wiki/Network_outage>.

_____.2007gg. "Process Architecture" (September 16). <http://en.wikipedia.org/wiki/Process_architecture>.

_____.2007hh. "Knowledge_management" (September 16). <http://en.wikipedia.org/wiki/Knowledge_management>.

_____.2007ii. "Organizational Learning" (September 17). <http://en.wikipedia.org/wiki/Organizational_learning>.

_____.2007jj. "The_Fifth Discipline" (September 17). <http://en.wikipedia.org/ wiki/The_Fifth_Discipline>.

_____.2007kk. "Social Comparison Theory" (September 18). <http://en.wikipedia.org/wiki/Social_comparison_theory>.

_____.2007ll. "Resource Dependence Theory " (September 18). <http://en.wikipedia.org/wiki/Resource_dependence_theory>.

_____.2007mm. "Cognitivism (psychology)" (September 21). <http://en.wikipedia.org/wiki/Cognitivism_%28psychology%29>.

_____.2007nn. "Chemotaxonomy" (September 22). <http://en.wikipedia.org/wiki/Chemotaxonomy>.

_____.2007oo. "Classical Elements" (September 22). <http://en.wikipedia.org/wiki/Classical_elements>.

_____.2007pp. "List of Particles" (September 22). <http://en.wikipedia.org/wiki/List_of_particles>.

_____.2007qq. "Neural Networks" (September 25). <http://en.wikipedia.org/wiki/Neural_networks>.

_____.2007rr. "Architecture" (September 01). <http://en.wikipedia.org/wiki/Architecture>.

_____.2007ss. "Information" (September 01). <http://en.wikipedia.org/wiki/Information>.

Windschuttle, Keith. 1997. "Absolutely Relative." <http://www.nationalreview.com/15sept97/windschuttle091597.html>.

Wolfram, S. 2002. *A New Kind of Science*. Champaign: Wolfram Media.

Wynar, Bohdan S. 1976. *Introduction to Cataloging and Classification.* Littleton, Colorado: Libraries Unlimited.

INDEX

•C•

•I•

•N•

Printed and bound by CPI Group (UK) Ltd, Croydon, CR0 4YY

03/10/2024

01040435-0013